Food Culture in
Scandinavia

Food Culture in
Scandinavia

HENRY NOTAKER

Food Culture around the World

Ken Albala, Series Editor

GREENWOOD PRESS
Westport, Connecticut • London

Library of Congress Cataloging-in-Publication Data

Notaker, Henry.
   Food culture in Scandinavia / Henry Notaker.
         p. cm. — (Food culture around the world, ISSN 1545–2638)
   Includes bibliographical references and index.
   ISBN 978–0–313–34922–5 (alk. paper)
   1. Food habits—Scandinavia.   2. Cookery, Scandinavian.   3. Scandinavia—Social
life and customs.   I. Title.
   GT2853.S33N67   2009
   394.1'20948—dc22   2008038955

British Library Cataloguing in Publication Data is available.

Library of Congress Catalog Card Number: 2008038955
ISBN: 978–0–313–34922–5
ISSN: 1545–2638

First published in 2009

Greenwood Press, 88 Post Road West, Westport, CT 06881
An imprint of Greenwood Publishing Group, Inc.
www.greenwood.com

Printed in the United States of America

The paper used in this book complies with the
Permanent Paper Standard issued by the National
Information Standards Organization (Z39.48–1984).

10   9   8   7   6   5   4   3   2   1

The publisher has done its best to make sure the instructions and/or recipes in this book
are correct. However, users should apply judgment and experience when preparing recipes, especially parents and teachers working with young people. The publisher accepts no
responsibility for the outcome of any recipe included in this volume.

Contents

Series Foreword

The appearance of the Food Culture around the World series marks a definitive stage in the maturation of Food Studies as a discipline to reach a wider audience of students, general readers, and foodies alike. In comprehensive interdisciplinary reference volumes, each on the food culture of a country or region for which information is most in demand, a remarkable team of experts from around the world offers a deeper understanding and appreciation of the role of food in shaping human culture for a whole new generation. I am honored to have been associated with this project as series editor.

Each volume follows a series format, with a chronology of food-related dates and narrative chapters entitled Introduction, Historical Overview, Major Foods and Ingredients, Cooking, Typical Meals, Eating Out, Special Occasions, and Diet and Health. (In special cases, these topics are covered by region.) Each also includes a glossary, bibliography, resource guide, and illustrations.

Finding or growing food has of course been the major preoccupation of our species throughout history, but how various peoples around the world learn to exploit their natural resources, come to esteem or shun specific foods, and develop unique cuisines reveals much more about what it is to be human. There is perhaps no better way to understand a culture, its values, preoccupations, and fears, than by examining its attitudes toward food. Food provides the daily sustenance around which families and communities bond. It provides the material basis for rituals through which people celebrate the passage of life stages and their connection to divinity. Food preferences also serve to separate individuals and groups from each other, and as one of the most powerful factors in the construction of identity, we physically, emotionally, and spiritually become what we eat. By studying the foodways of people different from ourselves we also grow to understand and tolerate the rich diversity of practices around the world. What seems strange or frightening among other people becomes perfectly rational when set in context. It is my hope that readers will gain from these volumes not only an aesthetic appreciation for the glories of the many culinary traditions described, but also ultimately a more profound respect for the peoples who devised them. Whether it is eating New Year's dumplings in China, folding tamales with friends in Mexico, or going out to a famous Michelin-starred restaurant in France, understanding these food traditions helps us to understand the people themselves.

As globalization proceeds apace in the twenty-first century it is also more important than ever to preserve unique local and regional traditions. In many cases these books describe ways of eating that have already begun to disappear or have been seriously transformed by modernity. To know how and why these losses occur today also enables us to decide what traditions, whether from our own heritage or that of others, we wish to keep alive. These books are thus not only about the food and culture of peoples around the world, but also about ourselves and who we hope to be.

Ken Albala
University of the Pacific

Introduction

This book is about food culture in four Scandinavian countries: Denmark, Iceland, Norway, and Sweden. Finland is left out, partly because of the difficulty with sources, as most of them are in Finnish, a language very different from the other Scandinavian languages, and partly because Finland has many similarities to food culture in Russia.

The Scandinavian countries do not have a uniform food culture, but given the close contact between these countries through the centuries, certain important similarities are evident. In this book these similarities will be pointed out as well as the many different traditions, due to variations in nature and climate and in social, cultural, and political history.

Food habits are quickly changing. Studies in the 1980s and 1990s showed a great stability in meal structures and food choices, but some new trends were detected among the young and urban. In the first decade of the new millennium the changes seem to be faster and more visible. Most important is the impact of the supermarket, offering a wider and wider range of convenience foods. Fast food restaurants, kiosks, gasoline stations, and take-away outlets are increasingly important in the distribution of food. These trends strengthen standardization and reduce the real choices for the consumers.

At the same time an interest in food culture is growing, which has led to experiments with both national and foreign food traditions. Many old national or regional products have been revitalized and are often produced and sold by small local companies. A new small-scale production has also begun in food products, animal species, and fruit and vegetable types that had almost disappeared through standardization in agriculture and demands for uniformity in supermarkets in the twentieth century.

In the cities the new immigrants from southern Europe and Asia have introduced new ingredients and dishes through shops and restaurants. A high proportion of the Scandinavian population travels to foreign countries and adapts more easily than before to new foods and preparations. A new wealthy elite, often representing prosperous enterprises in finance and industry, is the client base for a new group of luxury restaurants of very high quality. A strong interest in healthful food and, particularly in Denmark, for production of organic foods is also evident.

LAND AND CLIMATE

The interior parts of Norway and Sweden have a continental climate, characterized by cold winters and warm summers. The coastal areas of Norway, as well as Denmark, Iceland, and the other North Sea islands, are influenced by the warm Gulf Stream and have a more humid climate with less temperature differences between summer and winter.

Scandinavia has long coasts to the North Atlantic and the Baltic Sea. There are deep fjords, long and narrow valleys, rivers and lakes, thousands of islands, enormous forests, high mountains, rolling hills, tundra, glaciers, geysers, volcanoes, and flat fertile plains.

The total (ice-free) land area is 600,000 square miles (compared with three and a half million in the United States), but in addition are ice caps and glaciers, in Greenland alone covering more than half a million square miles. Arable land makes up 18.8 percent of the ice-free area, about the same as in the United States, but big differences exist among Denmark (with 54% arable land), Sweden (8%), Norway (3%), and Iceland (1%). The natural conditions for farming are particularly harsh in Iceland, Greenland, and the Faroe Islands.

In the agricultural sector, small holdings of less than 75 acres dominate, and most of the large holdings are in Denmark. Denmark produces three times as much food as its inhabitants need and has an important food export.

Historically, a dividing line went between a southern area (Denmark and southern Sweden), where grain was the most important product, and a northern area (Iceland, Norway, and northern Sweden), where milk was the most important product. Through the ages, other lines became more important, between coast and inland, between town and countryside.

POPULATION

Scandinavia today has a very high standard of living, and the percentage of very poor is low. Life expectancy is 77 years for men and 82 for women, a little higher than in the United States. The gross domestic product (GDP) per capita is 31,855 euros, and the total taxes, as a percentage of the GDP, 48.2 percent (United States: 26.8%). People spend an average of 13 to 14 percent of their total household expenses on food.

Denmark (population 5.4 million) is 10 times as densely populated as Sweden (8.9 million), Norway (4.5 million), and Iceland (0.3 million), and more Danes live in big towns and cities. The populations of Greenland and the Faroe Islands are each about 50,000.

A very low percentage work in the primary sector (agriculture, fishing, hunting), most of the workforce is in the tertiary (service) sector, about 30 percent in the public sector. The average hours worked per week is between 35 and 38 hours (United States: 41 hours).

NATIONS, STATES, AND LANGUAGES

Sweden (with Finland as an incorporated part since the mid-twelfth century), Denmark, and Norway were independent kingdoms until the late fourteenth century, when they were united in the Kalmar Union. Sweden ended the union by breaking out in 1521, but Denmark-Norway, under the Danish king, continued as an entity until 1814, when the Norwegians declared their independence. After Napoleon's defeat, Sweden had to cede Finland to Russia but was compensated with Norway. Norway was united with Sweden under the Swedish king until 1905, when full independence was established.

Iceland and the Faroe Islands were colonized by Norwegians in the Viking Age and passed some centuries as independent areas, but they were brought under Norwegian rule in the high Middle Ages. The same happened to Greenland, colonized by Icelanders from the tenth century. In the late fourteenth century, all these areas were brought with Norway into the Kalmar Union and subsequently under Danish rule. Iceland remained part of Denmark until 1944, when independence was declared. The Faroe Islands obtained status as autonomous territory in 1948 and Greenland in 1979. Sweden, Denmark, and Norway are kingdoms, Iceland a republic, but all have democratic constitutions and parliamentary systems. Sweden and Denmark are members of the European Union (EU); Norway and Iceland participate in the European Economic Area (EEA).

Scandinavian countries are represented by three language groups. Most important are the Germanic languages of the Indo-European group: Swedish, Danish, Norwegian (two different forms), Icelandic, and Faroese. Swedish is spoken in Sweden, in Åland an island, and in some coastal regions of Finland. The Samic language dialects, spoken by groups in northern Scandinavia, belong (as does Finnish) to the Finno-Ugric languages. Greenlandish (Kalaallisut) is related to other languages in the Inuit-Aleut family, spoken in Canada and Alaska.

THE CONCEPT OF SCANDINAVIA

The word *Scandinavia* is derived from names used by classical writers in the first centuries A.D. One such name is *Scadia* or *Scandia,* probably used originally for the southern tip of Sweden, still called Skåne. The meaning of the name is disputed.

The Scandinavian Peninsula is a designation of the region consisting of Sweden and Norway, but the name *Scandinavia* is generally used today to designate the Nordic countries, or *Norden,* as the region is called in Danish, Swedish, and Norwegian. Scandinavian cooperation is led by a Nordic Council, where the members are Sweden, Norway, Iceland, Denmark (with the autonomous territories Faroe Islands and Greenland), and Finland (with the autonomous territory Åland).

ACKNOWLEDGMENTS

To write a book like this, covering many aspects and several countries, has only been possible thanks to research in various fields by Scandinavian scholars. The Select Bibliography provides a sample of these works and is also to be considered a credit to these scholars.

More particularly I want to express my gratitude to Unni Kjærnes and Annechen Bahr Bugge at the National Institute for Consumer Research in Oslo (SIFO) for their ideas and suggestions; Ove Fosså (Sandnes, Norway), who has read my book in manuscript and come up with important criticism and advice; Barbro Henning (Stockholm, Sweden) and Lone Jensen (Årup, Denmark), who have helped me with national traditions described in chapters 4 and 6; and Lars Johansson at the Norwegian Directorate of Health for his invaluable comments on the material in chapter 7. I also want to thank Beate Velde Koren, Atle Koren, and Kari Anne Hoen for their generous help with some of the illustrations. The recipe for fish cakes on page 124 is from Liv Grønningssæter.

Timeline

12,000 B.C.	Reindeer are hunted in southern Scandinavia.
9000 B.C.	Elk are hunted.
8000–6000 B.C.	Pre-Boreal and Boreal period with fishing, hunting, and gathering of nuts and starch-rich roots.
7000–3000 B.C.	Kitchen middens of sea shells and early examples of pottery can be traced to this period.
4000–3000 B.C.	Beginning of the late (Neolithic) Stone Age, with introduction of animal husbandry and agriculture.
1800 B.C.	Beginning of Bronze Age, with land more intensely exploited for cultivation, fishing and seal hunting along the coasts, and the import of bronze vessels.
500 B.C.–800 A.D.	Iron Age, with agrarian societies spreading north and more contact with Europe.
500–1 B.C.	Pre-Roman Iron Age, with increased importance of animal husbandry and agriculture (barley, oats, a little rye); in the North combined with hunting, fishing, and gathering.
1–400 A.D.	Roman Iron Age, strong influence from Roman culture, more social inequality, elite importing bronze vessels, glass beakers, and high-quality kitchenware and tableware pottery.

400–800	Germanic Iron Age, introduction of new tools had resulted in a more efficient cultivation and an improvement of the methods, for example, through crop rotation; founding of town and commercial centers; imports of cereals, wine, and spices.
800–900	Export of stockfish (dried cod) from Norway documented.
800–1000	Viking Age (preserved meat and fish, porridges and gruels, and curds are dietary staples).
1000–1100	Christian laws against consumption of horse meat.
1000–1349	High Middle Ages (imports of luxury foods to the elite).
1100–1200	Herring fisheries in Danish towns along Ôresund.
1283	First law regulating inns along the roads.
c. 1300	First known recipe collection in a Scandinavian language.
1300–1500	Water mills and thin, flatbreads found in the North.
1348	*Gravlaks* (cured salmon) mentioned in a medieval document.
1349–1350	Black Death and beginning of the late Middle Ages.
1500	Sami nomads start domestication of reindeer.
1538	The Swedish *ostkaka* (cheesecake) mentioned for the first time.
1540	Dried cod in lye *(lutefisk)* mentioned in Sweden.
1555	Publication in Rome of Olaus Magnus's Scandinavian history, *Historia de gentibus septentrionalibus*, where lutefisk and flatbread are described.
1565	Orangerie built in royal gardens in Stockholm.
1600–1700	Strong alcohol (spirits) become more and more common.
1616	First printed Danish cookbook.
1642	*Spettkaka* (a pyramid cake of eggs, sugar, and flour) mentioned for the first time in Sweden.
1650	First printed Swedish cookbook.

1664	First French cookbook in Scandinavian (Swedish).
c. 1700	Production of *Klipfisk* (dried salted cod) starts in Norway.
1710–1720	First coffee house in Sweden.
1733	The drink *punch* mentioned in Sweden for the first time.
c. 1750	Potatoes introduced and grown in Scandinavia.
1774	Treatise about traditional Norwegian milk products.
1787	Operakällaren restaurant opens in Stockholm.
1791	First inn opens in Iceland.
1800	First printed Icelandic cookbook.
1800–1850	Coffee is a daily drink in most cities and towns.
1814	Norway in union with Sweden.
1831	First printed Norwegian cookbook.
1870s	Norwegian brown cheese is commercially produced.
1876	The first margarine factory, Aug. Pellerin Fils & Co., Oslo, opens in Scandinavia.
1879	Publication of Scandinavia's most prestigious cookbook, the Swedish *Kok-konsten*, by Ch.-Em. Hagdahl.
1886	First café opened in Iceland.
1901	Publication of the twentieth-century Danish cookbook classic, *Frøken Jensens Kogebog*.
1903	First Swedish Vegetarian Society (Svenska vegetariska föreningen) is founded.
1905	Norway becomes independent from Sweden.
1914	Publication of the twentieth-century Norwegian cookbook classic, *Stor Kokebok*, by H. Schønberg Erken.
1945	Iceland becomes independent from Denmark.
1958	The Swedish Gastronomic Academy (Gastronomiska akademin) is founded.
1964	The Danish Gastronomic Academy (Det danske gastronomiske akademi) is founded.

1973	First McDonald's opens in Scandinavia (Sweden).
1991	First Scandinavian medal won in the Bocuse d'Or world cuisine competition (silver, Norway).
1993	The start of the Meal House in Grythyttan, Sweden, with academic culinary studies.
	First Scandinavian gold medal winner won in the Bocuse d'Or world cuisine competition (Norway).
2000	Opening of the Cookbook Museum in Grythyttan, Sweden, with a collection of ancient European cookbooks.
2004	The Manifesto for a New Nordic Cuisine is published by Scandinavian cooks.
2008	First European Bocuse d'Or is held in Stavanger, Norway.

Sweden. Cartography by Bookcomp, Inc.

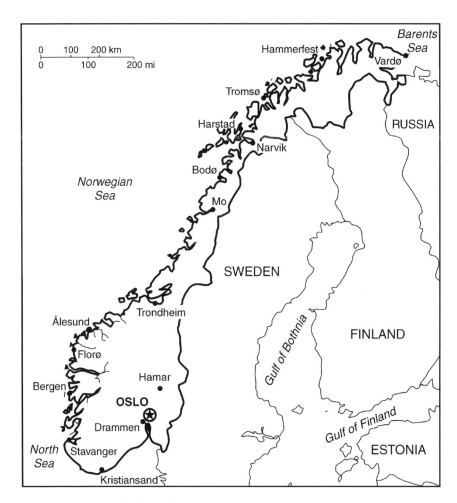

Norway. Cartography by Bookcomp, Inc.

Denmark. Cartography by Bookcomp, Inc.

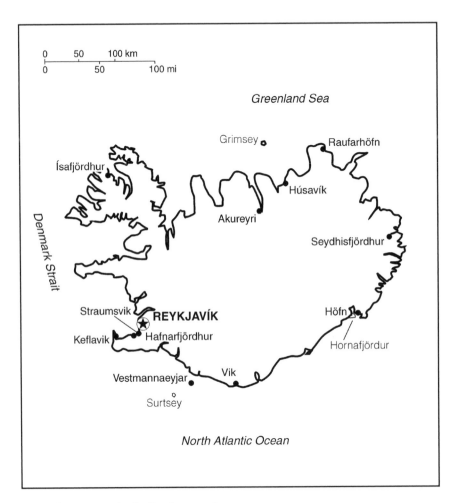

1

Historical Overview

The sources for food culture in the prehistoric period are primarily archaeological, and the culinary practice may be concluded from a general knowledge about how different foods were prepared by simple means in early civilizations. More specific details about diet and cooking are easier to obtain through the written sources available from the Viking Age and in particular from the Middle Ages.[1]

VIKING AND MIDDLE AGES (800–1500)

A quick profit was a strong motive behind the Viking raids into eastern and western Europe. There were goods of immense value to rob and bring home, also culinary goods that could not be produced in Scandinavia. Wine is one example, and treaties with French towns demanded delivery of wine as a condition for withdrawal. But extortion and plunder were not the sole forms of Viking activity. Swedish, Danish, and Norwegian Vikings settled in the British isles and in western France as merchants, artisans, or even farmers. Many of them mixed with the local population and became gradually integrated. One of the reasons for the expeditions and emigrations across the seas was a strong population growth. In Scandinavia itself this growth led to the clearing and preparation of new areas for agriculture.

The cultivation of grains was most successful in the southern parts of Scandinavia, but livestock was important also here, not only to give food, but the necessary manure. Animal husbandry became, nevertheless, of particular importance in the areas where there were natural obstacles to an effective cultivation of the land, such as steep and rugged terrain, cold and rough climate, and less fertile soil. These conditions were especially the case in the northern and western areas, in the fjords, the mountains, and the vast forests.

Scandinavian Nations

The Viking Age ended in the early eleventh century. At that time Scandinavia had already started a political development, and a patchwork of small kingdoms became large national entities with central administrations, as had occurred in other European states. The geographical borders established in the process were roughly the same as they are today, with certain small but important exceptions. The introduction of a new religion, Christianity, led to the building of churches and cathedrals and the establishment of a professional clergy with ideas that would affect the food culture for centuries.

During the last part of the twelfth and the beginning of the thirteenth century the Scandinavian kingdoms entered the European scene as strong powers with dominion over large areas. At the same time the aristocracy strengthened its position. It was not as in the Viking Age with a group of chieftains and powerful farmers, but a chivalry in the European tradition, with privileges assigned by the king and a court culture of their own. Next in rank came the peasantry, who constituted the large part of the population. At the bottom of the hierarchy were the thralls (slaves), who since the Viking Age had been an important economic factor, but from the thirteenth century slavery disappeared and was substituted by different forms of hired, paid labor.

Like many other areas, Scandinavia went through a demographic crisis at the end of the Middle Ages, mainly as a consequence of the Black Death (bubonic plague) and later epidemics. Large parts of the population were exterminated and many farms were laid waste. The political unrest that followed the crisis ended in an attempt to create a large political entity, partly as a result of dynastic factors. The Kalmar Union between Norway, Denmark, and Sweden lasted until the beginning of the sixteenth century.

Written Sources of Food History

The Viking Age is a transitional period when written documents begin to supplement the archaeological evidence from prehistoric time. But it is difficult to interpret the old texts, particularly poems and religious literature, where the purpose is not first and foremost to describe historical facts. The Icelandic family sagas probably reflect daily life better than any other medieval Norse literature, but they started as oral traditions and were written down a long time after the events they describe. The food culture these texts reflect may therefore be more typical of the food culture of the time of writing, normally the thirteenth century. Most of the law texts—another important source—are also from this period. But with the necessary reservations in mind, it is still possible to point out some foodstuffs that certainly were eaten during the Middle Ages, and many of them seem to have their roots in traditions going back to the Viking Age or earlier. From the fourteenth and fifteenth centuries, the source material is much richer in account books, wills, inventories, and purchase records.

A Culinary Poem

The social hierarchy in medieval Scandinavia is described in an intriguing way in one of the old mythological poems. It is called *Rigsþula* and relates the story of the god Rig, who in his earthly wanderings visits three different houses, each representing a different social category: the slave, the farmer, and the nobleman.[2] The three houses are characterized by the number of livestock, the interior decoration, and dress and food. In the first house, Rig is given a hunk of coarse bread filled with husks and a simple broth. In the next he receives a bowl with boiled veal. But in the last house, the table is laid with linen and silver, and he is served thin loaves of white bread, wine in adorned goblets, and meat consisting of juicy pork and roast birds on silver platters.

The description of the noble table may be taken from some of the chivalric novels that were translated into Old Norse. However, many other sources describe early imports of luxury foodstuffs, and there are small recipe collections in Scandinavian languages with refined dishes from the thirteenth century. These sources clearly show that an elegant cuisine existed, but as the *Rigsþula* poem demonstrates, there were deep social differences at the time.

MAIN FOODS

Cereals

Two sorts of bread are mentioned in the *Rigsþula*, the white loaves of wheat in the home of the nobleman and the heavy loaves of coarse bread in the thrall's cabin. Very little wheat was cultivated in Scandinavia, and importing it was necessary. Wheat products were very exclusive and primarily enjoyed by the elite for festive occasions, and wheat was used in the holy bread at the communion table in the churches.

Neither was rye extensively cultivated, even if this grain, so well suited for bread baking, steadily increased in importance, especially in Denmark and southern Sweden, where it has dominated since c. 1500. The cultivation of rye was accompanied by new baking techniques, the use of leaven and ovens. The first and simpler ovens were made of brick, but solid stone ovens were built in palaces and manors, and also in the northern parts. From the late Middle Ages commercial bakeries and guilds of professional bakers are documented.

The coarse loaves in the poem may be representative of the earliest breads. As in other parts of the world, they were simply made by shaping a flat cake of dough, made from flour or crushed grains kneaded with water or another liquid, and put in the ashes or on the embers or on a flat stone beside the fire. This process is a natural interpretation of names such as *ashen bread* and *ember cake*, words used in both Norwegian and Swedish.

Early on, these breads were mainly baked from oats and barley, and they were unleavened because those two grains don't contain the necessary gluten for leaven baking. In hard times they might be unsavory and coarse in poor homes because of the substitutes for grains added to the dough: husks, crushed and dried bark, and in Iceland also reindeer moss.

Barley is the oldest grain in Scandinavia and dominant in the North and in the mountainous regions, while oats were introduced in more humid areas. Barley or oats were also the basic ingredient in porridge and gruel, the most common of daily dishes, and the main source of starch besides bread in the nutrition of ordinary people. Porridge was considered so important in the diet that the old medieval Borgarthing law defined it as *hælagr* (sacred or legally protected),[3] which meant it was permitted to be cooked on religious holidays when other forms of work were banned.

Meat from Domestic Animals

Cattle were kept over the entire region, but meat from hogs (pork) had a higher status. Animal bones found during archaeological excavations in Oslo indicate that pork constituted only 10 percent of the total meat consumption. A proof of the high opinion of pork is the fact that it is the food eaten in paradise (Valhall) in the old Norse myths: "But never is so vast a multitude in Valhall that the flesh of that boar shall fail, which is called Sæhrímnir; he is boiled every day and is whole at evening."[4]

Goats played an important role and were primarily kept for their skin, which was important for the production of clothing, but also for parchment. Gradually sheep got a more important place, giving both wool and skin.

Goat meat, particularly kid, was eaten. Mutton was rather common, while dishes made from the more tender lamb meat were most highly prized. Sheep were kept all over Scandinavia, especially in Iceland and the Faroe Islands (the name means Sheep Islands).

Regarding poultry, geese and hens were kept, most extensively in the South, and they gave meat, eggs, and feathers.

Most meat was preserved after the slaughtering, dried, smoked, or salted. The usual culinary preparation was boiling. The Norse word for the broth in the thrall's kitchen is *sod*, past participle of the verb *sjúda*, which means "to boil." Such boiled dishes were common in all social groups, but the amount of meat varied according to the means. In its simplest form broth was a thin soup based on bones or slices of meat with grits or roots, for example, rutabaga or turnip, added. Richer forms of *sod* contained different meats and more exclusive vegetables. There are also a few descriptions from the Middle Ages of roast meat, but then it is generally in a literature influenced by foreign court culture.

Game

The introduction of agriculture and animal husbandry did not stop hunting and fishing, which had been practiced since Paleolithic times. One of the motivating forces behind the human immigration into Scandinavia after the Glacial period was the hunting of reindeer.

Around the end of the Viking era, several visitors to Scandinavia were stunned by the abundance of wild animals in the region. Adam from Bremen wrote around 1070 that almost the entire population could take their food from the birds and the game in the woods.[5] German travelers in Denmark in 1128 relayed that hunting, fishing, and animal husbandry made up the wealth of the country, but there was little grain production.[6] Hunting of grouse was described in one of the medieval chronicles, and capercailzie and black grouse are mentioned in the oldest law texts. Also meat from sea birds was eaten and their eggs were collected and eaten as well.

Elk was hunted for its skin and horns, which were commercial products. The meat was generally eaten locally. The reindeer were valuable because of skin and horns, but toward the end of the Middle Ages groups in the Sami population started to domesticate the animals and make them the foundation of their economy. The meat and blood were used in several culinary ways, while the milk was mainly used for cheese production.

Sea mammals, such as whales and seals, had been eaten since prehistoric times. Seals were hunted while whales occasionally stranded on the shores. Oil made from the blubber was used not only for lamps and for greasing of skins and hides, but also as a substitute for butter. The meat was eaten and the seal meat was particularly valued as it had a taste not too different from farm animals. In the Gulf of Bothnia the seal was called the *coastal pig* because like the pig it gave meat, blood, and fat. The Samis on the northwestern coast of Scandinavia were particularly dependent on the seal because they did not have reindeer, as did the Sami of the plains. It is not quite clear whether seal was eaten during fast days, but whale meat was clearly regarded as Lenten food.

During the Middle Ages, the growth of an aristocracy with large properties limited the access to game for ordinary people. Particularly in the South, hunting was a privilege for the rich. As in other European regions, game dishes were among the most treasured on the banquet tables. Archaeological digs show much more bones from game birds and animals in castles and palaces than in the towns.

Fish

Food from the sea is a matter of course in a region with so many coasts, rivers, and lakes. Shell middens, consisting of heaps of oysters, mussels shells, and clams, document early culinary use of these foodstuffs back to prehistoric times. Danish archaeologists were the first to discover the value of these middens for historical research, and the scientific term is still *køkkenmødding*, the Danish word for a kitchen midden.

All available sorts of fish were consumed, fresh or more often in preserved form, dried, smoked, fermented, or salted. The inland fishing played a far more important part than today. In the North where access to lakes and rivers was free, ordinary people could get food through fishing, but in areas where rivers belonged to nobility or monasteries, there were often conflicts between the owners and commoners. The nobility also maintained fish ponds to provide supplies for the fast periods.

Sea and estuary fishing were more important than the inland fishing and more rewarding commercially. Trade with herring, cod, salmon, and other fish started early and got an extra push during the Middle Ages because of the Catholic regulations for fast days and Lenten fare. Around the Gulf of Bothnia salmon fishing brought affluence, with catches being taken to Stockholm and partly exported from there. Also culinary delicacies such as pike and eel were caught in this area.

Scandinavian herring fisheries took place in several ocean and coastal areas. The herring markets along Öresund, the strait between Skåne and

Sjælland, are documented from about 1200, and they attained a greater importance when they started to produce salted herring instead of dried as earlier. But this required a constant supply of salt, and the supply of high-quality salt from Lüneburg was controlled by the merchants in Lübeck, Germany. The fishing trade soon became a tempting object, not only for Lübeck but for the other towns of the Hansa League in northern Germany. They were more advanced in economic management and expanded their activity in Scandinavia from the thirteenth century. They also secured the control of the stockfish from northern Norway through the most important export town, Bergen.

Vegetables and Fruits

Roots, pulses, and some vegetables have been cultivated since the Viking Age or longer: beans, peas, turnip, rutabaga, cabbage, onions, and angelica. Wild apples were found in the Oseberg ship—one of the best preserved Viking ships—and different berries and wild plants were used in cookery.

The establishment of a Christian, European culture resulted in a stronger emphasis on horticulture, promoted first of all by monasteries and nunneries. Cultivation of greens of all sorts was important because of the many days in the Catholic calendar when animal products were banned. Also many herbs were used in cookery, even if the main reason for their cultivation was dietetic or medical.

It is not known for sure how old the cultivation of the different plants are, and what exact role the monastic institutions played. In the example of fruits, there may be an indication in the names. Apple is called *epli,* an old Norse word, while the names for pears, plums, and cherries in the Nordic languages all are borrowed from Latin or romance languages.

The medieval law books have many rules about horticulture and particularly about theft of garden products. It seems as if many families—not least in the towns—grew vegetables for private use on garden plots, and this may have started long before the monks brought new plants with them from southern and central Europe.

Milk

Very important in the Scandinavian diet were the milk products from cows, ewes, goats, and reindeer. Caesar writes in his history of the wars in Gallia that the Germanic peoples live on milk, cheese, and meat,[7] and this was very true for the northernmost Germanic tribes.

The most important products were butter and cheese. Butter became a successful commercial product and was also exported at times. Being so valuable, it was only used for cooking in the wealthiest families and by peasants mainly for festive occasions. Lard, goose fat, and suet were used as substitutes for butter. Bread and porridge were enriched with spreads of different products such as sour milk, boiled skimmed milk, and liquid residues after the cheese and butter production, such as whey and buttermilk.

The early cheeses in Scandinavia, at least in the northern parts, were made from sour skimmed milk without the addition of rennet.

Drink

The only drink mentioned in *Rigsþula* is wine. The prestige of this drink is demonstrated in another mythological poem, *Grimnismál*, where wine is described as the only form of food and drink consumed by the god Odin. This was such an exclusive drink, so difficult to provide, that a Norwegian bishop asked the pope for permission to use beer in the Eucharist, but he was turned down.[8] Wine was very rare until the late Middle Ages, when it was served at feasts of the court, in aristocratic houses, and increasingly in city wine cellars.

Water was a natural drink where the supply of fresh and clean water was good, but in many areas the wells and creeks were polluted and the water a health danger. Daily drink in the northern areas with an important milk production was a mixture of water with sour (fermented) whey or buttermilk called *blande* (blend, mix). In the South where grain production was more widespread, ale of a low alcoholic content was a common drink. In Denmark the expression "food and ale" was synonymous with "food and drink."

Strong good ale was required for all great feasts, family occasions, and religious holidays. Ale commonly had been at the center of the celebrations of religious rites in the Norse religion and was continued with Christianity. Particularly before Christmas (the old yuletide) and weddings, the brewing of ale was considered not only a necessity but a duty. Imported beer was also consumed, and German beer had a very high prestige but not as high as mead and wine.

Mead was produced from fermented honey with spices added. Most of it was imported and, consequently, expensive. In one of the royal chronicles, *The Saga of King Sverri*, an incident from 1181 is related. King Magnus was in Bergen, many of the guests were served ale, and they were very upset when they learned that the royal guards were dining in a special room and served mead with the food.

CULINARY PREPARATIONS

Few sources from this period include detailed instructions on how the different foodstuffs were prepared for the table. There is reason to believe that many dishes from the popular peasant cuisine described under the early modern period had their roots in the Middle Ages, but there is little exact documentation. However, a collection of recipes from the thirteenth century survives, and this may throw some light on the culinary practices of the Scandinavian elite.

The recipes are found in small manuscript leaflets, and they are among the oldest in European cookbook history.[9] There are only about 35 recipes, very little compared to contemporary manuscripts in other parts of Europe with more than a hundred recipes. Four copies are known of this particular cookbook, two in medieval Danish, one in Icelandic, and one in Low German. The original is thought to have been written by a doctor from northern Germany who had studied in Montpellier in the south of France, a famous center of medical science.[10] The recipes seem to be influenced by the Mediterranean cuisine of that period.

The cookbook gives instructions for the preparation of almond dishes, sauces, dishes based on milk and eggs, and dishes with chicken and deer marrow. The absence of fish, game, and other meats may be explained by the medieval habit of spit-roasting. The accompanying sauces served to give the dishes their aroma, and the sauces in the cookbook may serve this function. The recipes are brief as most recipes from that time, meant as suggestions to professional cooks in princely courts or aristocratic houses. The following examples give an idea of the form and the contents:

How One Makes Almond Oil

One should take almond kernels and place them in hot water to peel them and then dry them over hot coals with a cloth and pound them in a mortar and squeeze them through a cloth. The oil is good for all kinds of foods.

How One Prepares a Sauce for Lords

Take cloves and nutmeg, cardamom, pepper, cinnamon, that is, *canela*, and ginger, all in equal amounts, except that there should be twice as much *canela* as the other spices, and throw in an equal amount of toasted bread, and pound them all together, and grind with strong vinegar, and place it in a jar.

How One Prepares a Dish Called White Mush

One should take whole milk, and well-crushed wheat bread and a beaten egg, and well-pounded saffron, and let it boil until it becomes thick. Then place it on a dish, and throw in butter, and sprinkle with powder of cinnamon. It is called white mush (hwit moos).

How One Prepares a Pie of Deer Marrow

One should boil bones of deer, and crack them open when they are cold, and make a dough of wheat flour and cold water, and add to it salt and pepper and cinnamon, and add the marrow and make pie of it, and bake it in a hot oven.

A Different Way to Prepare Chicken

One should cut a chicken in pieces and grind pepper and cinnamon and cardamom, all in equal amounts, and take the white of hard-boiled eggs and cut it small. And add the whole egg yolk, saffron and vinegar, and thicken it with egg yolks and salt it adequately.

The dishes were meant for people of considerable wealth, since almonds and oriental spices had to be imported. For most people, seasoning came from domestic herbs or roots such as marjoram, cumin, anise, onion, and angelica. Pepper, ginger, and other spices from Asia were out of reach for ordinary people. But they were known, which is demonstrated in medieval law texts about the sale of spices and fines for adulteration. These exotic spices are also mentioned in inventories from royal courts in the fourteenth century.

FOOD HABITS

Meal Times and Rules

The two principal meals from old were the morning and the evening meals. The first took place at the beginning of the day but was later put off till mid-morning, and a smaller meal was served at daybreak. Another light meal might be served in the afternoon. The names of the meals and their relative importance changed with regions and over the centuries. At the end of the Middle Ages, a so-called mid-day meal consumed at noon was introduced.

Food might be eaten anywhere, for example, by the fireplace where it had been prepared. In bigger households the meals were served at a long table, where the seating was important. The master of the house had his place in the "high seat," either at the end of the table or at the middle of one of the sides, and people were seated near him according to rank.

In rich houses, as in the aristocracy, the guests were given water to clean themselves before eating. The elegant table described in Rigsþula was representative of a very small elite only. Table linen was not common, but in the fourteenth century a wealthy farmer is reported to have given his daughter a fringed tablecloth as dowry.

Wooden cups, spoons, plates, and bowls were common, but from the thirteenth century pewter tableware was imported, and silver was very rare.

Fast Days and Lenten Food

The (Catholic) Church in Scandinavia followed the dietetic rules established by Rome, with abstinence from animal food certain days in the week and certain periods during the year. Lent, the long fast before Easter, was the most important during the year, beginning Ash Wednesday and ending Easter Eve, but there were also fasting periods before Christmas and other Church holidays.

Abstinence from meat did not always imply frugality and abstinence from pleasure, particularly not among the elite, even the clerical elite. Detailed descriptions exist of the food served around 1500 in the household of Bishop Brask in Linköping, Sweden. On Christmas Eve, before the fast ended at midnight, he had a *maigre* (meager) meal consisting of cured salmon, salted herring, small boiled herrings, fried herrings with mustard, dried cod with raisins and almonds, fresh and dried pike and ling, apples and nuts.[11] Even if there is no trace of the elegant preparations from early Italian and French cookbooks of the Renaissance, this meal was well above the average diet in Scandinavia.

The Christian laws introduced in Scandinavia banned all flesh of horse, cat, and dog for human consumption and imposed heavy penalties on those who broke this law. Horse meat was eaten in pre-Christian Scandinavia and probably also consumed in religious rites.

EARLY MODERN PERIOD

The Kalmar Union between the Scandinavian kingdoms lasted until the 1520s when Sweden broke out. For almost three centuries to come Scandinavia would be dominated by the conflicts between two strong rival powers: Denmark-Norway, still in union under the Danish king and with North Sea possessions (Iceland, Faroe Islands) on one side, and Sweden (with Finland) on the other.

In both kingdoms the Protestant Reformation came out victorious in the early sixteenth century. The Catholic Church was replaced by national Lutheran churches under royal supremacy, a development that ended certain culinary traditions such as the regulation of fasting days.

Politically the period was characterized by rivalry between the king and the aristocracy. In the seventeenth century both kingdoms followed the

European trends and became absolutist. The dominant economic ideology in most of the period was mercantilism, but in the last part of the eighteenth century liberal ideas prevailed. The economic, social, and cultural ideas of the European Enlightenment gradually permeated intellectual life and practical politics: A new urban bourgeoisie secured power over much of the commercial businesses. The first towns had grown up in the Viking Age, particularly in the South, but towns now became more important and dynamic centers in the economy of the countries.

When the Napoleonic wars broke out, Denmark-Norway took the French side, Sweden the English side.

Regional and Social Differences in Cooking

The cuisine of the early modern time continued many of the medieval traditions. Some of the dishes and preparations described in this chapter were probably common long before the Middle Ages ended, but they are treated here because they are better documented in this period and were probably developed into their modern forms in the seventeenth and eighteenth centuries.

It is difficult to establish a valid menu for the whole region during the early modern period. The food was not the same in 1800 as in 1600. Trade increased the importation of foods and ingredients, many of them new to the Scandinavians. There were also important variations between regions, depending on their main food products. An extreme example is the situation in Iceland and a few places in northern Scandinavia where grain were so scarce that bread was hardly eaten at all. Rich in supply of fish and milk, people buttered bits of dried cod and ate it as bread.[12]

Apart from regional variations, big differences in food consumption still existed between the various social groups. There were differences in the *amount* of food consumed, but the court, the aristocracy, and rich merchants in towns and cities generally also had a more varied diet and enjoyed the more prestigious, exclusive, expensive, and often imported products, lobster and crawfish, game and birds, spices, sugar, and wines. Their preparation methods were also more differentiated, due to a better technology and foreign recipes. In addition, the elite differed from the ordinary citizen, who as a rule ate preserved foods, in its increasing taste for fresh meat and fresh fish, particularly for festive occasions.

The diet of the majority, living in rural areas or in small towns, was in general much simpler, based on homegrown products, and the cheapest and simplest of these products, that is, what was less attractive to the market and therefore cheaper. The dishes were hardly varied, partly because the food had to be prepared in a cauldron over open fire or on a flat stone or a griddle. It is significant that breads of different qualities sometimes were given names such as *lord's bread* or *master's bread* and *servant's bread* or *journeyman's bread*.

The social differences existed not only between a small elite and the rest of the people but between groups within the rural population. Rich farmers had more and better food, and some of them tended to pick up culinary habits from the elite. In contrast, laborers, servants, and different groups of landless poor had very little to add to the daily porridge. But with these reservations in mind, it is still possible to see some similarities in the way the different foodstuffs were prepared and combined in meals.

Most people in the countryside started the day with staple foods such as bread or porridge, combined with a fatter and often stronger flavored relish, either milk or cheese, or a salted herring, or a slice of cured meat. The last meal of the day was almost without exception a porridge. There were generally two other meals during the day, one simple, not too different from the breakfast, and one richer with meat or fish served with groats, roots, peas, or greens.

Preservation of Food

Most Scandinavians rarely ate fresh food. Preservation techniques are well known in many cultures, but they were of particular importance in the North where snow and low temperatures made it impossible for animals to graze in winter, and fodder was a constant problem. Every autumn a substantial part of the livestock was slaughtered, and a stock of meat and other victuals was secured. This is the background for the prominent role of the Scandinavian *storage culture*. Fishing was also a seasonal activity, and fish transported over long distances to be sold or consumed had to be preserved.

In regions with long and cold winters, it was possible to keep meat for long periods in frozen condition, as is documented in sources from the eighteenth century. In general the cold was not of any help, but rather a problem to be protected against with proper housing and warm dress. Meat and fish were therefore usually treated with special preservation techniques.

Drying is probably the oldest of these techniques, and in certain areas it was maintained as the only method because of scarcity in salt supply. The price of salt in some of the interior and more inaccessible regions sometimes increased to four times as much as the price on the coast. The

Sami population used drying for their reindeer meat and also for offal, for example, the heart.

Drying was used to preserve fish and meat, fruits and vegetables. Among the most successful fish products in European commerce were the stock-fish and halibut from northern Norway and pike from the rivers flowing into the Gulf of Bothnia, particularly the so-called Finnish pike.

But fish was not only dried for sale. In all coastal areas people continued the tradition of drying all sorts of fish, even herring, for their own consumption. They would hang the fish on poles, fasten them on the walls of their houses, or put them to dry on cliffs and beaches.

Drying in combination with salting was a method particularly successful when used on cod on the northwestern coast of Norway, and from the eighteenth century it ousted the stockfish from most countries in Europe.

Salting became more and more common, and salted herring continued to play a basic part in the Scandinavian diet. Cod and other fish were also salted.

Pork was well suited for salting, and salt pork, either dry salted or in brine, has been a very important element in Scandinavian cuisine, particularly in the southern regions. In Denmark goose meat was preserved by a light salting and made an attractive commercial product.

Fish and meat were also smoked, above all in the southern regions, while another special preservation technique through controlled fermentation of lightly salted fish was developed in the northern regions. Because of the strong smell many people considered that the fish was rotten, and an old name used in Dalarna, Sweden, *lundsfisk*, meant exactly this.

Food was also preserved in a strong vinegar solution, sour beer, whey, or lingonberry juice.

MILK AND CHEESE

Milk was produced in all parts of Scandinavia, but cattle were relatively more important in the northern areas and Iceland, where the diet consequently was more lacto-animal than in the South.

A characteristic feature of dairying in the northern area is the mountain grazing in summer. The background for this is the short and hectic grazing period that had to be taken advantage of as efficiently as possible. While the fields around the farms were used for production of hay—fodder for the winter—the animals were brought up to higher mountain areas where the grass was extremely rich and nutritious. In these more or less remote places small mountain farms were erected, called *fäbod* in Sweden, *støl* in western Norway, and *sæter* in eastern

Norway. The hard work was done by women, dairymaids, who milked the animals and prepared different products from the milk.

Milk was not drunk fresh or sweet as today; this only became common in the twentieth century. Sour or curdled milk of different qualities and consistencies was used with porridge and gruel and even with meat and fish dishes.

Most milk was from cows, but milk from ewes and nanny goats (and reindeer among the Sami) was also used, mainly for cheeses. A special dish of sour milk from ewes, eaten in southern Sweden and eastern Denmark, seems to go back to the late Middle Ages. Sweet milk was boiled and set aside to curdle and was kept for consumption in winter. The name *syltemjölk/syltemælk* (salted milk) indicates that salt may have been added earlier, possibly to help preservation.

The most important milk product was butter and some exclusive cheeses. These served to pay for taxes, duties, or tithes or were sold to give cash for the necessary products that could not be made on the farm: salt, spices, tools, and later coffee.

Cheeses

Cheese was produced in Scandinavia as elsewhere in Europe by adding rennet to the milk, heating it until it curdled, and then separating the curd from the whey. The fresh cheeses might be sprinkled with spices and put aside to dry.

In the North, more specifically in the *fäbod/sæter* areas, another and probably older method was followed. The basis was sour milk that coagulated without the help of rennet. The process was brought about during the heating by the lactic acid itself. The curd was taken out of the whey and put in a cloth and shaped into certain forms. Some of these cheeses were eaten relatively fresh, others after months of storing.

The production of firm, yellow cheeses in the Swiss and Dutch tradition was introduced on big estates in Sweden and Denmark from the seventeenth and eighteenth centuries, but large-scale industrial production only came with the dairy factories in the nineteenth century.

Cheeselike Dishes

In the southern parts of Sweden *ostkaka* (cheesecake) was made from the curds that separated from whey when rennet was added to the milk and heated. The curd was mixed with cream, sugar, eggs, and almonds and baked in an oven.

In Denmark thick sweet milk mixed with buttermilk was heated and put aside so the whey could drip off. Then it was smoked and named *rygost* (smoked cheese).

In Norway several variations of a curdled milk dish were produced, some for daily use, others for festive occasions. The preparation was similar to the cheese-making process until the milk curdled. Spices, raisins, eggs, and sugar might be added. The names differed from region to region, but *gomme* and *dravle* were the most widely used.

A Special Scandinavian Milk Culture

As a general rule the sour milk in Scandinavia curdled naturally or by addition of old sour milk. But there also exists a special milk culture comparable to kefir and yogurt in other societies. The milk is made by adding remains from the preceding production in a similar process to the way sourdough is used in baking. It was called *tätmjölk* in northern Sweden (and western Finland) and *tettemjølk* in Norway. The names refer to a plant, the *tätgrass/tettegras*,[13] which in popular tradition was thought to bring about the fermentation in the milk. The milk has a consistency that makes it possible to form it into long threads or ropes, and it is called thick milk, long milk, or sticky milk.

Buttermilk and Whey

After the production of butter and cheese, the thin liquid residues were put to culinary use. The residue after the churning, buttermilk, was mixed with flour and made into a porridge or gruel. Culinary use of whey, which was left after the cheese production, had a central position in the old diet in Norway and Northern Sweden. Whey butter and whey cheese were used on porridge and gruel or as a sandwich spread instead of butter in the less fortunate parts of the population. The whey cheese from sour milk was the cheapest one, but so hard that it was impossible to cut slices from it. Chips had to be scraped off. The sour whey was also used as a substitute for vinegar in various dishes.

BREAD

Scandinavian breads were of many sorts and forms: round or oblong, thin or thick, leavened or unleavened. They were baked from many different grains. Barley and oats were common in the North, rye in the South, whereas wheat bread—in the early modern period as in the Middle Ages—was primarily eaten by the elite, at festival time, and in church rituals (holy bread). Iceland had to import most of its grains, normally Danish rye.

Unleavened breads were baked on stones (slabs of rocks), griddles, or small frying pans. They had in common that they could not be kept for more than a few days. It is possible that the need for preservation was one of the motivating forces behind the very thin dry and crisp breads that could be stored for years. They are typical of northern Scandinavia, and their capacity to maintain a good quality over time is reported in different written sources since the Renaissance.

In northern Scandinavia the grains had been ground on manually operated rotary querns, but in the late Middle Ages the millstones worked by stream water were introduced, and larger amounts of grain could be ground in a shorter time. But these mills depended on a good flow of water, which mainly occurred in spring and in autumn. And these two seasons were just the seasons for the baking of the thin crisp bread.

Oven-Baked Bread

Bread with sour dough and later with other leaveners has a long history but had certain limits in Scandinavia, both regional and social. There were certain experiments with a simpler technology, types of primitive "ovens." Leavened bread was baked between iron sheets, or on a sheet inside a pot turned upside down and covered with embers, or in a pot with a tight lid. But the quality could not be compared with that of bread baked in real ovens.

In the northern parts of Scandinavia, where the crisp flatbread was daily fare, the leavened oven-baked bread was considered a special festive bread. The Swedish naturalist Linnaeus calls it a "bread for guests." But in southern Sweden and in Denmark this rye bread was the daily bread. Here the wheat bread was used for festive occasions.

The rye in the oven-baked bread was often mixed with barley for economic reasons. It was baked once a month, more often in the summer. In these areas grains could be ground more often, because in addition to water mills they had windmills, typical of the flat plains of northwestern Europe. When stored, these breads got gradually drier and drier, even if they were carefully kept in bags of cloth or in the grain bins. But dry breads were also more economical. To eat fresh bread was considered a luxury. Therefore new baking was started when there were still three large bread loaves left in the storeroom.

A special preparation was used to make leavened oven-baked bread more durable. This was particularly necessary for ships' crews on long voyages. The product offered was *kavring*, or *tvebak*, meaning "baked twice,"[14] and this also eventually became a popular bread in the rest of the population.

Breads and Cakes for Special Occasions

Many small breads, cakes, and cookies were prepared for special occasions. One way to make ordinary breads more exclusive was by coating them with cream, milk, or egg. The Swedish *vispebröd* (whip breads) were small, thin flatbreads made from rye flour and coated with egg whites to get a shiny surface. Norwegian *gullbrød* (golden breads) were thin flatbreads coated with a mixture of egg and milk before the baking had been finished. Danish *knepkager* (crack cakes) were normally baked of barley flour mixed with fat or butter and put in the oven covered with a batter made from egg yolks and cream. They were very hard and cracked when eaten.

Waffles are well known since the Middle Ages in Europe and became very popular in Scandinavia. Along with waffles, many other wafer-thin cakes were prepared the same way, between two iron sheets with different patterns engraved. Another European tradition imported to Scandinavia was the deep-frying of small cakes with beautiful patterns or special shapes. Small hard *pepper cakes* and *pepper nuts*, a kind of ginger cakes, had been imported from Germany to Scandinavia since the sixteenth century, but were also baked in private homes. The small crisp *kringle*, like a German *pretzel*, was baked in the ovens after having first boiled in water.

Bread from Bakeries

Guilds of professional bakers existed in the late Middle Ages in some Scandinavian towns, and the authorities strictly regulated product offerings, prices, and categories.[15] In Denmark the bakers were required by law to have at least three varieties available: (1) ordinary rye bread called *coarse bread*, round or oblong; (2) a finer *sift bread* of sifted rye flour, also called *skonrok* after a German word meaning "fine rye"; and (3) white wheat bread.

The German influence in this trade was strong. Many bakers were educated in Germany, as were so many other artisans at that time, and German breads were imported.

OTHER GRAIN DISHES

Porridge

Porridge has been one of the fundaments of Scandinavian food culture from prehistoric times until the twentieth century. In some areas it was served two or three times a day, eventually as a thinner soup, or gruel. The quality depended on the ingredients, the type of grain as well as the liquid in which it was boiled. The most exclusive porridges were made from grains of rice or semolina, but such porridges were only for festive occasions. Porridges based on grits were in general more exclusive than flour porridges, which prices may explain: pearl barley was more than twice as expensive as barley flour.

Barley flour boiled in water, or *water porridge*, was the most simple. Milk and cream were only used for Christmas and special holidays. But liquids were not only something in which the grain was boiled. Different liquids were also added to the porridge itself. Most common was sour milk. When the porridge was served warm, freshly prepared, the milk was cold, but when the remainders of the porridge was served cold, at the next meal or even the next day, the milk was warm.[16] In areas where the supply of milk was scarce, other liquids might be used, for example, ale in the grain-growing areas in the South.

Jumble, Kams, and Dumplings

Very widespread and probably with roots far back in the Middle Ages or earlier were dishes combining grains and fat in various ways.[17] One of the simplest was prepared in many areas under the name of *mulle, mölja, mylja* (jumble). It consisted of bread put in a bowl with fat. The kind of bread varied with the different regions: crisp in the North and soft in the South. The liquid was either milk or broth. Meat broth was most common, but in certain coastal areas they used fish broth with the fish liver added.

A group of flour dishes more like porridge was called *kams*, after a verb meaning "to knead." Flour was kneaded with fat of a type easily available at the local level, for example, milk, blood, leaf fat, seal blubber, cod liver, or roe. Sometimes the whole mass was put into the head of a fish and boiled. Many of the names of these dishes contain the word for "head": in Norway *kamshau,* in Sweden *kampelhuvud,* in Denmark *kroppehoved,* corresponding to similar dishes in the North Sea area, for example, the Scottish *crappit head*. It is possible that these dishes go back to before the era of bread baking, because they represent a simpler use of grains.

Balls or dumplings with a firmer consistency are related to similar dishes in other parts of Europe, particularly the German-speaking area, something many of the names indicate. They are made of flour mixed with water or some sort of fat, boiled in salt water, milk, or another liquid. They were often eaten with meat or fish; they had, in other words, the same function as bread.

OTHER POPULAR DAILY DISHES

Many simple dishes were based on products grown on the farm or available in the local environment. A very important period was the slaughtering season. The *storage culture* in the rural economy meant that these animals were killed when they were at their fattest, in the autumn when the summer grazing ended. Pork and geese might be fed extra until November or December so they were ready for consumption at Christmas.

The meat was partly for private consumption and partly a means to provide an income for the household. The most exclusive parts of the animals were in great demand and sold to butchers in the towns or directly to wealthy people or to industrial entities, for example, mines with German engineers used to a continental cuisine. Some parts were sold fresh; other parts were salted, for example, hams and geese. Also meat, blood, and offal from seals and whales were prepared as dishes similar to those for the meat of domestic animals.

Offal Dishes

Most of the meat that the peasants kept for themselves was preserved after the methods described earlier. But some parts, particularly internal organs, were not suited to the traditional preservation techniques without special preparations. These preparations used to be done in connection with the killing, and they meant very busy times on the farms.

One of the most common ways of using the offal and extra tough parts of meat was to chop it or mince it and put it in animal guts, stomach bags, or other forms of sausage casings. Spices were added, often also groats, and the sausages were put in brine and later dried. That much of what was put away in such a manner would not have been eaten otherwise can be concluded from the many proverbs, such as this from Denmark: "You ought to know well the housewife whose sausages you eat."

Heart, liver, and kidney were also chopped and boiled with spices and apples to a dish called *finker* (finches). Meat from the head of swine was boiled and chopped and made into press brawn, a sort of brawn or headcheese spiced with pepper and cloves. The head and other meat of sheep were boned and rolled up into a brawn roll or collar and boiled. Meat from newborn calves, including head and feet, was boiled into a thick jellylike dish called *kalvost, kalvedans,* or *kalvesuss* in different parts of the region.

In Denmark the wings, feet, and neck of geese were used in a special rich soup, often with the addition of blood.

Blood Dishes

Blood was an important ingredient in the Scandinavian households and had to be taken care of immediately after the killing. It was mixed with groats and eaten as a soup or porridge as in the *kams* dishes, sometimes with lumps of meat as in a dish called *lummer*.

A very common use of blood, as of offal, was to make sausages, especially of pig's blood. The blood was poured into casings with flour or groats, dices of leaf fat, and spices or herbs, for instance, thyme or marjoram. The blood sausages were eaten cold or hot, often fried in a pan. Blood was also prepared without casings, as blood pancakes, blood puddings, or dumplings, where the blood was mixed with flour.

The culinary use of blood was widespread and not characteristic of the lower layers of society only. An early description of the importance of blood in the cuisine is given by a Polish officer who visited Denmark in the seventeenth century: "When they kill cattle, swine and sheep they don't waste a drop of blood, but pour it into a vessel with groats of oats or buckwheat. They fill this in the guts of the animal, boil it in a kettle, put the sausages in a circle around the head of the animal, take it to the table and enjoy it as a delicacy. Yes, even in aristocratic homes they behave like this, and I was served it until I felt disgust and finally said that it was not suitable for a Polish person to eat such things, because I would fall out with the dogs, since it was their food."[18]

The Sami people had a special method to preserve blood. They freeze-dried it and ground it into a powder, so it could easily be transported and made into dishes when mixed with liquids.

Soups

One very common dish was a soup or broth with meat or fish and some sort of vegetables. These soups have been common in most rural societies as they might be prepared in a single vessel and save expensive fuel that way. This did not mean that it necessarily had to be eaten as a soup. The dish consists basically of four ingredients: the broth, the meat (or fish), the fat coming up to the surface, and eventually vegetables. The fat was often skimmed and used for other purposes, for example, frying in a pan. The broth was sometimes drunk separately, and the firm ingredients were eaten by hand.[19]

The meat and fish used in these dishes was normally salted or dried. In poor homes where very little meat or fish was available, perhaps only a piece of fat or a marrow bone, the expression was "to boil a soup on a nail."

As a general rule people made little use of vegetables. Greens of most sorts were called *grass* or *cow's food* and not considered worth eating. The more substantial roots and pulses (legumes) were more highly regarded. There was a certain difference between the South where peas, beans, and curly kale were used and the North where turnips and rutabaga were the most common.

RURAL FEASTS

As in all rural societies, festivals played an important part and consumed much energy and resources. Among the religious holidays, Christmas, Easter, and Whitsun were most solemnly celebrated, while many of the saints' days had lost in importance since the Reformation.

Christmas

Food played an extremely central role at Christmas, from Christmas Eve until the sixth of January. Everything had been carefully prepared. During slaughtering time good cuts were put aside for the holiday, pigs and geese were fed extra in the autumn months, and cakes and festival breads were baked in advance. This was a holiday with much food, but also with food of high quality: the fattest meat, the finest fish, and the best bread.

Porridge and preserved fish were ubiquitous, possibly relics from the Catholic times when they represented the *meagre* food. But fasting habits had waned since the Reformation, and fat food was already eaten on Christmas Eve.

Easter and Whitsun festival food was much the same as for Christmas, but the feasts did not last for as many days. Not much is known from this period about food during the other holidays.

Festivals and Rites of Passage

The most important feasts in addition to Christmas were held in connection with important transitions in life, the rites of passage, notably birth, marriage, and death. The festivals were held within a religious framework, but even if the central rituals were followed in the church, the festivals had their own vigorous life in the homes before and after.

The baptism ceremony was an important event, but just as important and much older was the visit to the house just after childbirth. The visitors were relatives and neighbors, always represented by the women in the households, never the men. They brought different kinds of food as presents, most often porridge, called *bed porridge*. This tradition may go back to the time before the Middle Ages and the Christian era, because in the Faroe Islands the porridge is called *nornagrautr* (norn porridge), the norns being deities in the Norse religion who span the life threads and were protectors of the midwives.[20]

To bring food as gifts was even more usual at weddings and funerals. The number of guests might exceed a hundred and in the less densely populated areas with bad roads, particularly in the North, they could last for several days. The first day the guests arrived, many of them from distant places and therefore were given a place to sleep. The next day everybody went to church, often many miles from the home and only reachable by boat or horse. The dinner was served at the return from church, and the guests stayed at least until the next day.

A lot of food was needed, butter, cheese, fish, meat, porridge, cakes, and so on. Very few in the pre-industrial rural societies had the means to provide all this alone, and an ingenious system of give and take had developed, so that the giver knew that he would be paid back when it was his turn. This was of course only possible for land-owning farmers; landless laborers and servants had to settle for more modest kinds of celebration.

Butter and cheese were not always eaten but put up in pyramids as table decorations. Some of the butter lumps were sculptured, an example of popular art in Norway and Sweden. The butter was formed in wooden molds or cases with carved patterns of flowers and animals on the inside. The cases had hinges, so they could be removed after a while, when the impressions were left in the butter.[21]

Some Swedish descriptions explicitly emphasize that the pyramids were meant to stand on the table as an adornment and should not be touched:

First illustration of flat bread baking in Scandinavia, 1555. From Olaus Magnus, Historia de gentibus septentrionalis, Rome, 1555.

"The cheese and butter are brought back home after it has served as show-pieces."[22]

In Denmark and southern Sweden there are descriptions of the *salt meat plate*. In 1620 a French visitor to Denmark remarked that even if there were a lot of game in the country, a large plate was served with ham, salted and smoked meat, pig's ears and trotters and several sausages.[23] A Dane who returned home after a longer stay in southern Europe remarked that he started to sweat at the sight of these plates. It was only in the homes of gourmets that fresh food was served, he said, because this was "against the old Danish custom."[24]

URBAN MENUS

The population in the towns was not a homogeneous group but showed important social, economic, and cultural differences. On the top was a small elite (see Chapter 2), which was followed by a middle class of arti-sans and shopkeepers (burghers) with city privileges, and beneath them the majority (50–75%) consisting of working people of all kinds: journey-men, apprentices, errand boys, removers, shop assistants, servants, maids, sailors, soldiers, and many others.

Little is known about how these last groups prepared their food, but there was certainly not much of it, and it was hardly very elegantly cooked. The middle classes also probably ate relatively simple food, except for special occasions. Among the sources to the culinary practice in towns, the most complete are the detailed instructions given to the management of institutions, boarding schools, for example. Most likely the menu lists reflect what was considered a correct daily diet within the middle classes, where these schools recruited their pupils.

The *menus* list which dishes should be served for the two main meals. Apart from a light breakfast there was one meal at noon and another in the early evening. As a general rule the meals seem to consist of two dishes, one simple based on cereals or vegetables and one with meat or fish. In the institutions, as in the private homes, the amount of fish and meat compared to the other ingredients indicate different levels of wealth or poverty. In many homes only a simple porridge was served as an eve-ning meal.

One example of a menu from an institution is a list of dishes to be served for schoolboys in Roskilde, Denmark, in 1668:[25]

Sunday, Tuesday and Thursday had the same food: kale with pork at noon and buckwheat porridge and beef in the evening.

Mondays and Wednesdays the meal at noon consisted of a gruel (buckwheat or barley) and fish (herring or salt cod), the evening meal of porridge and lamb.

Friday noon: peas and gooseflesh, evening: barley porridge and salt cod.

Saturday noon: boiled tripe and herring, evening: flour porridge and cod.

Another menu from the Cathedral School in Christiania (Oslo), Norway, from 1735 shows a similar structure with two main meals, each with two dishes, one of them a soup or porridge and one of them meat or fish.[26] The difference is that there is more roast meat and that the soups and porridges tend to be sweet, for example, with honey added. These two differences probably indicate a higher social level; among these pupils were also children of burghers with more wealth but not rich enough to have private tutors.

ELITE FOODWAYS

The court, the aristocracy, big landowners, rich merchants, and crown officials constituted an elite in the Scandinavian countries. They shared certain ideals, in gastronomy as well as in other matters, and they had access to a rich variety of food products. Many of them had meat from their own properties; oxen were slaughtered every second week and poultry when needed. They had vegetables and fruits from their own gardens, particularly from the eighteenth century onward when horticulture became increasingly popular in higher circles. They had fish from their own rivers or ponds, or it was delivered to them by fishermen's wives. Imported luxuries were purchased in the big cities or in the ports.

This elite had the necessary technology, for example, ovens for the baking of bread, tarts, pies, and cakes. They had wide hearths where birds, small game, and chunks of lamb and venison were roasted on a spit. They had professional cooks and servant maids for the most time-consuming kitchen tasks, for example, the chopping and mincing of meat for forcemeat to dumplings and stuffings. And they had cookbooks, more often than not foreign, or translated from French and German, diffusing new recipes into the Scandinavian cuisine.

Foods from the Woods

Game was treasured food. In most of Europe, and also in the southern parts of Scandinavia, hunting was a privilege for the landowning elite. The law in Denmark established that priests, civil servants, burghers, and farmers had no right to own hunting dogs or to shoot game. Poachers were severely punished. In the northern areas, with large uninhabited forests, hunting was more or less free for everybody, but since the upper classes paid good prices for game, the peasants preferred to sell what they shot instead of eating it. Particularly birds such as capercailzie, grouse, black grouse, and hazel grouse were in high demand and were exported from northern Sweden to Stockholm and from Norway to Copenhagen.

Berries had a similar exclusive position: blueberries, lingonberries, cranberries, and the yellow arctic cloudberries. Certain traditions existed for their use in the popular diet, partly as a remedy against scurvy. Lingonberries and cloudberries could be preserved without the use of sugar because of the acid contents. But gradually the berries became very popular with the elite, who made use of them the same way they did with the different garden berries, for wine, liqueurs, and jams. Many commoners sold berries they picked, and the most prestigious berries were exported from the northern areas to southern cities.

Feasts

Many members of the elite ate rather simple food on a daily basis but always rich and hearty meals. At festive occasions, however, there was great refinement, dinners and banquets with lots of dishes, and an extravagance that intended to show off wealth and status but was criticized by the moralists.

The gastronomy of the court was of course a model for all others. But it is possible to detect an increasing refinement in the food eaten at the Scandinavian court in the early sixteenth century and the early seventeenth century. During the reign of the Danish king Christian II (1513–1523), the menu is solid, but relatively simple. This is before the Reformation, and the distinction between meat days and fast days is still apparent. On meat days (Sunday, Tuesday, Thursday), the following dishes were served: roast beef, roast lamb, boiled hen, roasts of game, salted meat with mustard, cabbage, and pork. On the fish days, the following were served: herring, dried or salted fish, and boiled cod with eggs and butter.[27]

A hundred years later a detailed description of the food served at the Swedish royal court on February 8, 1623, shows that the king, who ate his lunch alone, could pick from the following dishes: roasts of turkey, goose, small birds, hazel hen, veal, beef, lamb, ox tongues, olives, almond soup, cherry soup, beef soup, beef with rice, lamb with mace, hen in broth, black deer tongue, black hare, egg cake, trout in wine, fermented bream, pike with pork, perch with butter, grouse pie, cherry mousse, and pastry.[28] The evening meal was an official dinner for the ambassador of the German duchy of Mecklenburg. Two services consisted of 24 dishes each, many of which were roasts, but they were prepared with somewhat different sauces, based on lemon or raisins.

In both periods, but particularly in the oldest one, it is possible to see a strong German influence, many centuries old. Gradually other influences made themselves felt, particularly from the seventeenth century onward. During its Golden Century, Holland exerted a strong influence over the southern and western parts of Norway, for example, in Bergen, where many Dutch words entered the language, from the culinary field *snop* (sweets), *puspas* (hotch-potch), and *spekulasjer* (cookies).

The French influence was already strong in Sweden from the seventeenth century, when the philosopher Descartes came to Stockholm, invited by Queen Christina. The French culinary dominance can also be recognized in the names of dishes taken up in the Scandinavian cuisine: *kotelet, kompot, gelé, frikassé, ragu, saus,* and *sky (jus)*. In the eighteenth century the French influence was felt so strongly in Denmark that the great playwright Ludvig Holberg ridiculed the phenomenon in a comedy about a Francophile Dane who calls himself Jean de France, follows all French fashions, and says that if there were no French cook in Copenhagen, he would die of hunger.

With the Enlightenment the foreign influences became even stronger. Describing the society in general, it has been stated that the "styles and tastes of the cultivated came from the continent, especially France, Rome and England."[29] This was certainly true for gastronomy. The English influence was particularly strong in eastern Norway and on the Swedish west coast, demonstrated by the early use of tea in the Gothenburg area.

The Early Cookbooks

The first printed cookbooks in Scandinavian languages were in Danish (1616) and Swedish (1650). Until the mid-eighteenth century most of them were translations of foreign works, most of them German. Three Swedish and two Danish books were abridged and adopted versions of French books, but two of them were based on German translations instead of the French originals.

After the European Thirty Years' War (1618–1648), the German states were strongly influenced by French fashions in all fields, cuisine included, and this is reflected in the Scandinavian cookbooks of the period. The preparation methods are mainly French, and the names of the dishes are often given in French, probably because no similar dishes are known.

In the latter half of the eighteenth century, when cookbooks by Danish and Swedish authors are published, the French influence is still strongly felt, but recipes for simpler dishes based on local ingredients and cooking traditions are also included.

DRINK

As in the Middle Ages fermented whey and buttermilk mixed with water (*blanda*) was a daily drink in the northern areas. In the South ale with low-alcoholic content was the daily drink. In all areas a stronger and more potent ale was brewed for Christmas and family celebrations.

German beer and ale, considered to be of a higher quality than the Scandinavian ones, was imported to the towns. Mead was still drunk at festivals in the early eighteenth century but soon lost out completely in the competition with wine. Wine became increasingly the festive drink of the elite and was also made the basis for mixed drinks with sugar and spices.

Strong spirits under the name of *aqua vitae* were introduced in the Renaissance, first as a medical remedy sold by apothecaries but soon as an exclusive drink among the affluent. The spirits reached the popular classes in Denmark in the sixteenth century and in Sweden and Norway in the seventeenth century and became a notable social problem in all three countries in the eighteenth century. Spirits, either distilled in Scandinavia from grain or imported, were used for different liqueurs and mixed drinks containing sugar and juice from fruits and berries.

Tea, coffee, and chocolate were new drinks introduced in the sixteenth century and made into daily drinks for the elite in the eighteenth century.

NINETEENTH AND EARLY TWENTIETH CENTURY

During the nineteenth and early twentieth centuries, Scandinavia went through profound changes in demography, economy, political system, social and cultural relations, and manners, diet included.

A strong population growth led on the one hand to emigration of three million Scandinavians, most of them to the United States, and on the other hand to a rapid urbanization. The population of Copenhagen increased in the nineteenth century from 150,000 to 370,000, Stockholm from 80,000 to 300,000, Oslo (Christiania / Kristiania) from 10,000 to 250,000, and Reykjavik from 475 to 6,500. This growth had a great effect on the food culture, with new restaurants, cafés, and food stores.

Democratic systems were established within constitutional monarchies. Suffrage was gradually widened to all groups, women included; parliamentary and local elected government were introduced; and the political process was led by parties, a free press, and strong popular movements and organizations.

Economy

This period is characterized by a rapid industrialization. New communications, railroads, and steam engines helped to build the economy and were crucial for the imports of cheaper consumer goods, not least sugar, flour, and meat. Distribution of foodstuffs was taken care of by a network of general stores in the rural areas. Agriculture became less and less important in the total economy, except in Denmark, where agricultural products were produced for export.

Agriculture went through efficient modernization in the nineteenth century, with better livestock because of new breeding methods, better yields because of crop rotation and the use of fertilizers, and later mechanization. One of the important new machines was the cream separator, which made the work easier and the exploitation of the milk more efficient.

Social Groups

The crown officials who represented the central powers on the regional or local level (civil administrators, judges, tax collectors, bishops, and priests) still constituted an elite together with the aristocracy and rich landowners. They were easily recognizable by their big houses, carriages, dress, and lavish dinners. These dinners were held in large dining rooms, furnished with chairs and tables of the most modern style, and the banquet table was laid with silver and glass and porcelain from Meissen or Limoges or one of the new factories in Scandinavia.

It was a stratified society where everybody had to be aware of his or her place. But during the nineteenth century a new rich middle class demanded to be heard, and a growing body of white-collar officials and employees wanted their share of the increasing prosperity and political decision making.

Differences between rich and poor had always existed in the rural communities. But there were of course also others in the middle, and in the nineteenth and twentieth century a strong group of farmers with a relatively high standard of living developed in the most fertile agricultural areas.

The rural poor consisted of the cottagers who leased small plots of land from farmers and had to work hard and long hours for it, the itinerant workers who had no firm employment but worked as seasonal labor, and the servants at the farms, often young men and women from the cottages but also from the richer farms, where the oldest brother was the heir to the farm. From all these small and poor groups came many of the recruits to industry in the twentieth century.

The ever-stronger working class put forward their demands through trade unions and social liberal and socialist parties, and by the mid-twentieth century the welfare state had made them part of a common culture by reducing social inequality.

A Changing Diet

Scandinavia came out of the Napoleonic wars with a diet for the majority that was not too different from the one in preceding centuries. Around 1815, 90 percent of the population still lived in rural areas and had agriculture as their main occupation. They ate preserved food (dried cod, salted herring, dried mutton, smoked geese, salted pork), bread and porridges, soups with pulses, roots and grits, and they had curdled milk dishes and fresh cheeses. There were regional varieties of course, more milk products in the North and more use of beer in the South, soft leavened rye bread in the South and crisp barley bread in the North, more beef in the North and pork and goose meat in the South, more dried products in the North and more smoked products in the South. But it was basically a traditional, popular cuisine, distinctly different from the cuisine of the elite and to a certain degree also from popular urban cookery.

People started their day with bread or porridge accompanied by a relish of fat or proteins. The last meal of the day was almost without exception a porridge, as in the centuries before. The two other meals of the day would have a more substantial part of meat or fish.

During the late nineteenth and early twentieth century this Scandinavian cuisine changed in a fundamental way: It became more uniform. This change toward uniformity does not mean that the social differences disappeared. There was still an elite enjoying food of the best quality and luxuries from abroad and a growing middle class imitating the fashions of the elite. The average peasant or town dweller could never hope to eat as well as them, but they gradually turned to the same foodstuffs and above all to their preparation methods.

This development was caused partly by lower prices on several of the imported goods and partly by industrialization, which made a new technology accessible to a large segment of the population. But there was also a question of cultural diffusion; new recipes were picked up in schools, from cookbooks, and through practical experience.

Many young girls from the countryside worked as housemaids and cook maids in wealthy families in the towns or at the manors, and they returned home with new ideas, new attitudes, and new recipes. In the last decades of the nineteenth century, domestic science and household management were taught in elementary schools and in courses for future housewives. At about the same time the cookbook industry exploded, and books were often adapted to the needs of simple households and poor families.

Even if there were still regional differences, it is possible to point out important similarities in the changes that took place within this period:

- potatoes served as basic staple with meat and fish
- more fresh (or canned) fish and meat
- meat dishes were more often fried
- increased consumption of fruits and vegetables
- more use of rye and wheat
- more oven-baked breads and cakes
- less use of porridge
- new and more varied sandwich spread
- margarine as substitute for butter
- more use of sugar
- coffee as a daily drink

Potatoes

One of the most revolutionary changes in the Scandinavian food culture was the introduction of the potato. It secured a more prominent position in the diet here than in any other area outside Ireland. A statistical survey from 1896 showed that in Norway the consumption of potatoes per person per year was 144 kilos (315 pounds) and in Paris 22 kilos (48 pounds).[30]

Culinary use of the potato began in the latter half of the eighteenth century, but only during the first part of the nineteenth century did a real breakthrough for potatoes as popular food take place. The slow process is explained by the fact that this root, as elsewhere in Europe, was considered as a surrogate for grain, not as a new valuable foodstuff. Because potatoes were meant to substitute for grain, people first made flour of them. But they gradually understood that the roots might be eaten boiled and eventually mashed and served as a staple in hot meals with fish or meat, where bread earlier had been the common accompaniment.

In the early years potatoes had a certain image as the poor man's food, but very soon recipes appeared in the cookbooks for the preparation of potato soup, potato pudding, potato stew, and even so-called French-fried potatoes. But there was a difference. The wealthy ate them as one of the many dishes that contributed to the variation of their diet. For poor people potatoes constituted the center and basis of their diet.

The Cooking Stove

In the last part of the nineteenth century, the cast-iron stove invaded the kitchens of more and more homes in Scandinavia. The stove was fired with wood, later also with coal, and had an enclosed oven and a top plate with room for pots and pans. This new technology made it easier to prepare several dishes at the same time and facilitated meal preparation without the help of maids.

Danish cast iron stove. From the catalogue of N.A. Christensen & Co, Iron Foundry, Denmark.

One of the important changes in the cuisine was the preparation of sauces. In popular cuisine it had been usual to put a bowl with fat, milk, broth, mustard, or vinegar on the table, and everybody could dip a piece of fish or meat in this liquid to give it taste. The new sauces were made after French and continental models, gravy thickened with flour and butter, and they were served at the table in a sauceboat or directly on the plate.

At about the same time the use of fats for cooking changed. Production of margarine started in the 1870s and substituted for the different fats that had been used traditionally, lard, goose fat, tallow, suet, and to a certain degree the expensive butter.[31]

Dishes of fried or roast pork became increasingly popular, especially in Denmark. In the sixteenth century pork was 150–300 percent more expensive than beef, but around 1900 this had changed, and ordinary Danes ate pork at least once a week, more often in the countryside. In the other Scandinavian countries pork became more accessible as well, but later than in Denmark.

In the southern areas where the status of pork had diminished, the middle and upper classes appreciated the more expensive good cuts of beef and veal, and they prepared them in and on the new stoves as gratins, roasts, fillet steaks, and chops, or in stews such as fricassee or ragoût, and in sauces such as *karri* (curry). In the areas where pork was scarce, mutton and lamb were appreciated; they could be served roasted, fried, or boiled with cabbage and roots in the type of hodgepodge dish known around the North Sea.

Birds had been eaten by the elite, while peasants kept hens in order to sell eggs and chickens. Only old and no-longer-productive hens were eaten, after hours of boiling in a *hønsekødsuppe*. Chickens were served as festival food same as duck, goose, turkey, and game birds.

Consumption of eggs, an earlier luxury, increased in the twentieth century. Eggs were more common in the South, where they were prepared as omelettes and other egg dishes.

Game still had high prestige, and roasts of deer, elk, reindeer, and game birds were prepared for banquets among the elite.

The Meat Grinder

Technological innovations also made forcemeat more available for an increasing number of people. Until the last part of the nineteenth century servants in large kitchens chopped and minced meat with different special knives. But with the introduction of the mechanical meat grinders at reasonable prices, a growing number of families could prepare dishes based on forcemeat.

Chopped and ground meat was used in sausages, which now became much finer in consistency. But more important was the success of some dishes that had been eaten only in wealthy households earlier, such as meatballs and ground-meat patties.

Fish

Much salted fish was still eaten, both herring and klipfish, but it became more common to serve fresh fish boiled, poached, fried, or baked. The heads of fish were particularly enjoyed in some areas and reserved for the husband, the head of the family. Apart from this symbolic meaning, it is worth noting that the head normally was the fattest part of the fish, important at a time when fat was judged valuable. In central Sweden the head of large bream was extra sought after, but also pike. In northern Norway the same was true for the head of halibut, in the rest of the country cod's head.

Fruits and Vegetables

A lot of vegetables were grown in the kitchen gardens on the big properties of aristocrats and crown officials: peas, parsley, carrots, spinach, beetroots, cucumber, asparagus, horseradish, beans, celery, leeks, salads, cabbage, onion, shallots, cauliflower, kohlrabi, and many others. But in the population as a whole the consumption of such products was minimal. The majority ate kale, peas, rutabagas, turnips, and potatoes. A statistical survey from 1896 found that Norwegians ate 10 kilos (22 pounds) of vegetables per person per year, compared to 118 kilos (260 pounds) eaten by people in Paris.[32]

But at about this time things were beginning to change. Horticulture became a widespread activity, not only in the countryside but in the gardens of suburban villas, in the small allotment gardens owned by townspeople, and in the school gardens. Professional gardeners started delivery of a much wider selection of vegetables to markets and general stores.

Some vegetables were used in soups or stewed in milk sauces, but many of the products were not consumed immediately. They were canned and bottled according to modern preservation methods, often in vinegar and spices. Pickled gherkins and sweet-and-sour beetroot were popular trimmings with cold as well as hot meals.

Fruits and berries from gardens and forests were preserved in sugar. A decrease in the price of sugar, partly a result of the newly introduced cultivation of sugar beet in Denmark and Sweden, made it possible to prepare a series of new dishes. A sweet soup with fruit syrup and sugar, eventually with groats added, was popular all over. Prunes were also popular for this kind of stewed fruit, and one recipe entered an American cookbook in 1896 under the name *Norwegian Prune Pudding*.[33]

Different fruits had been preserved as marmalades and jams since the sixteenth century, for example, Seville oranges and quinces, but some of the northern berries were also well suited for this. They included black and red currants, strawberries, raspberries, and gooseberries from the garden, lingonberries, blueberries, cranberries, and cloudberries from the forests and moors.

Jams were from the beginning very popular with elite women, who served them with a glass of wine. In the nineteenth century jams were served with small cakes and cookies, but lingonberry and red currant jams were also commonly served with roasts and forcemeat balls. In the twentieth century all these jams became common as spreads on sandwiches.

Open Sandwich

Bread and butter form an old and well-known combination in northern Europe, but in the twentieth century this combination took on a new importance with the use of many more spreads beside the butter. The words *smørrebrød* and *smørgås* are the terms generally used for what in English is called an *open sandwich*. A great variety of different spreads were used: slices of beef and pork sausages, salted or smoked, paste or mousse of pork liver, boiled ham, cheese, and canned fish products such as cod roe, smoked sprats in oil, and mackerel in tomato sauce.

Pastries

All different kinds of breads, cakes, and tarts that had been made in the old ovens now became possible to bake for the general public who had acquired a stove. At the same time new baking powder from the United States was introduced in letters from emigrants and in new cookbooks, many of which had whole sections with *Amerikanske kager* (American cakes) from the 1880s. Small cookies of every kind became popular for Christmas, but in the twentieth century also for weekends or with the afternoon coffee. Many big cakes were also baked in the oven, round or oblong or high towers, with chocolate, fruits, and berries mixed into the dough or put on top with cream as decoration. Special kinds of bread and cakes that required more professional skills were also bought in the bakeries.

Drink

The most important change in culinary habits in Scandinavia after 1800, apart from the establishment of the potato as the dominant staple food, was probably the use of coffee as a daily drink within all social groups. This process did not extend to the most remote areas until around 1900, but it started much earlier in the cities and towns.[34]

The elite had made coffee a daily drink during the eighteenth century, but already in the early nineteenth century this drink became popular among all classes in the cities and towns. The strong increase in coffee drinking coincided with the acknowledgment of alcohol consumption as a great social problem in Scandinavia. New temperance movements ran a very active propaganda against abuse of strong drink, and the existence of a stimulating but not inebriating alternative made the transition easier when free distilling was made illegal, in Norway in 1845 and Sweden in 1859.

Syrups made from garden fruits and berries were not only used in sweet dishes but were mixed with water into drinks. The strong restrictions on

Coffeemakers in Scandinavian cafés are like those in any other country, a long way from the first primitive grinders of the nineteenth century. Photo by Atle Koren.

distribution of alcoholic products and the strong position of the temperance movements in the twentieth century made these soft drinks an alternative to beer and wine. Even at festive dinners fruit juice was served with cooked fish and meat.

Bourgeois Dinner Parties

The new merchant classes during the nineteenth century mixed with crown officials and the aristocracy in dinner parties with a high culinary profile. In Europe the first part of the nineteenth century was the period when the serving changed from *service à la française*, where a large number of dishes were placed at the table, to *service à la russe*, where the dishes were served one after the other, such as today.

Whether the new serving method was introduced by Russian nobles in France around 1830 or by French cooks who had worked in Russia is disputed. There are also few known sources to this tradition. A German visitor is reported to have written about it in 1606.[35] One Russian food historian claims that the system started in the late eighteenth century,[36] while another one gives a menu for a dinner from that time, with twelve dishes, apparently served one by one.[37] The Russian service was observed in Scandinavia around 1800, by one visitor to Trondheim, Norway, and another to Christiania (Oslo).[38] In 1838 a French lady visiting Norway wrote to a friend in Paris that the food was served *à la russe*.[39]

What were they served? Printed menus from the 1870s onward show a similar pattern in all the countries, in fact, patterns that were also known in France and other European countries. The structure of a meal was almost without exceptions the following:

1. Small appetizers, oysters, or pies with lobster or game
2. Soup, often a turtle soup or mock-turtle soup
3. Fish, for example, salmon or cod
4. Boiled or cured meat, ham, or tongue
5. A light vegetable dish such as asparagus or artichokes
6. The roast, very often game birds or domesticated birds
7. Cheese, ice cream, desserts, fruits, or sweets

The general rule was to serve a different wine with each new dish. Madeira and sherry were served with the first two dishes, white wine (even sweet) with the fish, burgundy with the boiled meat, mineral water with the vegetables, and champagne was the favored drink with the roast.

From around 1900 the number of dishes became reduced. It was now common to serve either appetizers or soup, and the dish with boiled or cured meat was dropped. The vegetables were rather served as a side dish to the roast, and the roast tended to be more substantial, for example, saddle of lamb or roast beef. It followed as a matter of course that a rich red wine replaced the champagne.

In Scandinavia as elsewhere, white wine was served with fish dishes; the only exception was Norway. Foreign visitors to Norway are still surprised when they are given claret with cod. This seems to be a very special tradition, documented as early as 1860, when it was explained that while white wine was good with red fish, red wine was good with white fish.[40]

Festival Food

Religious holidays and family events were celebrated in rural areas much the same way as in earlier centuries until about 1900 or even longer. It is, however, possible to see an increasing diffusion of elite and urban habits into rural feasts, particularly in weddings when new trends and fashions were important to follow. In Sweden, for example, fresh fish was eaten instead of lutefisk, roast beef instead of boiled, macaroni pudding instead of stewed peas, and creams and soups made from fruit juices and sweetened with sugar. In Norway the old sweet milk dishes lost in importance to fancy cakes from the town baker.

This tendency to more uniform culinary habits was increased when urbanization brought more people from the countryside into direct contact with manners in towns and cities. From 1900 more families left to cafés, hotels, and restaurants the responsibility of meals after weddings and funerals, and this lead to an even stronger standardization of festival food.

This is not to say that the different regions and countries dropped their special traditions. Many dishes were thought of as special wedding dishes, and also in funerals some old food rituals were followed. Some of the Christmas culinary traditions were centuries old, but there are also examples of novelties from the nineteenth and twentieth centuries that have acquired the status of *traditional*.

Baked products of every kind were abundant. In Sweden a special tradition was the Christmas heap, different types of breads and cakes piled up in a big pyramid with the smallest and most exclusive on top. The breads were often decorated with religious symbols, or given the shape of a cross or of goats and pigs, important in older mythology.

A special sort of festivity in areas with grain production was the meal organized for servants and laborers by big farmers and landowners at sowing and harvesting times. This was considered part of the salary for the work done. Porridge of the best quality was considered a compulsory dish, and the traditions go back to before 1800.

Eating Habits

The transformation of habits in a European context is partly true also for the Scandinavian elite, who eagerly followed European fashions. This includes the use of individual forks, plates, and so on. Porridge was eaten from a common plate or bowl until about 1900 in certain remote villages.

Tableware of high quality was imported from abroad and used in manors from very early on and in the urban bourgeoisie before 1800. But most tableware was made from wood in the north and earthenware in the South until the second half of the nineteenth century.

Traditionally the farmer and his family ate at the same table as the servants and laborers. But from around 1800 rich farmers started to eat in a separate room. This was an imitation of the pattern established in manors, rectories, and other elite homes. The immediate consequence of this separation was a difference in the quality of the food itself.

Cookbooks

During the nineteenth century the cookbooks relate more and more to the new middle classes in Scandinavian towns and cities. The prefaces emphasize that they are alternatives to the earlier cookbooks, which are described as too influenced by foreign models and too extravagant in their recommendation of expensive ingredients. A few ingredients are also mentioned as "foreign" to Scandinavian taste: garlic, strong spices, and oil.

Economy—how to prepare good food without spending too much money and how to make the most effective use of the foodstuffs—was one of the most important aims in many of these books. Even if sophisticated dishes for formal dinners were included in these cookbooks, they also contained simpler preparations from the traditional cuisine, such as the Danish ale bread and the Swedish herring pudding.

Iceland and Norway got their first printed cookbooks in 1800 and 1831, respectively, and they reflected the Danish culture that had impregnated the elites in these countries for centuries.

The authors of the Scandinavian cookbooks in the first part of the period were housewives, housekeepers, or professional cooks in restaurants or royal kitchens. Around 1900 a new group emerged, the well-educated (female) teachers in the new school kitchens and schools of domestic science. The emphasis was still on economy, but another aspect became at least equally important: health. New developments and discoveries in medical science and chemistry brought forth a greater understanding of the dietary functions. and this new knowledge was channeled into the cookbooks.

At the same time the books became more didactic, with a systematic approach to the measures and cooking times and a more pedagogical and straightforward language. These changes served partly to facilitate a widening of the market to new social groups.

The first cookbooks for poor people had been printed in Sweden around 1800, but the mass production of such books started a hundred years later when the working classes became an important segment of the Scandinavian societies.

Typical of the twentieth century is diversification and specialization, cookbooks on budget meals and for great dinners, cookbooks with fruit recipes, rabbit recipes, tomato recipes, on French and Italian cuisines and

Title page of the first printed Scandinavian cookbook, published in Copenhagen, Denmark, in 1616.

"recipes from the whole world," cookbooks for singles, for men, and for vegetarians.

The production of cookbooks slowed during World War II but saw a new expansion from the 1980s onward. Today production is still big, but more and more people look up recipes on the Internet.

NOTES

1. The basic historical facts about the Viking era and the Middle Ages are taken from Knut Helle (ed.): *The Cambridge history of Scandinavia: Prehistory to 1520* (Cambridge: Cambridge University Press 2003). The description of food history until c. 1500 is based on the encyclopedic work *Kulturhistorisk leksikon for nordisk middelalder*, vols. 1–21 (Oslo: Det Norske Videnskaps-akademi/ Jacob Dybwad 1956–1977), and Fredrik Grøn: *Om kostholdet i Norge indtil aar 1500* (Oslo: Gyldendal Norsk Forlag 1926).

2. These mythological poems are collected in the *Edda*, often called the *Elder Edda*. One original version is printed in Jón Helgason: *Eddadigte II: Gudedigte* (Copenhagen: Munksgaard 1965), pp. 72–79.

3. *Norges Gamle Love*, vol. 2 (Christiania, 1846), p. 349.

4. The quotation is from *Gylfaginning*, the collection of myths made by the Icelandic historian Snorri Sturluson in the thirteenth century, but he is referring to an old Edda poem, *Grimnismál*.

5. *Mester Adam Canikens i Bremen Beskrifning om Swerige, Danmark och Norig* (Stockholm: Almqvist & Wiksell 1978), p. 36. This is a reprint of the Swedish translation, printed in 1718, of *Descriptio insularum aquilonarium*.

6. Jacob Langebek (ed): *Scriptores rerum Danicarum medii aevi* (Copenhagen: Godiche 1772–1878), vol. 4, p. 219.

7. Caesar: "[M]aiorque pars eorum victus in lacte, caseo, carne consistit." in *The Gallic War* (Cambridge, MA: Harvard University Press 2004), vol. 6, chap. 22.

8. Letter from Pope Gregor IX to Archbishop Sigurd of Nidaros, May 11, 1237, *Diplomatarium Norvegicum*, vol. 1 (Christiania: Malling 1847), p. 15.

9. Manuscripts no. 66, Ny Samling, Det Kgl Bibliotek, Copenhagen.

10. The manuscripts are presented and analyzed in Rudolf Grewe: "An early 13th century Northern European cookbook," in *Current research in culinary history* (Boston: The Culinary Historians of Boston, 1986), pp. 27–45.

11. Charles-Emil Hagdahl: *Kok-konsten som vetenskap och konst* (Stockholm: Em. Giron 1891), pp. 13–14.

12. "Viaggio del Magnifico messer Piero Quirino," in Giovanni Battista Ramusio: *Navigationi et viaggi*, vol. 2 (Venetia 1559), fol. 148r. Nils-Arvid Bringéus: "Matkulturen i jämförande perspektiv i 1700-talets Norrland," in *Maten meir enn halve føda!* (Arendal, Norway: Arendal Historielag, 1998), p. 29 (referring to a description from the eighteenth century by A. A. Hülpers).

13. *Tätgrass/tettegras* are classified as *Pinguicula vulgaris*.

14. *Kavring*, or *tvebak*, is similar to the biscuit (French *bis-cuit*).

15. Axel Steenstrup: *Dagligliv i Danmark i det syttende og attende århundrede: 1620–1720* (Copenhagen: Nyt Nordisk Forlag 1969), p. 412.

16. Mette Skovgaard: *Bondens køkken* (Copenhagen: Nationalmuseet 1984), p. 17. Henry Notaker: *Mat og måltid* (Oslo: Aschehoug 2006), p. 41.

17. Alfa Olsson: *Om allmogens kosthold* (Lund, Sweden: Gleerup 1958), pp. 99–101.

18. Stanislav Rosznecki: *Polakkene i Danmark 1659 efter Jan Paseks erindringer* (Copenhagen: Gyldendalske 1896), p. 33.

19. Olsson: *Om allmogens kosthold*, pp. 94–96.

20. Nils-Arvid Bringéus: *Livets högtider* (Stockholm: LT 1987), p. 15.

21. Ragnar Pedersen: "Smørformen: En diskusjon om å analysere kulturell kompleksitet," *Dugnad* 2 (Oslo: 1996), pp. 3–28.

22. Nils-Arvid Bringeus: "Skåderetter," in *Gastronomisk kalender* (Stockholm: Prisma 1997), pp. 40–41.

23. Steenstrup: *Dagligliv*, p. 421.

24. Niels Siggaard: *Fødemidlerne i ernærings-historisk belysning* (Copenhagen: Nilsen & Lydiche 1945), p. 12.

25. L. Engelstoft (ed): *Universitets og Skole-Annaler* (Copenhagen: Seidelin 1806–1813).

26. *Kongelig Fundats for Christiania Skoles Kommunitet eller det saakaldte Christiani 6ti Stipendium, med tilhørende Spisereglement.2.9.1735*, Reglement, hvorefter Christiania Communitets Alumni, Norwegian National Archives.

27. Troels Troels-Lund: *Dagligt Liv i Norden i det sekstende Aarhundrede*, vol. 5 (Copenhagen: Gyldendalske Boghandel s.a.), p. 31.

28. Hagdahl: *Kok-konsten*, pp. 18–19.

29. Byron J. Nordstrom: *Scandinavia since ca. 1500* (Minneapolis: University of Minnesota Press 2000), p. 121.

30. Amund Helland: *Hvad vi spiser i Norge og hvad der spises i Paris* (Oslo: Statsøkonomisk Tidsskrift 1896), p. 46.

31. Else-Marie Boyhus: *I lære som kokkepige* (Frederikshavn, Denmark: Dafolo 2000), pp. 75–76.

32. Helland: *Hvad vi spiser*, p. 50.

33. Fannie Farmer: *The Boston Cooking-School cook book* (Boston: Little, Brown and Company 1896), p. 349.

34. Beate-Cornelia Matter: *Die Eingliederung bürgerlicher Elemente in die ländlichen Mahlzeiten Norwegen* (Frankfurt am Main: Peter Lang 1982).

35. Peyerle from Augsburg, quoted in R.E.F. Smith and D. Christian: *Bread and salt* (Cambridge: Cambridge University Press 1984), p. 115.

36. V. V. Pokhlebkin: *Natsionalnie kuchni nasjikh narodov* (Moscow: Tsentrpoligraf 1978), p. 10.

37. P. V. Romanov: *Zastolnaja istorija gosudarstva rossijskogo* (St. Petersburg 2000), p. 87.

38. Jacques-Louis de la Tocnaye: *Promenade d'un français en Suède et en Nor-vège*, vol. 2 (Brunswick: Fauche 1801) p. 133. A. Lamotte: *Voyage dans le nord de l'Europe* (London: Hatchard 1813), p. 33.

39. Léonie d'Aunet: *Voyage d'une femme au Spitsberg* (Paris: Hachette 1854), p. 91.

40. Løken, Haakon: *Landsens liv* (Oslo: Aschehoug 1911), p. 36.

2

Major Foods and Ingredients

The Scandinavian kitchen is typically well stocked with the staples of bread, potatoes, milk, and coffee. But a closer look reveals rapidly changing patterns, for example, in the choice of different breads and curdled milk products and in the preparation of potatoes. More important is the increasing variation in fruits, vegetables, and spices. Only a few decades ago, many ingredients were not on the market, some of them were hardly known at all, and others were considered exotic because they were consumed only during vacations or on business trips to foreign countries. Today *globalization* is a favorite word used to describe the internationalization of economy and commerce, and it is certainly a word that makes sense when the shelves in the supermarkets are inspected. Variation is a key word, variation in brands, in tastes, in countries of origin, and not least in prices. Sauces and seasonings, for instance, are offered in hundreds of different cans and bottles, from the simplest ones to luxury items.

The media have been quick to observe these changes, but with a general tendency to overestimate the real dimension and focus more on the new and sensational than on general trends. Media are therefore not reliable sources about what really happens in this field.

There is also the question of whether all the variation is real. Even if there are many new and hitherto-unknown exotic fruits, there is also a smaller selection of national apples and pears. Many of the products sold are the same but appear in different packaging. Special foods made by artisans are hard to come by in the jungle of mass-produced foods.

Most of the information in this chapter is based on material from the national statistical institutes, from the ministries of agriculture and fishing, from official organs in the health and nutrition sector, from institutes of consumer research, and also from certain big companies in the food processing industry that undertake projects for market research. For comparison between the countries, the *Nordic Statistical Yearbook* and EU statistics have been helpful.

One problem is that all statistics are not based on the same methods or the same parameters. Some are collected through surveys among a representative selection of the population; others are based on sales or on a comparison between production, export, and import figures of different foods. Some of the statistics only cover private households and do not include the consumption in cantinas, restaurants, and institutions.

But in spite of these difficulties, statistics are able to provide a broad picture of availability and consumption. It is possible in these statistics to see common features and patterns on the one hand and on the other hand differences that still exist between the different regions.

CEREALS

Wheat is the grain with the absolutely highest production and human consumption in Scandinavia. It is used for the baking of different breads and cakes primarily. Bread is still the fundamental foodstuff, the *basis alimentorum*, as the Swedish naturalist Linnaeus called it. Porridge, the other traditional basic dish, has lost its former prominent position in the daily diet and is substituted by modern and often imported breakfast cereals.

Pasta made of hard wheat (durum) is of increasing importance. The same is true of rice, which over the last 50 years has made room for itself in the daily diet with about 12–15 pounds consumed annually per capita.[1]

Of the 14 million tons of grains produced every year, two-thirds are grown in Denmark, where the yield per area unit is bigger than in the other countries.[2] Norway has always had to import some of the grain it needs, and Iceland depends totally on imports because grains are hardly grown at all. The Danes and Norwegians consume a lot more grains than do Swedes and Icelanders.

Wheat and Rye Bread

The variety of breads available in Scandinavia is bigger than ever before: ordinary breads for open sandwiches as well as the sweet breads and cakes that are so important for the afternoon snack or a family reunion. This is a totally new situation compared to what was usual only 50 years ago, when the selection was much more narrow.

Many foreign breads have become popular and are imported or baked locally based on foreign recipes. This means that there are certain tendencies toward uniformity in the area as a whole, even if significant national and even regional differences in bread consumption still exist.

One general tendency is to use wheat flour instead of rye. This corresponds to the sharp rise in wheat production and the rapidly declining rye production. At the same time there is a tendency to use more whole-grain flour. Traditionally the finest breads in Scandinavia were made from sifted flour of wheat or rye, made from the endosperm only and ground very fine. Other breads were made from a flour ground with bran, germ, and endosperm. In the whole-grain flour the grains are only partly ground, so some whole-grains remain. All these types of flour are available to the consumer. Norway has the highest consumption of whole-grain breads, and Denmark has the highest consumption of white breads.

Most breads are made in big factories, a smaller amount from local bakers, but a rapidly growing number of breads are now offered through the so-called bake-off system. Doughs or half-baked breads are produced by factories and transported to the supermarkets where employees in a small bakery section finish the baking, so that the products are still warm when the customers buy them. There is no need of a professional baker in the shop and adaptation to demand is easy, because the products take about 10 minutes to get ready. Such bake-off products are also sold in gas stations and convenience stores like 7-Eleven.

Swedish VR Classic

In Sweden the most common bread is the VR-limpan, even if its share of the market today is only 25 percent versus more than 50 percent in the 1960s.[3] The letters VR stand for vete (wheat) and råg (rye), the flours used in this bread, which also contains syrup and spices. The syrup is the reason that it sometimes has been called sweet bread or syrup bread. This very special tradition has its roots in flour shortage during World War I, when the authorities decided that bakeries should increase the energy value in bread by adding beet sugar, a commodity Sweden produced and did not need to import. This bread has normally been made from fine-sifted flour, but in recent years whole grain has also been added.

Danish Rye Bread

In Denmark the classic bread for open sandwiches is rye bread, for centuries the standard bread in Danish households, and also the common oven-baked bread in Iceland, where Danish influences were strong. But the consumption of rye bread in Denmark has been halved during the last 20 years.[4] Today there are many different categories of rye bread, some of a darker and some of a lighter color. There are also whole-grain rye breads. A new organic soft rye bread has been on the market in recent years. In this bread, linseed and sunflower seeds are added to the dough.

Norwegian Dark Breads

In Norway the traditional dark bread was called *household bread* or *sour bread* and in Bergen *long bread*, and it was made from fine-sifted rye flour. In the latter half of the twentieth century it met with competition from breads made with coarse whole meal, *kneipbrød* and *grahambrød,* named after the diet reformers Sebastian Kneipp (Germany) and Sylvester Graham (United States). They are still sold, but today there are a lot of other breads; some of them made from spelt flour, but also increasingly from rye flour; many of them are darker and coarser than Norwegian breads normally have been.

White Breads

Wheat breads are popular in all countries, and they have names indicating that they once were considered foreign. In Denmark and Sweden white bread is called *French bread*, in Norway *loff* (a Low German word) or *wittenberger* (after the German town). Some of these breads are sprinkled with poppy seeds, often called *berkis,* or *barkis,* a word that originally was the Yiddish name of a Jewish *shabbath bread* with poppy seeds. There are also small breakfast wheat breads, and today wheat or hard wheat (durum) is used in all sorts of foreign inspired breads, for example, Italian *ciabatta,* French baguette, Greek pita, Indian nan, American bagel, in addition to pizza crusts and buns for hot dogs and hamburgers.

Wort Bread

This special sweet bread is popular in Sweden and Norway. It is a sort of malt loaf, baked with a dough of rye or wheat, where beer wort is one of the ingredients. Spices are added (anise, sweet fennel, ginger, cloves) or molasses, bitter oranges, and raisins. It was documented in Sweden in the seventeenth century by the French ambassador Ogier, who complained that the bread "tasted terrible for all of us, since wort and fennel had been added." It started out as a bread for the elite, but spread to the broader circles, especially in central Sweden. Today it is sold as a festival bread, first of all for Christmas, but in Sweden also for Easter.

Thin Crisp Breads

A special tradition in the northern part of Scandinavia is the baking of thin crisp breads. The north Swedish *tunnbröd* (thin bread) is baked from barley flour, the Norwegian *flatbrød* (flatbread) traditionally from barley or oats flour, but today both rye and wheat are used. These breads are flat and thin and crisp and are sold in family-size packets.

More important is the leavened thin bread traditionally baked in the central parts of Sweden. A hard bread, made from rye flour, it is thicker than the thin breads of the North and goes back to the round *hålkakor*

Knäckebröd, the Swedish leavened thin crisp bread. Photo by Atle Koren.

(hole cakes), with a hole in the middle. This hole made it possible to store them on long poles fastened under the ceiling in the kitchen. These have been known since the Middle Ages and from the seventeenth century also in the variety called *knäckebröd*. They are thinner than the other hole cakes but still thicker than the northern breads and more like a cracker. The *knäckebröd* industry is big in Sweden and the breads are exported, but the consumption in Sweden has recently been falling.[5]

Thin Soft Bread

The quality of the flatbreads depends on what sort of flour is used. The same is true for the soft thin bread often known as *lefse/levse/läfsa*. It was usually baked for feasts, and rye or wheat was then preferred (from the nineteenth century, potatoes too). In some areas the soft breads are soft from the beginning, because they are fried less than the crisp ones, but in most places the *lefse* is made the same way as crisp bread and stored. When it is prepared for use, it is sprinkled with water to become soft. At festive occasions *lefse* is buttered and folded according to certain established rules, which are different from region to region. Up until the early twentieth century people baked *lefse* in the homes, but today a lot of small bakeries deliver the crisp kind in cartons or the soft kind in plastic bags. A special small variety of Norwegian soft bread is the *lompe*, used for coffee with a cheese or jam filling, but above all known as a wrapping for hot dogs instead of bread.

Pastry and Cakes

A lot of cakes, cookies, biscuits, and pastry are made from flour, some of them for special occasions such as Christmas, others for daily consumption or a Sunday treat. One special sort of pastry, sold the whole year in all countries, has been known internationally under the name *Danish pastry*. The Scandinavians call them *wienerbrød*, literally "Vienna breads." No satisfactory explanation is given for the choice of this name by the Danish bakers who started to produce them from the 1840s.

MEAT

Meat is part of the daily diet and on Sundays and holidays, and fresh meat plays a much more important part than earlier when preserved products were more common. Denmark has a high production of meat

Arne Ploug-Jacobsen, who has worked at La Glace bakery for 40 years, prepares Danish pastries at the famed bakery in Copenhagen, Denmark 2006. AP Photo/ John McConnico.

and exports mostly pork and pork products to other countries, including Scandinavian neighbors. But Scandinavia depends to a large extent on imports of meat from Ireland, Germany, Brazil, Argentina, and New Zealand. Meat products play a central part in the food processing industry.

Meat Consumption

As a result of growing wealth the consumption of meat has risen in the latter part of the twentieth century. In the 1960s around 120 pounds were consumed per person per year. Today consumption has risen to between 160 and 200 pounds, with the highest in Denmark and lowest in Norway. Pork is the preferred meat. There has been a strong increase in pork consumption over the last decades, except in Denmark where pork historically has played a more prominent part than in the other countries. The largest quantities of pork are eaten in Denmark and Sweden, around 85 pounds per person per year, but the most sensational change has taken place in Iceland where consumption has gone from 4 pounds in 1965 to 40 pounds in 2005. Iceland is also the country where the increase in poultry consumption is the most dramatic, from 1 pound in 1965 to 45 pounds in 2005. The consumption is almost as big as in Denmark, the number-one chicken-eating country.[6]

The increase in pork and chicken consumption in Iceland has led to a drop in the traditional mutton and lamb consumption from 100 pounds to about 55 pounds. Nevertheless, these numbers still stand out compared to the other countries in Scandinavia. Norwegians eat 12 pounds a year, Denmark and Sweden only 2–3 pounds.

Beef and veal still are prestigious, and the consumption level is about 55 pounds in Denmark and Sweden, which is a little more than Norway and about the double of that in Iceland.

Reindeer meat from the domestic reindeer flocks owned by Samis in the northernmost areas is very popular. It has a taste similar to that of game, but the products are rather expensive and not easily available.

Horse meat was eaten in the old pre-Christian societies but was prohibited by the Catholic Church in the Middle Ages. In the early eighteenth century a campaign against the waste of this nutritious meat was started and encouraged by the authorities, but horse meat never managed to compete with other meats. Nevertheless, in Iceland it is still eaten in various culinary preparations, in Sweden smoked horse meat is sold under the name *hamburgerkött,* and in all four countries the meat is used as an ingredient in salami-like sausages.

Liver, blood, and other offal played an important part in the diet until after the mid-twentieth century. A lot of different products were made from pig's blood after the slaughtering, such as balls, sausages, and pancakes. Liver sausages can still be bought, but the main liver product is the liver paste, used as a sandwich spread or a dish on the *smörgåsbord* and lunch table. In recent years there has been a higher appreciation of the culinary value of certain offal, and many restaurants serve sweetbreads (of calves and lamb).

Chicken

As a result of production in high-density factory farms, the rapid increase in chicken consumption has been stronger and faster than any other change in meat consumption in Scandinavian history. Systematic farming of chicken started in the early twentieth century, but the chickens were normally raised out of doors until the 1960s when the large confinement operations were started, inspired from similar enterprises abroad. Instead of separating pullets and cockerels, the first for egg production and the second for meat production, a special broiler breed was now developed through scientific feeding and controlled environment. This led to lower prices and a constant supply the year round.

Young people growing up in Scandinavia today, where chicken is a very common dish, both at home and in fast food restaurants, are surprised when told about the prestige and status this bird had less than 50 years ago. Chicken was known from elegant preparations in the seventeenth and eighteenth centuries, and in the nineteenth century veal rolls were cooked with chicken recipes and called *mock chicken*.

Even if the new broilers were tender and juicy compared to the old hens, consumed in soups and stews after they no longer produced eggs, it was obvious that the industrial products had less taste and flavor than earlier chicken. In recent times an increasing number of poultry farmers have for this reason raised chicken on grass ranges. These pastured poultry are more expensive for the average consumer and still cover only a small segment of the market, but it is highly appreciated in the restaurant sector.

Other kinds of poultry cannot be compared quantitatively to chicken. Denmark has a long tradition of goose, but today this animal has mostly been replaced by duck. Turkey is also eaten more in Denmark than in the other countries, where it is above all considered as Christmas food. Turkey and chicken are used in sausages and canned "hams" for the breakfast table (sandwich toppings) as an alternative to darker meats.

Egg consumption is between 20 and 30 pounds per person per year in Scandinavia, highest in Denmark, and lowest in Iceland.[7] Eggs are important in the daily diet, especially in Denmark, but are also essential in the baking of various cakes. A growing part of the sales come from so-called ecological farms with open range where no pesticides are used.

Game

The total consumption of game per person is of minor importance, but this meat is highly appreciated in the cuisine. Even if most of the 600 to 700 hunters in Scandinavia don't hunt as a means to provide food, the hunters nevertheless like to prepare and eat what they have killed. Much of what is shot is therefore kept for private consumption or given or sold to friends. But there are also more professional hunters who sell to the market and especially to restaurants, where the interest in game is considerable. Some restaurants will pay extra to get the meat of really rare species such as bear. Only about 100 per year are killed because of conservation laws.

Because much of the meat is kept by the hunters themselves, the consumption has a tendency to be local; most meat is eaten in the country where the animals are killed. Moose is hunted in Sweden and eastern Norway, and between 100,000 to 150,000 are killed each year. They have an average weight of 1,000 pounds, but the biggest may weigh 2,000 pounds. That means they are more important in terms of meat consumed than are the roe deer, even if more than 250,000 of these deer are killed, the largest numbers in Denmark and Sweden. Sweden is also the main country for fallow deer, while red deer has its stronghold on the western coast of Norway. Wild reindeer is a more rare animal, hunted in Greenland (10,000), Norway (5,000), and Iceland (1,000). Of smaller game, hare is the most important.[8]

In Denmark hunting of game birds is a popular activity, notably of pheasants (735,000), different sorts of duck (800,000), and wood pigeons (276,000). But there are also other gastronomic delicacies such as snipe, woodcock, partridge, and wild geese. Geese and duck are hunted in the other Scandinavian countries as well, but not in the same numbers.

Sweden and Norway have many black grouse and capercailzie, but above all ptarmigan, both willow ptarmigan and rock ptarmigan. Rock ptarmigan is also hunted in Iceland, where it has become a national Christmas dish.

Sea Mammals

The northwestern part of Scandinavia (Norway, Iceland, Greenland, Faroe Islands) has long traditions in the hunting and catching of sea mammals. Seal used to play a fundamental part in the lives of the aboriginal societies in Greenland, and seal hunting was both a part of daily life and a commercial activity. Today hunting of seal and whale is banned with some exceptions. Many seals and whales are declared endangered species. The big catches of seal take place in Greenland (130,000 in 2006), where the major part of the meat goes to animal fodder, but also is an important part of the human diet. Seal hunting is highly controversial, partly because of hunting methods used on young seals, so hunting has been subjected to strong restrictions, both in the quotas and in the hunting methods.

Whaling, once a big industry, still continues for some species, but the animals caught today can be counted in hundreds. In 2006 about 800 pilot whales were caught in the Faroe Islands, and minke whales were caught in Greenland and Norway, but in numbers far below the national quotas.[9]

Whale meat was a very important foodstuff in the years after World War II but almost disappeared from the market. Today some cooks and gourmets have tried to revitalize the consumption of whale meat and invent new recipes.

Meat Cuts and Ground Meat

Chicken meat is distributed fresh or frozen, normally whole and ready to put in the oven, but also in packets with either breasts or legs, practical for the many single-person households. The most exclusive cuts are the breast fillets, with bones and skin removed, ready for cooking. Pork is sold in fillets, chops, roasts, or ribs. Beef and veal are sold as steaks of different qualities and tenderness, boneless roasts, and smaller cuts for ragouts and casseroles. Lamb is sold as chops, rack, roast, and smaller cuts for stews.

A lot of meat is ground and sold as forcemeat. Beef, pork, or a mixture of the two is the most common. Recently forcemeat of lamb and poultry has also been made available. Forcemeat is an important ingredient in a lot of dishes both in Scandinavian homes and in the food processing industry. The various kinds of meatballs are almost considered national dishes. Such products are sold frozen or canned. Forcemeat is also used in sausage production. Some of these sausages are sold in fast food restaurants, but there are also typical dinner sausages common in many family dinners. In Denmark the most popular is *medisterpølse*, made from a mixture of fat and lean pork, which is either finely or coarsely chopped, providing two different products for the market. In Sweden the smoked *falukorv* is one of the winners on the dinner table. It is made with a minimum of 40 percent pork and beef. The name is protected and has its origin in the late nineteenth century in the area of the Falun copper mines where German miners had started production of sausages from smoked meat several centuries earlier.[10] In Norway a smoked dinner sausage is made from 50 percent beef and pork plus 7 percent meat from the heads of cows and pigs.

Preserved Meat

Even if the consumption of preserved meat has dropped, such products are still produced and appreciated. Smoked foods have been exposed to the fumes from burning wood. It seals the surface with an antiseptic coating and gives both a special aroma and a special color to the meat. It is usually combined with another preservation method, either drying or salting. Smoking is used in southern Scandinavia and in certain areas of the Norwegian west coast to preserve meat such as lamb and goose. In Iceland the smoked lamb meat par excellence is *hangikjöt* (hung meat). The temperature should not be higher than 20–25 degrees Celsius (68–77°F) as the heat reaches the meat. The fire is made from wood, and birch, willow, and juniper are considered best, but in some places sheep dung and straw from the pens are used instead, continuing an old tradition.

When meat is dried, salted, or smoked, a curing process called *speking* may take place. This means that certain enzymes start a hydrolysis of the protein molecules. The texture is transformed, so that the food will be easier to chew and new tastes are developed. The result is that the food may be eaten "raw," that is, without any further culinary preparation. Ham and other parts of pork are particularly popular, but not particularly Scandinavian; they are known in many other cultures. One Norwegian preparation called *fenalår* is more rare because it is made with leg of lamb.

The method of keeping food pickled in a strong vinegar solution or in sour beer has been used in Scandinavia, but the most characteristic acid preservation in the food culture of this region is the use of fermented whey. The Sami people used it for both meat and fish, and in several districts in Norway game was put in whey during summer. Iceland had great problems with the supply of salt and kept several different foodstuffs in whey after boiling: fish, meat from whale and seal, sausages, and many parts of the mutton such as the head, offal, and testicles. This is still a common way to preserve foods in Iceland.

FISH

The North Atlantic is one of the world's most important fishing areas. Between Norway and Iceland the warm Gulf Stream meets the cold nutrient currents from the Arctic, and these waters offer very favorable conditions for marine life. There are rich fishing grounds with unpolluted water, and fish from this area has acquired a considerable reputation in the countries of the European Union, where it is considered to be of high quality and of eminent taste. The biggest fish imports to the EU countries therefore come from this area.[11]

The major part of the fishing is carried out by fishermen from the countries bordering on these waters: Iceland, Norway, and to a lesser degree, Denmark. Norway is the most important of these nations, with the biggest fleet, in number of vessels and fishermen, engine power, volume of catches, and economic value.[12] Denmark and Sweden also have access to the Baltic Sea, but fishing there is on a smaller scale and cannot be compared to what goes on in the North Atlantic.

Fishing has been an important activity for many people in Scandinavia since the Middle Ages, but modern fishing is very different from tradi-

Fish dish from the late nineteenth century. From Ch.-E. Hagdahl, Kok-Konsten, 1879.

tional fishing. To many people fishing used to be a part-time occupation. They spent most of the year cultivating small plots of land and only went to sea during the relevant seasons. Today fishing is a full-time occupation, and much of it is carried out from big mechanized vessels, even if the majority of boats still are less than 30 feet long.

In Iceland and even more in Greenland and the Faroe Islands, fish is so important that it has put its stamp on the whole culture of these societies. In Iceland the part of the population employed in fishing and the fish processing industry has diminished from 27 percent in 1930 to 6 percent today, but in many of the small communities along the coast the fishing sector is a major source of income and employment. More than half of the export articles and export value stems from fishing. In Greenland fish is really the hub of the economy, accounting for 90 percent of the export value. Fishing has always had a considerable impact on the economy in Norway, but this industry has been dwarfed by the powerful petroleum industry.

More than half of the ocean fish caught by the Scandinavians go to animal fodder or the fish meal and oil industry. These are first of all blue whiting, capelin, sand eel, and part of the Danish sprat catches.

Consumption of fish is highest in Iceland and Norway, lowest in Denmark.

Codfishes

Of the total six and a half million tons of ocean fish caught by the Scandinavian countries, the most important for human consumption is the Atlantic cod, one of the most sought-after fish because of its culinary value. Most of the fishing is done by the Icelanders and Norwegians, who also consume great quantities of cod. Other codfishes of importance are saithe and haddock, followed by hake, ling, and pollack.

Herring and Mackerel

More than one million tons of herring are caught each year. About 80 percent is Atlantic herring, the rest is Baltic herring. Herring has a special place in Scandinavian gastronomy because of all the different dishes prepared for the Danish lunch table and the Swedish *smörgåsbord*.

The herring may be eaten fresh as fried, or it may be salted, cold smoked, hot smoked, or fermented. The mackerel is also smoked or canned with tomato sauce. Fresh mackerel is very popular along the west coast of Sweden, in Denmark and on the southern and southeastern coasts of Norway, where thousands of small private boats go out to follow the shoals of mackerel in the late spring or early summer months. In the North and West of Norway old prejudices are tied to this fish, which was once thought to consume drowned persons.

Herring has been an important part of the Swedish diet since the Middle Ages. From Olaus Magnus, Historia de gentibus septentrionalis, Rome, 1555.

Flatfish

More than one million tons of flatfish are caught each year, and the small Greenland halibut constitutes the bigger part. Not only Icelanders and Norwegians catch it, but above all the Greenlanders themselves, and it is widely exported. The catches of this fish are about 20 times bigger than those of the ordinary halibut, caught around Norway and the Faroe Islands. Halibut has had a high reputation since the Middle Ages, when it was exported to Germany. It is normally sold fresh or frozen, and the Greenland halibut is also smoked.

Plaice is caught in substantial quantities, particularly by the Danes, who also catch a lot of other small flatfish, such as dab and flounder.

Other Ocean Fish

Visitors to Scandinavia may have discovered canned products called sardines and anchovy, but this fish has nothing to do with the European species with the same names. The fish in question is sprat, which is caught in large quantities. The *ansjovis* in Sweden are sprat fillets canned in a brine made of sugar, vinegar, and spices such as cinnamon, ginger, cloves, bay leaves, and sandalwood. This canned product is used to flavor some of the dishes at the *smörgåsbord*. In Norway the fish is called

Canned sardines (brisling). Photo by Atle Koren.

brisling, but is sold as *sardines* canned in oil and eventually with different spices added.

Two of the ugliest fish in Scandinavian waters have very fine meat and are excellent for cooking: wolf-fish caught in great quantities by the Danes, and angler-fish, or monkfish, a rare and expensive item caught in 13 to 16 thousand tons.

Uer, in English called redfish or sea perch, is a fish found in deep waters, between 1,000 and 3,000 feet deep. Only about 15,000 tons are caught outside the northern coast of Norway and in the Barents Sea. It is appreciated for its culinary value, and sold fresh, but locally it is salted or lightly salted and dried.

Shellfish

About 137 tons of crayfish are caught in the Swedish rivers each year. From the ocean about 200,000 tons per year of crustaceans and mollusks are caught. Greenland and Norway catch a lot of prawn/shrimp and some crab. More than 100 tons of lobster are caught per year, but in Denmark there are big hauls of Norway lobster (Dublin Bay Prawn), known by the Danes as *jomfruhummer* (virgin lobster). Blue mussels, horse mussels, and cockles are popular, particularly the blue mussels eaten fresh everywhere during summer or canned during winter. A new species of shellfish has entered Norwegian waters the last decades, the *kongekrabbe* (king crab).[13] This is a Pacific Ocean crab that Russian researchers introduced to the Murmansk area in the 1960s, and from this area it has spread west to the Norwegian coast.

Freshwater Fish

Sweden and Denmark catch more than 1,000 tons of *ål* (eel) per year, and in addition they import about 100 tons from Norway. For most Norwegians eel has traditionally been considered a form of snake, and the consumption is still minimal; the eel never managed to enter the popular gastronomy. In Denmark and southeastern Sweden eel has been considered a delicacy for centuries and it is prepared in various ways, both fried and smoked. The eel has recently been redlisted in Norway and Sweden as critically endangered.[14]

Laks (salmon) is caught in Swedish and Norwegian rivers, but the catches are minimal compared with that of the farmed salmon. The quality of wild salmon is appreciated by gourmets, something reflected in the price.

Sweden is the absolutely most important country for commercial fresh-water fishing, and there are a lot of different species. By far the most important is *gös* (pike perch). Another popular fish is the *siklöja* (vendace), called *lagesild* in Norwegian. Pike, perch, and whitefish are also much appreciated in the cuisine. Roe from the *siklöja* is called *löjrom* and is a sort of regional caviar with a great commercial success. Also the roe from other fish is used for caviar substitutes.

Farmed Fish

Fish farming developed into a big industry the last part of the twentieth century and has made trout and salmon, exclusive products in the past, available to everybody. The aquaculture is increasingly important, above all in Norway, where the production has tripled in 10 years and constitutes more than a third of all fish farmed in the 25 EU countries. More than half of the Norwegian fish export now consists of farmed fish.[15]

The most important farmed fish is salmon, with a production of more than half a million tons per year. It is very popular on the local markets, but a lot of it also goes to export, not least to sushi bars around the world. Smaller amounts of cod and halibut are also farmed. Rainbow trout is farmed in all the Scandinavian countries, with Denmark and Norway as the biggest producers. Denmark also farms eel. Aquaculture is not big in Iceland, but the prospect is good; in addition to ordinary fish farming in the ocean, it is possible to farm fish from warmer waters, for example, sea bass, in the hot springs.

Fresh and Frozen Fish

Preserved fish—salted, dried, smoked, fermented—dominated the Scandinavian diet for centuries. Only a small elite and fishermen along the coasts had the privilege of eating fresh fish. This has changed over the last 100 years, and the consumption of preserved foods is down, while fresh-fish consumption is increasing. This trend was helped by better distribution systems in the first part of the twentieth century; *fish cars* with fresh fish kept in containers with ice cubes were driven round to small towns and rural communities and offered new culinary possibilities. From the 1950s a new revolution took place when the development of a frozen fish industry coincided with the spread of freezers in most homes.

The frozen fish is sold in small plastic bags with fillets or in packets with rectangular cuts, some of them ready battered. Almost half of the fish caught for human consumption is sold frozen, while one-fourth is sold

Drying and salting of fish in the sixteenth century. From Olaus Magnus, Historia de gentibus septentrionalis, Rome, 1555.

fresh. Independent fishmongers are fewer now, but many supermarkets have established their own fish shops. They sell fish whole, in fillets, and in chops, but also minced fish products, cakes, balls, and puddings.

Some fish products are also canned: such as fish cakes and balls, cod roe, tuna, sprat, and mackerel.

Preserved Fish Today

About 20 percent of the fish for human consumption is preserved. Some of the traditional methods for preservation are very old, and drying is probably the oldest one. One of the ideal places for drying of fish is northern Norway where big shoals of ocean cod come to the coast every winter. Here the stockfish industry started more than 1,000 years ago. When the head and gut has been removed the fish is hung up on a wooden rack called *hjell* in Norwegian. The average temperature is relatively low, and dry air and wind blow the humidity out of the fish, so that after about three months the weight is only one-fifth of the original. Much of this fish is still exported, but some is consumed in Scandinavia, particularly for the specialty *lutefisk* (lye fish), which is stockfish softened in lye and water before it is cooked. It is an important pre-Christmas and Christmas dish in Norway and Sweden, in Norway based on cod, in Sweden on ling. Pollock, haddock, and tusk may also be dried this way, but in much smaller quantities. Lutefisk is also popular in some areas of the United States, where there are many descendants of Scandinavian immigrants.

Fish hang out to dry on racks in Svartsengi, Iceland, 2002. AP Photo/Virginia Mayo.

A more modern method of drying is done in combination with salting. On the northwestern coast of Norway dried and salted cod has been produced for export since around 1700. The fish was dried on the cliffs after it had been sprinkled with salt, and it was originally known as *klippfisk* (cliff fish). Today it is produced in scientifically outfitted drying houses. It is an important export fish, known in France as *morue* and in Spain and Portugal as *bacal(h)ao*. It used to be a Christmas and New Year dish in Denmark, but consumption fell when fresh cod became more easily available.

Fermented fish is the result of a salt-saving preservation method going back to the Middle Ages. If fish is slightly salted, the enzymes and microorganisms will still be active, but the biochemical activity may be controlled by regulating the temperature. The result is a fermentation that gives the fish a certain soft consistency and a strong aroma. In the valleys of eastern Norway there are lakes and rivers with trout and other fat freshwater fish well suited to such fermentation (*rakefisk*). In Sweden a little Baltic herring, *strömming*, is caught in the spring and fermented in brine for 6–8 weeks and made into *surströmming*. Today almost all *surströmming* is sold canned. The fermentation continues in the tins and makes them bulge. One of the crucial moments in *surströmming* consumption is the moment when these tins are opened. In Iceland a similar method is used for skate and the Greenland shark.

DAIRY PRODUCTS

Consumption of milk is very high in Scandinavia, actually one of the highest in Europe, if not in the world. Of European countries only Finland, Ireland, and the Netherlands have a higher consumption of liquid milk products.[16]

Milk has traditionally played a central part in the Scandinavian diet. It has been particularly important in Iceland, where almost no grain was cultivated, but also in Norway and northern Sweden where there were rich summer pastures in the mountains.

Today almost all milk products come from cow's milk. Milk from goats or sheep, in much smaller quantities, is mainly used in the making of cheeses. Cheese made from reindeer's milk was a tradition among the Sami population, but is no longer practiced because it demands too much time and labor to make it worthwhile. The old system, where cheese and butter were made on the farms, started to change in the last part of the nineteenth century, when dairies were established, often as farmer cooperatives. Today most milk is collected from the farms and brought to big dairy factories, even if a few farmhouse producers still exist, mainly concentrating on a single or a few traditional local products. Some farms deliver organic milk.

Sweet Milk and Cream

Until the beginning of the twentieth century most milk was curdled or fermented if it was not used to produce butter or cheese. But during the last hundred years fresh sweet milk has become common, not least for children and young people. Since the 1930s milk has been promoted by the authorities for its nutritional value, and during the last decades with emphasis on the low-fat products.

The milk is sold in cartons in the supermarkets, pasteurized and homogenized, and there is a selection of different liquid milks with varying fat content. The skimmed milk has 0.1 percent fat; a semi-skimmed, generally called *light milk*, has between 0.5 and 1.5 percent (there are certain differences here between the countries); and a sweet or full milk has between 3 and 4 percent fat. There is also a small distribution of what is called original or old-fashioned milk, which is pasteurized, but not homogenized, and where the natural fat is left, between 3.7 and 4.4 percent. In Denmark they also sell some buttermilk with the designation *old-fashioned butter-*

milk. A small portion of the milk is also sterilized for long-term conservation (three months) or prepared as powdered and condensed milk.

In all the Scandinavian countries there has been a reduction in the consumption of milk over the last decades, but more important is the shift due to a stronger consciousness of the health effects of a high intake of animal fat. This has had led to a sharp rise in the consumption of the skimmed and semi-skimmed varieties and a corresponding reduction in whole-milk consumption. On the other hand an increasing part of liquid milk is flavored with fruit or chocolate and is particularly popular among the youngest.

Consumption of fat milk has been reduced, but not of cream. This product is as popular as ever, poured over berries in summer, eaten with canned fruits or used in cooking, where it is considered essential. Cream is also used to produce ice cream, most of it commercially, but many people prefer the homemade taste of the ice cream from their own freezer. As with milk there is a choice of different fat contents, among them a low-fat cream for coffee.

Sour Milk Products

The most successful cultured milk product in Scandinavia today is of the yogurt category. Introduced to the region from the 1960s, it has established itself as a breakfast classic, used instead of milk with the grains and cereals or just eaten alone with a spoon. Yogurt is also eaten as a dessert or as a snack between meals. It is sold either with its natural sour flavor or with a lot of sweeter flavors, most of them based on fruits and sold with different fat contents.

Yogurt is made from special bacteria. Other Scandinavian fermented products are made with the addition of various other different bacteria. The Swedish *filmjölk*, produced since the 1930s, and the thicker *långfil*, is fermented with bacteria that produce less lactic acid than the yogurt bacteria.

The Icelandic *skyr* is a cultured milk preparation based on skimmed milk of sheep or cow and with bacterial cultures and rennet added. The way to add a bacteria culture is normally to use a little of already-made *skyr*. The mixture curdles and the whey is removed through a strainer. The similarity to yogurt has inspired producers to market it with different flavors, such as fruit or vanilla. It is eaten the same way as yogurt with breakfast cereals but is also eaten as desserts with fruit and berries (blueberries are particularly popular) and cream or honey. *Skyr* is still very much appreciated in Iceland and considered a national dish. Its history goes back to the first centuries of colonization 1,000 years ago.

Sour cream also plays a part in gastronomy. The most popular today is the French-inspired *crème fraîche*, introduced in the 1960s, but with a rocketing success from the 1980s. It is very useful as an ingredient in many dishes but is also served with cakes and desserts.

In Norway the traditional sour cream *rømme* is produced in its original form with 37 percent fat, but also in a light variety with 20 percent fat. It is served with several preserved meat and fish dishes and with sweet berries.

Cheese

The most common cheeses in Scandinavia are the yellowish semi-hard or hard cheeses of the Swiss and Dutch type made from cow's milk. Some of them contain caraway seeds, a tradition that probably goes back to the early imports from Holland. These cheeses are used as spread on sandwiches and are cut with special slicers, different in Norway and Denmark. They are also popular on grilled cheese sandwiches and on pizzas.

Fresh cheese is the most original of all cheeses and has been made in Scandinavia for thousands of years. Today one of the best-selling fresh cheeses is cottage cheese, inspired by American recipes. It was first introduced to Scandinavia in the 1950s when Danish dairies produced it for U.S. troops stationed in Germany. By the 1960s the Danes themselves had acquired a taste for it and it has spread to the whole area. It is used as a sandwich spread, in salads, and in cooking when low-fat milk products are needed. There are also other fresh cheeses continuing national traditions. In Denmark some of these fresh cheeses are smoked and have a rich and fascinating flavor.

A rich variety of cheeses is on the market, both imported and Scandinavian made. For many years there has been a high consumption of soft processed cheeses, in reality made from melted hard cheeses, called *melted cheese*, soft enough to spread on the sandwich like butter and with different flavors added (for example, shrimp).

Most cheeses are delivered from the big industrial producers, but there is a growing market for farmhouse cheeses, where an emphasis is put on the variation in taste.

The old Scandinavian cheese-making was done without rennet by heating sour milk. One of the traditionally important cheeses in Norway is the *gammelost* (literally, "old cheese"), a semi-hard product with grainy texture and brown or dark brown color, often with a pungent flavor reminiscent of ammonia.[17] There has been a new interest for this cheese among connoisseurs, but the production is down.

Brown Cheese

Whey has always had a very central place in the northern and western areas of Scandinavia. In Iceland it was put to a lot of uses. In Norway and the North of Sweden they boiled it until it became a thick soup or porridge, called whey butter. After further cooking it thickened even more, only to be put into molds where it hardened into whey cheeses, looking like small bricks. Sometimes they were made in cylindric form, a tradition followed today in some of the classic strong goat cheeses. The cheese was brown in color and firm in consistency. The brown cheeses made today represent a continuation of this tradition, but since the whey has been boiled with milk and cream, they are much fatter and have a richer taste. The brown cheese needs no maturing, and it is more durable than other cheeses.

The brown cheeses are made with cow's milk, goat's milk, or a combination of the two and are characterized by a sweet caramel-like taste, some milder and some stronger in flavor.[18]

Ekte Geitost (genuine goat cheese) is made entirely with goat products: whey, cream, and pasteurized milk. A particular *støl* brand is browned so hard that it gets a more burned taste.

The most popular is *Gudbrandsdalsost* (Gudbrand's valley cheese), made with whey, cream, pasteurized cow milk, and some pasteurized goat milk. In this cheese the caramel-like flavor is kept, but the taste of goat is less prominent.

Brown goat cheese and Norwegian cheese slicer. Photo by Atle Koren.

Mysost (whey cheese) is made entirely with cow products: whey, pasteurized milk, and then a certain amount of cream depending on the content of fat desired.

Butter, Margarines, Fats, and Oils

Butter is sold in different salted and unsalted varieties. It is still important in cooking, in sauces and in the baking of cakes and pastry, and it is used as a spread on sandwiches. But the consumption has been reduced in recent years, partly as a result of health propaganda recommending a lower intake of products with high saturated fat and cholesterol content. The most common substitute for butter is margarine, of which there is a big consumption in Scandinavia.

When margarine entered the market in the second half of the nineteenth century it represented a cheaper alternative to butter. Even farmers sold butter and bought margarine to make a profit. In recent years the price of butter has been less important in these rich welfare societies and health considerations more important. This has also inspired the margarine producers to develop new polyunsaturated and low-fat margarines based on vegetable oils. Some producers have combined the margarine with butter to obtain a fuller butterlike taste without increasing the fat content too much. Some of these products are also softer in consistency and thereby better suited to spread on open sandwiches. This change is very important, because margarine was for a long time the greatest source of trans fatty acids, as the margarine industry used hardened vegetable and marine oils.

Animal fats from pigs and sheep are much less used than before, with butter or margarine or vegetable oils substituted. Vegetable oil consumption is up. The selection of olive oils, sunflower oils, and others in the supermarkets is large, but vegetable oils still constitute a small part of the total fat consumption.

VEGETABLES

There has been a sharp rise in vegetable consumption.[19] Over the last 50 years it has doubled, in Iceland even tripled. This is a total change from the situation foreign travelers used to describe after visits to Scandinavia in earlier centuries. They saw no vegetables on the table except for a few side dishes of roots eaten with meat or fish. As late as in 1965, when vegetable consumption had already changed dramatically since the nineteenth century, an American visitor observed the scarcity of vegetables and salads, but he also predicted an improvement because of the growing canning and freezing industry.[20] These industries have obviously been instrumental in increasing consumption, but so has the construction of hothouses. One explanation of the enormous growth in vegetable consumption in Iceland is the establishment of geothermically heated greenhouses. In spite of a relatively high production of vegetables in the Scandinavian countries, many vegetables are also imported fresh from Europe and other continents. The rise in vegetable consumption is partly due to long and strong campaigns from the authorities.

Potatoes

These roots, completely unknown in Scandinavian cuisine until the last part of the eighteenth century, are still the basic staple in the hot meals of all the countries in the region. Most people buy the potatoes fresh, but the sale of frozen potatoes and of prepared potato dishes has increased. Also on the rise is the sale of other, different potato products such as French fries and chips. In spite of this, the total consumption of potatoes has been going down since the 1970s, but it is still between 55 and 85 kilograms (120–190 pounds) per person per year, highest in Sweden and Norway. The drop in consumption may partly be explained by the growing popularity of other staples such as pasta or rice and of new meal types (pita, pizza, taco) where such staples are substituted by the bread in the dish itself. One explanation may also be that staples play a relatively less important part compared to meat, fish, and vegetables than before.

Roots and Cabbages

The rough climate and short seasons made it difficult to grow certain plants in Scandinavia, and the most common were turnips and rutabaga in the North and curly kale in the South. They contained vitamin C and were probably one of the reasons scurvy was not more widespread.

Turnips and rutabaga are among the oldest cultivated plants in the northern regions and played an important part in the cuisine before the introduction of the potato.[21] Other roots became common during the nineteenth and twentieth century, for example, carrots, celeriac, and parsley roots.

The curly kale was highly resistant to the cold, and it could be harvested any time during the winter. In Denmark it was almost in daily use in soups and other dishes, but is less frequently consumed today. It has been replaced partly by many other variations, such as cauliflower, broccoli, and Brussels sprouts.

Peas and Other Pulses

Peas and beans had the advantage that they could be kept for long periods in dried condition. To prepare them for a meal, they were soaked in water during the night and boiled until tender and served as a soup, often with meat added. Pea mash or pea stew was also served as a side dish with salted or smoked meat or fish, sausages, herring, and dried cod. It was popular in the towns as well as in the countryside and on board ships, in military camps, and in public institutions.

Green and yellow (ripe) peas are still sold dry, but canned and frozen peas have taken over an important part of the market, because they don't need to be softened in water before cooking but are just heated and served.

Today a wider range of pulses is available in Scandinavia than ever before—all sorts of beans and lentils, both dried and canned, and not the least to be found in the grocery stores of immigrants. This change may partly be explained by an increasing interest in ethnic recipes, but also an increasing awareness of the healthful aspects of pulses, which have a lower glycemic index.

Other Vegetables

The most popular vegetables today are tomatoes and cucumber, followed by onion and carrots, but also lettuce and sweet peppers. Onion has been one of the most useful vegetables for centuries and is a basic ingredient in many dishes. Leek and other onion varieties also play an important part in the cuisine.

Many vegetables are sold frozen, often in packets with different combinations, for example, peas, cauliflower, and carrots. Tomatoes are sold canned, and so is corn, which is mainly used in salads, and olives, pickled gherkins, small onions, beetroots, and so on.

Mushrooms

From the late 1900s mushrooms became increasingly appreciated as an ingredient in various dishes, casseroles, stews, and sauces or just fried as a separate serving. Historically mushrooms had a much lower status in Scandinavia than in the southern and eastern parts of Europe, and the inhabitants of Copenhagen were highly surprised when a foreign diplomat in the seventeenth century sent people out to gather champignons. In the nineteenth century various private groups started to promote the con-

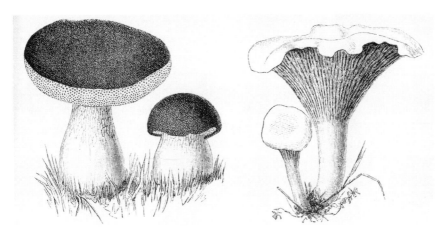

Chanterelles and other mushrooms are tasty ingredients in many dishes. From Ch.-E. Hagdahl, Kok-Konsten, 1879.

sumption of mushrooms, and mushroom recipes entered the cookbooks, but it didn't change the basic attitudes. Even in years with hunger, when the peasants helped themselves to other foods from the forest, they left the mushrooms untouched.

Today many Scandinavians collect mushrooms in the wild during the late summer and early autumn months, but most of the consumption is based on cultivated white champignons and a few other imported species.

FRUITS AND NUTS

Partly due to campaigns from the health authorities, the consumption of fruits has risen in all social groups, and more particularly, fresh fruits. The highest consumption is in Sweden. Measured in per capita consumption, three fruits or fruit groups top the list: apples, citrus fruits, and bananas.

Apples and Other Scandinavian Fruits and Berries

Apples are by far the most consumed among homegrown fruits. Pears, plums, and cherries are also eaten but do not play such an important role as apples. These fruits used to be grown in many private gardens, but today gardens tend to be more decorative than utilitarian. Most of the fruits are produced by big gardening companies, and the highest production is of apples. Many different apple variations are still grown, but only a few of them are important in a commercial sense, as products sold in supermarkets and other shops. Apples comprise a large import from other countries and continents.

A lot of berries are imported. Among the berries cultivated in Scandinavia strawberries are the most important, followed by raspberries and black currants, while red currants and gooseberries play a minor part. Also cranberries, blackberries, cloudberries, and other fruits and berries are eaten fresh, used in jams, juices, desserts, and a lot of cakes.

Citrus Fruits

Among the citrus fruits oranges are by far the most important product and are eaten fresh. Oranges are also important in the juice industry, sold in cartons or bottles in every shop and supermarket. Grapefruit is eaten fresh or consumed as juice, but to a much lesser degree. Lemons are used for flavoring fish and meat dishes and wedges are often put on the plate as a garnish or decoration, for instance, in prawn dishes. The zest and juice of lemon are used in many desserts, cakes, and in icing for cakes. Lemon slices are used to garnish several mixed drinks.

When imports of lemons started in the seventeenth and eighteenth centuries (depending on the region), it was more than anything else in order to flavor the popular drinks of the time, consisting of sugar and wine or brandy. The most famous of these drinks was *punch*, which still holds an important place in Sweden where it is sold in bottles as an already mixed drink. It is popular at certain traditional festivals.

The most important use of citrus fruits, apart from juices, is as marmalade. Scandinavia's production of orange marmalade very seldom uses bitter oranges, and therefore exclusive English marmalades are also imported.

Other Imported Fruits

The most appreciated tropical fruit in Scandinavia is the banana, with about as large consumption as apples. Bananas have been imported since the early 1900s, but it was during the last part of the twentieth century that the fruit really became widely popular. A banana, easy to peel and eat, is often eaten as a snack between meals, but it is also used sliced as an ingredient in fruit salads (*macedonias*).

Various sorts of canned fruits used in fruit salads are still popular, for example, pineapples, peaches, and apricots, but the fruits are now just as often imported and eaten fresh. Papaya and mango and other tropical fruits are also imported fresh today, but in less significant quantities. Kiwis were for some years very often used to garnish dishes, but are now mainly eaten as other fruits. Melons are served as starters, usually with cured ham, and grapes are popular with cheese or just as fruit after a meal.

A lot of dried fruits are imported. Raisins play an important part in the diet, partly as an ingredient in breakfast cereals, partly in buns and cakes. Prunes used to be one of the most popular ingredients in fruit puddings, but they have lost this prominent position. Some dried fruits, such as figs and dates, are particularly used at the Christmas table or in Christmas fruit cakes.

Nuts

Many nuts are used in cooking, first of all almonds, raw material for marzipan, but also hazelnuts and walnuts. Various kinds of nuts—and a nutcracker—are something everybody expects to find on the Christmas coffee table. Some nuts, for example, peanuts and cashew nuts, are salted and roasted and consumed as snacks, often with alcoholic or nonalcoholic drinks.

FLAVORING AGENTS

Vinegar

Vinegar has been widely used in the kitchen for a long time, but until the last decades the selection of different vinegars was not very exciting. Most common was spirit vinegar, either colorless or artificially colored. Wine vinegar was more exclusive, but is sold today in red and white varieties and with many natural flavors added. Balsamic vinegars are imported and much appreciated by private consumers and in the restaurant business.

Mustard and Sauces

Mustard has been eaten with salted meat and fish since the Middle Ages. It is often used to flavor food, and it is an absolute necessity for hot dogs. Most Scandinavian mustards have been of a smooth consistency, rather mild and sweet in taste, but there are exceptions such as the Swedish *Skånsk senap* (mustard from Skåne), which is stronger and with a coarse-grained texture.

Mustard is the base in the sauce for gravlaks, and it is also used in other sauces and dressings. A lot of bottled sauces ready to pour on various dishes are available, and the most common is tomato ketchup. Soy sauces and other Asian sauces are more and more popular in new Eastern-inspired dishes, and British sauces such as Worcester sauce and Cumberland sauce are also imported.

Spices and Herbs

Pepper is the most common of all spices and used to flavor a lot of foods. Traditional spices for baking are first of all cinnamon, allspice, nutmeg, and cardamom. Mace, cloves, and ginger are used in a variety of dishes. For many years most of these spices were only available dried and ground into a powder, sold in small packets or jars. Today it is possible to purchase gingerroots and cinnamon bark. Hot peppers and chili varieties are also offered fresh. Other popular spices are saffron and turmeric, which also bring a golden color to Christmas buns and Mediterranean dishes. A lot of other Chinese and Indian spices or spice mixtures are for sale in the supermarkets and in immigrant shops. All these different spices have acquired a new importance along with the increasing interest in Eastern, Mediterranean, and Caribbean food.

A lot of fresh herbs are also for sale: basil, cilantro, rosemary, and sage, just to mention a few.

New uses of exotic herbs, pepper, *ingefær* (ginger), *kanel* (cinnamon) and *nellik* (cloves). Photo by Atle Koren.

Sweeteners

Sugar—long an exclusive article—flooded into the Scandinavian market from the end of the nineteenth century. Most of the sugar consumed today is made from sugar beets, grown in Sweden and Denmark. Iceland and Norway import all their sugar and are therefore more vulnerable to price fluctuations. Refined white sugar represents the highest consumption, even if the healthier brown sugar is available everywhere. Confectioners' sugar is used for icings and sprinkled on certain cakes.

Refined sugar has experienced a drop in sales, but a lot of sugar is consumed through candy and sweetened carbonated drinks.

Molasses, the poor man's sugar, is less consumed than earlier because price is not as important as it once was. It is still needed in certain Scandinavian cakes.

Honey is used as a sandwich spread or as a sweetener in tea.

Artificial sweeteners are used in some processed foods and in coffee and tea for diabetics and people who want to keep their weight down. The value and side effects of artificial sweeteners in the so-called light soft drinks have generated much controversy.

BEVERAGES

Scandinavia is a coffee-drinking region. Tea plays a very small part in the daily diet of these countries. The consumption of coffee is among the highest in Europe, about nine kilos (20 pounds) a year per person compared to only five kilos (11 pounds) on average in the EU member nations. The most common coffee is arabica, imported from many different countries. Most coffee is drunk as filtered coffee, and instant coffee plays a very insignificant part.

All the Scandinavian countries have experienced a strong increase in the sales of carbonated soft drinks. The consumption has been doubled many times over the last 50 years, in Iceland actually 10 times over.

The market for bottled still water is also growing, surprisingly enough in an area where water can be drunk from the tap almost everywhere.

Milk is drunk more in Scandinavia than in most other places. A new tendency is to flavor it with fruit or chocolate. Milk shakes are still popular and recently many young people have started to drink the Italian-inspired latte, consisting of hot milk with very little coffee.

A wide selection of beers with a low-alcoholic content is available and, in recent years, with no alcohol at all. These changes are considered particularly necessary in Sweden and Norway, where driving under the influence of alcohol is severely penalized. A driver in these countries is considered to be under the influence of alcohol if the amount of alcohol in his or her blood is more than 0.2 per thousand.

Alcohol

The characteristic strong alcoholic drink in Scandinavia is *akevitt* (or aquavit, after aqua vitae). The akevitt is now regulated by the European Union and must be distilled from pure agricultural products and spiced with caraway seeds and/or dill. Typical of the Norwegian production is that it is primarily based on potatoes, while Denmark and Sweden primarily use grains. Another Norwegian tradition is to store the akevitt in sherry casks, something that gives the product a special flavor. This is also the reason that Norwegian akevitt normally holds at room temperature. The Danish and Swedish akevitt is served chilled. Iceland makes an akevitt like Brennivin from imported spirits.

Denmark has a much higher consumption of alcohol than Sweden, Norway, and Iceland. Statistics show that the total sales of all sorts of alcoholic beverages—measured in liters of pure alcohol per inhabitant—is about twice as big in Denmark as in the other countries. Denmark is in the top group in Europe with France, Spain, and Germany, consuming more than nine liters. Sweden, Norway, and Iceland consume between 4 and 6 liters.[22]

Real consumption in Scandinavia is probably higher. A significant amount of alcoholic beverages escape official registration. Home production of wines and beers is legally accepted, and people bring home alcoholic drinks from visits abroad. In addition there is an illegal distillation of spirits and a lot of smuggling. In Norway this unregistered consumption has been assumed to account for as much as 25–30 percent of the total intake of alcoholic beverages.[23]

As producers of beers and spirits, Scandinavians have traditionally consumed these drinks to a much higher degree than wine. But in recent years the most characteristic change in alcohol consumption is the increasing part played by imported wines. Between 1992 and 2003 consumption went down in great wine-producing countries in Europe (France, Spain, Italy, Austria). In the same years consumption increased rapidly in Scandinavia, by 50 percent in Denmark and Sweden, 100 percent in Norway, and 200 percent in Iceland. Sales are by far the highest in Denmark, about double the Swedish sales and three times higher than in Norway and Iceland.

At the same time a certain reduction is seen in the consumption of spirits. A little more than a liter, if measured in pure alcohol, is sold in the Scandinavian countries per inhabitant, only half of what is sold in Germany, and even less compared to France.

The sale of beer has dropped in Denmark and Sweden, the two countries where most beer is consumed. But sales in Denmark are still approximately twice as high as that in the other Scandinavian countries, around 100 liters a year per inhabitant. In Norway the sales have been relatively stable, but in Iceland they have tripled. The rapid increase in Iceland is explained by the very particular situation on this Atlantic island, where beer sales were prohibited until 1989.

Historically beer was produced in hundreds of local breweries. Today there are two distinct trends: the strong centralization in most of the beer industry under large international companies and a growing number of very small breweries, offering a wide range of special beers.

Sales of sweet drinks with alcoholic contents similar to those in beers make up a fairly modest portion of the total sales.

One of the characteristics of Scandinavian beer consumption is that such a great portion of the beer is consumed at home. Between 70 and 80 percent is even more than in the other north European countries with the same tendency, and this portion differs strongly not only from Ireland (12%) and the United Kingdom (35%) but also from several south European countries.[24] The cause may be the difference in price between beer purchased in a shop and beer consumed in a bar, which is very big in Scandinavia because of taxes.

With the exception of Denmark, all the Scandinavian countries have a long history of state intervention and control of the imports, production, and distribution of alcoholic beverages. Retail stores selling beverages with high-alcoholic contents for off-premises consumption are run by the state monopolies: Systembolaget in Sweden, Vinmonopolet in Norway, and Vinbud[25] in Iceland. Beer of alcoholic content lower than 4.75 percent in Norway and 3.5 percent in Sweden is sold in ordinary shops if they are licensed for it, but only to customers who can document that they are over 18 years old.

The background for the monopoly system is the strength of the temperance and anti-alcoholic organizations, historically supported by labor movements and religious groups. The purpose of their campaigns was to limit the overall consumption of alcohol in the population, which they saw as the roots to social problems, bad health, and in the case of religious groups, to low moral standards. The temperance movements argue that alcoholic beverages cannot be considered the same as other commodities that are sold for profit in an open market. The state authorities have to take care of the citizens as part of their social responsibility. This line of argument is the same as that used for tobacco.

To the customers the monopoly has as a consequence the following: shorter opening hours; no sales on Sundays and holidays; age limits for purchase; bans on alcohol advertisements; and high taxation resulting in high prices, which is thought to limit consumption.

The monopoly system of taxing based on alcoholic content and not on the value of the product has led to some apparently paradoxical situations where buying expensive products pays off better than buying cheap ones. Visitors from abroad will realize that some cheap wines and ordinary gin and vodka are more expensive than elsewhere in Europe, whereas high-quality wines and single-malt whiskies are priced lower than in other countries.

The prices are different in the Scandinavian countries, and many Norwegians cross the long border to Sweden to buy wines a lot cheaper than in Norway. In Denmark about 20 percent of consumption comes from alcoholic beverages bought south of the border, in Germany.

NOTES

1. *Nordic statistical yearbook 2007* (Copenhagen: Nordic Council of Ministers 2007), p. 117.

2. *Nordic statistical yearbook 2007*, p. 242.

3. "Brödkultur i förändring" (Stockholm: Brödinstitutet): www.brodinstitu tet.se.

4. Rye bread has also a strong position in the food culture of Finland.

5. Åke Campbell: *Det svenska brödet* (Stockholm: Svensk bageritidsskrift 1950).

6. *Nordic statistical yearbook 2007*, p. 117.

7. *Nordic statistical yearbook 2007*, p. 117.

8. *Nordic statistical yearbook 2007*, p. 253.

9. *Nordic statistical yearbook 2007*, p. 252.

10. Jan-Öjvind Swahn: *Fil, fläsk och falukorv* (Lund: Histoiska media 2000).

11. *Food: From farm to fork statistics* (Brussels: European Commission 2006), p. 19.

12. Arnold Farstad and Bjarne Medby: *Fiskeriene i Norden* (Copenhagen: Nordisk Ministerråd s.a.).

13. The *kongekrabbe* (king crab) is *Paralithodes camtschaticus*.

14. National redlists are made on the pattern of the international redlists from IUCN (International Union for Conservation of Nature and Natural Resources).

15. *Food: From farm to fork statistics*, p. 55.

16. *Mejeristatistik 2007* (Copenhagen: Mejeriforeningen 2007), p. 53.

17. Gustav Ränk: "Gammal ost," in *Gastronomisk kalender* (Stockholm: Prisma 1864), pp. 47–56.

18. The following information is from the main Norwegian producer, TINE. There are also other, smaller producers, among them some that don't use pasteurized milk.

19. *Consumption of vegetables, potatoes, fruit, bread and fish in the Nordic and Baltic countries*, The Norbagreen 2002 study, TemaNord 2003:556 (Nordic Council of Ministers 2003).

20. Nika Hazelton: *The art of Scandinavian cooking* (New York: Macmillan 1965).

21. Christina Fjellström: "Rova eller potatis—basknöl eller komplement-mat?" in *Gastronomisk kalender* (Stockholm: Prisma 2003), pp. 80–98.

22. *World drink trends 2005* (Henley-on-Thames: World Advertising Research Center 2005). *Nordic statistical yearbook 2007* gives 11 liters for Denmark and 6–7 liters for the other countries. The statistics in this part are from *World drink trends 2005*, if nothing else is said.

23. Anders Bryhni, Elin K. Bye, Ragnar Hauge, Øyvind Horverak, Sturla Nordlund, and Astrid Skretting: *Rusmidler i Norge 2007* (Oslo: Statens Institutt for rusmiddelforskning 2007), p. 22.

24. Figures for 2001 statistics in *Het Brouwersblad* (June 2005), p. 8.

25. The official name of Vinbud is ATVR—*Áfengis- og tóbaksverslun ríkisins* (The State Alcohol and Tobacco Company of Iceland).

3

Cooking

In Scandinavia, cooking in a broad sense is done in the home, in the big kitchens of the cafeterias, in private firms and public institutions, in take-away outlets, in cafés and restaurants, and increasingly in the food processing industry. Many factors have influenced cooking during the last half century. Cooking and kitchen work in general have become more efficient with new technology. The changes in food production and distribution have had a great impact on home cooking. Education in home economics, instructions in the preparation of new dishes in printed and visual media, and public information about nutrition and health have modified many traditional attitudes and practices. A very important factor is demographic change in family structures, size of households, and gender roles.

To understand the characteristics of the developments within cooking, a distinction has to be made between the cooking by professionals and the daily cooking in private homes. Most of this chapter describes home cooking; professional cooking is discussed in Chapter 5, Eating Out.

WHO COOKS?

Cooking may be interpreted as one of the most important tasks in a society, because it provides the body with the necessary nutrition and at the same time is fundamental in creating the basis for the social intercourse a meal represents. Cooking is a prerequisite for a meal; therefore the responsible person ought to be accorded a high prestige. However, this scenario has not been the case in family households. Traditionally the women have done the home cooking, and this unpaid work always has suffered from a lower status than paid cooking in cafés and restaurants where most cooks were male.

The Disappearing Housewife

Cooking was only one of the responsibilities of the so-called house-wife. But *housewife* is not any longer such a well-defined term as formerly when most married women did the housework while their husbands were employed in factories and offices outside the home. The woman had the responsibility for child-rearing, cleaning, washing clothes, shopping, and cooking and was expected to serve a dinner for her husband and children when they returned from work and school.

Today most married women have work outside the home, some of them part-time work, but a growing number have long working days, so they return home about the same time as their husbands. Many women and particularly feminists expected that this integration of women in the paid labor force would lead to fundamental changes in the traditional division of labor and household tasks. Who was now supposed to pick up the children in kindergarten and schools, do the shopping, and cook the food?

Gendered Division of Cooking

Studies from the 1970s onward show that equality in housework has not become a reality. In 1990–1991 Swedish women spent on average 6 hours 33 minutes per week on cooking and baking, while men spent only 2 hours 38 minutes.[1] In 2000 Norwegian women spent 5 hours 50 minutes on cooking, while men spent 2 hours 20 minutes.[2] This does not mean that no men are participating in any housework at all, but there are great differences between more and less active men. A study from 1996 of different forms of house work among Swedish couples revealed that women did the cooking in 73 percent of the households, men in 8 percent, and in the remaining 19 percent of the households, men and women divided the cooking.[3] Men were a little bit more active when it came to shopping (of food), but they did even less laundry than cooking.

A survey done in Denmark, Sweden, Norway, and Finland of the gendered division in cooking was published in 2001.[4] A representative selection of households was telephoned and asked about who had been responsible for the preparation, cooking, and serving of the hot meal the day before. This study showed clearly that cooking was still done largely by women, three decades after the new feminist movement accelerated the campaigns for equality. Among those asked, two-thirds of the women but only one-third of the men answered that they had done the cooking. Certain groups of men contributed more than others, particularly young partners and men with middle and higher occupational status.

Interest and Participation

The survey also studied the participation in kitchen work in relation to what interest the partners had in cooking. This showed some interesting differences. Among the men who said they had an interest in cooking, 60 percent had actually prepared the meal the day before. Among the men who were *not* interested, only 33 percent had cooked. However, among women who were not interested in cooking, 87 percent had cooked. In other words, men seem to cook mainly because they are interested, whereas women cook regardless of their interest in cooking. This finding probably means that when nobody in the couple is particularly interested, the woman steps in. A Danish survey shows that 70 percent of women in families with children feel a responsibility when a meal has to be cooked.[5]

The aforementioned Swedish study showed that when men participated in housework, they shared the cooking rather than other tasks. Much housework has often been considered negatively, as something repetitive, boring, and burdensome. But it seems that cooking is evaluated somewhat differently today. In a Norwegian survey women were asked how they judged different sorts of housework, and they put baking and cooking on top of the list, because they regarded these tasks as more creative.[6] Cooking has without doubt acquired a higher value in the Scandinavian societies the last decades, and not only through admiration for the celebrity chefs, but through a genuine increased interest in the art of cookery. On the one hand, the signals given in the studies indicate that further changes in the direction of greater gender equality are possible, even if the changes seem to be rather slow. On the other hand, Scandinavian men seem to be more active participants in housework if compared to the situation in other European countries. A study in 2000 of 15 countries showed that Swedish and Norwegian men between 20 and 64 years, living with women, are topping the list with 40 percent of the total housework, while Italian and Spanish men are at the bottom with about 25 percent. Men in Sweden do 34 percent of the cooking, Norwegians 31 percent, Italian 17 percent.[7]

The questions discussed are relevant only for households with couples and are leaving out important groups. Today more than half of the households consist of one person only, and in many households children are living with a single parent, usually the mother.

Cooking, Gender, and Education

Much of the gender division in cooking has its roots in established gender roles. From an early age daughters were taught cooking by their mothers in the kitchens. They were prepared for a future life as married housewives. This pattern had to change when women started work outside the home. There remained less time for long and patient hours in the kitchen. The schools therefore took over this responsibility and started to teach young girls the basic knowledge of a subject that was generally called household management, domestic science, home economics, or something similar.

Education in this field started in the last decades of the nineteenth century. Important changes in the society occurred at the time—industrialization, urbanization, democratization, and progress in science and technology. All this offered new challenges to housework. To master the new technical inventions, for example, the stove, instruction and more practical and theoretical knowledge were necessary. A new awareness and consciousness about the relationship between nutrition and health, based on discoveries in physiology and in chemistry, led to conclusions that were important to convey to new generations. The economic management of the home was becoming more complex when the barter economy—with many foods made on the farm—gradually turned into a full money economy, in which farmers delivered their goods to industrial mills, big dairies, and meat factories and purchased their necessities with cash. Under these new conditions the housewife, who was doing the shopping, had to learn how to plan and make a budget, in other words, how to read, write, and calculate. Schooling in general was in these years recognized as a necessity for all members of the society.

Teaching in housework started in the primary schools and continued in courses and schools for young women. The education was exclusively made for female students. Only since the 1970s was the gender division abolished, and boys and girls are now treated equally. Today education in primary schools is considered crucial in developing new attitudes in the children at an early stage. Gender equality is emphasized in the political programs of most parties, and a broad consensus exists on this topic in Scandinavia, even if the parties have different strategies for how to obtain the wanted goals.

New Focus in Cooking Education

The new teaching in home economics—after the integration of boys and girls in the same programs—changed the focus from preparation of future housewives to a wider understanding of food and food culture. Earlier the schools taught the basic practical skills and emphasized the value of nutrition and hygiene and the value of economic planning. The food had to be balanced based on the different food groups, and too much money should not be spent on food. Today more and more aspects have become part of the education. Cooking instruction is still based on certain technical skills, which are a part of the curriculum, but there is also much more theory. First of all nutrition is important as ever before, but in addition to knowing the protein value or number of calories of different foodstuffs, awareness of other factors that influence health is needed. Also necessary is knowledge about additives in the foods and an ability to read the information labels about contents. Education emphasizes that food products must be considered in relation to nature and ecology; cooking should not be practiced in ways that harm the environment or with the use of foods produced under unsustainable conditions. All this is called *consumer consciousness*, and it includes an ability to evaluate the massive advertising from the food producers.

The teaching enhances the social value of the meal, but in a context other than the old one. Even 100—or even 50—years ago the family dinner was a place where children were taught socialization, how to behave toward their parents, to ask politely for the salt, not talk too loudly, not to leave food on the plate, not to drink noisily, and so on. Today this patriarchal family context is no longer taken for granted. A stronger focus is put on communication, fellowship, equality—and not the least—gender equality.

With all its social and environmental consciousness the new education also is very open to cooking as a means to enjoy food. In the old schools the value of good taste and esthetic presentation was not neglected, but acknowledgment of the value of pleasure in both the cooking and the eating was absent. Many of the dietarily correct dishes were considered ordinary if not "boring." Today cooking is seen as an adventure, and a consequence is the search for new tastes, either by going back to old local and national traditions or by exploring exotic cuisines in immigrant communities or in other countries such as Spain, Greece, or Thailand when on holidays.

This way cooking is no longer the boring job a woman has to do to keep her family alive, but a source of common experiences for men and women alike.

Planning, Shopping, and Cooking

Shopping is closely connected with cooking, not only because most ingredients have to be purchased regularly in stores, but because these two activities are part of a broader context of planning the meals. The housewife of the past might do the planning, shopping, and cooking in one sequence during the day. Today, with no person at home taking these responsibilities, planning has to be done in the morning or the evening before. Such planning is not just a question of deciding what kind of food will be served. The cupboard, the refrigerator, and the freezer must be checked to establish what is available, how long the food will last, and what leftovers ought to be finished. In the words of a researcher in the field of diet and gender, one important reason for women shouldering the responsibility is that they have "the cupboard in their heads."[8]

Planning also has to do with variation. When the next meal is planned one has to remember what was served the days before, so there are no unnecessary repetitions. The meal must also be planned from an angle of taste; what do the different members of the household like and dislike? All this has to be settled when the working day starts, so the shopping in the afternoon may be done quickly and efficiently.

The New Retail System

Great changes in the distribution of food at the retail level have had both positive and negative consequences for the consumer. Earlier a lot of small independent shops offered different foods, some of them made by artisans. Even small towns had several grocers, bakers, fish dealers, and butchers, and in the marketplace gardeners and farmers sold their potatoes, vegetables, and fruits. This system more or less disappeared during the twentieth century. Today the supermarkets dominate the retail trade in food, and they tend to be only one part of larger commercial centers—enormous complexes where everything is sold. Also a strong concentration in the retail trade has resulted in a small number of companies controlling most of the distribution.

On the one hand, supermarkets and commercial centers offer a lot of advantages to the shopper. The square footage allows for a rich variety of different foodstuffs, and this makes shopping more efficient. Going to different shops to provide the necessary ingredients for a meal (meat at the butchers, vegetables at the market, bread at the bakers, cheese in the dairy shop) is very time-consuming work compared to just walking around in a big supermarket and picking various items down from the shelves, putting them in a cart, and paying for all at one counter.

Most commercial centers have good parking facilities, free of charge for at least a couple of hours and with easy access to the shops. This makes it possible to buy food for several days in one trip and have days free of shopping. Many couples do this extensive shopping together, for example, during weekends, and this contributes to more gender equality.

On the other hand, the new distribution patterns have as a consequence less-direct contact between the merchant and the consumer. The consumer must study the product, the declaration of contents, the expiring date, and so on. This also means that it is not so easy to send a child shopping with a piece of paper where the desired items are listed: 2 pounds of flour, 1 pound of sugar, half a pound of margarine. Many children did this when the shops were around the corner and the goods were easy to carry home.

The big commercial centers, often outside the towns and cities, create a dependence on cars. This makes shopping difficult for many older people. They therefore depend to a high degree on the continued existence of small neighborhood shops. Today many such small shops are run by immigrants. Because they are organized as family businesses. they are less dependent on labor regulations and they keep long business hours. Elementary distribution of basic foodstuffs is also done by gas stations, chains of small shops and stores, and places such as the 7-Eleven, open all day, nearly every day. But because of limited space the selection of foods is narrower. A reduced selection is also often the case in some of the discount stores. They belong to big chains that manage to lower the prices because they coordinate large purchases. But a consequence is often that the selection is more uniform than wanted.

This reduction in choice has led to a new demand from wealthy people who look out for more exclusive products. A lot of small specialty shops have started to offer French and Italian cheeses, Spanish and Greek olive oils of high quality, special breads, balsamic vinegar, and so forth. This has been observed by the commercial centers; they have taken up the challenge and invited the small shops into the centers. Some of the supermarkets in the upmarket category have counterattacked by expanding the selection of exclusive products. They have also hired butchers and fish dealers who can advise the customers in the use of the meat and fish products. Some supermarkets even employ sellers with an education as professional cooks, so they can provide the customer with both the fish and an adequate recipe.

These more demanding customers are still a minority. The majority seems to be satisfied with a limited selection and do not exploit the extremely wide range of foods and beverages that are now available.[9] Shopping is also related to private economy. On average the Scandinavians spend between

13 and 14 percent of their total household expenditure on food. But averages tell nothing about how the money is spent in different income groups. Prices are influential not so much in deciding the quantity of what is eaten, but in choosing certain foods instead of others. In a bad economy a cheap product may be chosen even if it is not considered the best one from a nutritional or taste point of view. Those who live on a tight budget will only spend more money on food at Christmas and other special occasions.

THE KITCHEN

Cooking is in many ways dependent on what technology is available. One-pot dishes were common in the old kitchens where cooking had to be done in a single pot over the fire. Minced meat demanded a lot of work and only had a breakthrough with the meat grinder. The development of the kitchenware industry has made kitchens into small laboratories with many instruments and machines for food preparation.

Stove

The rapid spread of stoves fired with wood or coal from the late part of the nineteenth century and with electricity and to a lesser extent gas from the early twentieth century opened the possibility for cooking several dishes at the same time. The stoves were built with three or four hot plates on top and an oven inside. The dominant fuel is still electricity, which has been rather cheap in Scandinavia up until recently. Some people have installed gas burners to better prepare certain dishes. Many stoves are also sold with two electric hot plates and two gas burners. Halogen rings were popular for a while, but today the induction cooktops are conquering the market. Apart from some of the same advantages as gas burners have, the induction cooktops heat quickly and lose heat quickly. Many stove manufacturers offer other options, such as grills, timers, thermostats, or auto-cleaning systems.

The microwave oven was introduced very rapidly from the 1970s onward and is still in use in many homes, but more often for defrosting frozen food products and ready-to-heat dinners than for actual cooking.

Kitchen Equipment

The meat grinder was a revolution in its time, but a new big step forward came with the food mixer and finally with the food processor, where all kinds of grinding, mincing, mixing, blending, and kneading became possible without extra physical exertion. This influenced cooking in a remarkable way, because so many new possibilities were opened.

Early meat grinder. From Grethe Haslund, Min Medhjæl, Kristiania, 1894.

Coffee machines for filtered coffee, electric kettles for the boiling of tea water, sandwich toasters, and electrical waffle irons are very much part of a modern kitchen today. Other machines and nonelectric equipment have had a tendency to come and go, and they are in less general use: bread bakers, espresso machines, pressure cookers, fondue sets, and woks. Deep-fat fryers have been popular in families for children who wanted French fries. The same clientele has been especially interested in ice cream machines.

With the electric stoves a wide selection of cooking pots in aluminum or stainless steel was necessary, but there were wrought iron options. But with the induction cooktops, new pots are necessary. For oven baking, terracotta and earthenware dishes are used to roast and bake Mediterranean and other specialties.

Storage facilities changed dramatically when refrigerators and freezers became common from the 1960s onwards. Earlier, food had been stored in larders and basements, and there were always problems with easily perishable foods. When freezers began to come on the market, many families purchased large quantities of meat, fish, and breads and froze them. But the freezers took up a lot of space, and when house prices rose, as they did in the biggest cities in particular, less room became available; thus the combined fridge/freezer became the natural choice. Room was also needed for the dishwashers, quite common in the late twentieth century.

Most kitchens today are planned as a total package, the producers furnish a so-called fitted kitchen where cupboards, benches, and shelves, are made to give adequate room for the stove, fridge, and other appliances. The only movable furniture is the table and chairs.

The kitchen used to be a living room in the nineteenth century, except in the upper and middle classes where it was important to separate the kitchen—with cooks and maids—from the dining room. In the twentieth century, when house servants gradually disappeared, the modern and efficient kitchen was the ideal but still separated from the dining room. A little corner of the kitchen was reserved for the daily family dinners. But during the last decades, with a renewed interest in food and gastronomy, the tendency is to make the kitchen into a living room again, an all-activities room, where reading takes place, the children do their homework, and food is prepared and eaten.

COOKING IN THE MEDIA

In the 1980s and 1990s the national broadcasting monopolies were dismantled in Scandinavia and a lot of private channels sprang up. The hosts of television cooking shows had already acquired a status as national housemothers, with serious recommendations of healthy food and efficient preparations. The new generation of national and international TV cooks were often as much entertainers as cooks, but at the same time they managed to convey practical hints as well as introducing new ingredients, new dishes, and new techniques. A few of these hosts have introduced Scandinavian cuisine to American viewers on PBS (Public Broadcasting Service).[10]

The change in the presentation of food shows over the years on Norwegian TV has been described as a development in three stages. The first is argumentative, in favor of healthy dishes; the second is descriptive, telling about food habits in various places nationally and abroad; and the third stage is narrative, with small histories about the cook himself, his experiences in the kitchen, meals with friends, and so forth. A common technique in all these stages has been the use of dialogue, conversations not only with specialists or locals but with anyone who could work dramatically and move the program forward.[11]

Cooking also plays an increasingly important part in the printed media and has conquered the daily press. Since the end of the nineteenth century, recipes were given in ladies' journals and family magazines, but today both tabloid and more serious newspapers print suggestions for the day's dinner. Some of these articles are furnished by food companies and marketing groups for meat and fish. Nevertheless, they give important new information to the readers and are without any doubt instrumental in furthering the changes in Scandinavian food culture.

Cookbooks flood the market as never before, offering recipes for all kinds of dishes, from all the cuisines in the world, suggesting new and fascinating ingredients, and using more and more creative presentation methods. Many of the books integrate the recipes into a text full of personal reflections, historical background, or humorous commentaries. Design is given high priority, and the photos often take up more room than the text. The books are read and looked through with pleasure, even if the readers don't try or even plan to try out the recipes.

SCANDINAVIAN COOKING

All demographic, economic, commercial, cultural, and technical developments have initiated changes in Scandinavian cooking traditions that will probably continue to be felt more strongly in the coming decades. In some areas and among some social groups these changes take place quicker and with wider consequences than in others. Many of the cooking techniques established after the introduction of the stove are still in use, but new preparations and combinations of ingredients gradually transform the image of Scandinavian cuisine.

Before a description of the basic cooking approaches is given, an analysis is necessary of the concept *domestic cooking* in relation to what is happening in food processing.

Convenience Foods and Homemade Foods

More and more of the food preparation have been transferred from private kitchens to the food manufacturing industry. This development started with the canning industry in the nineteenth century, but today it has gone all the way to the preproduced meals that are put in the oven and heated and then are ready to put on the table. There are even frozen packets where all the components are laid out properly, in order to be eaten without putting them on a plate.

In addition to these products offered by the food industry, it is possible to purchase not only ready-to-heat but ready-to-eat, already heated products in the take-away outlets. Many supermarkets have taken up this challenge by doing their own cooking in the shops where they sell hot grilled chicken, fish cakes, meatballs, and stews as well as potato or vegetable salads to go with it.

Studies of which convenience foods are most popular show an interesting tendency. People buy ready-made dinners that are similar to the ones they generally prepare or want to prepare in the home.

In analyzing the expanding growth of the food industry, there is no clear and distinct line between what is convenience food and what is homemade food. Today spaghetti with ground meat and tomato sauce is a popular dish. The spaghetti is boiled at home, but bought in a package in the shop, not prepared in a pasta machine in the kitchen. The meat is fried at home, but bought ready ground and not ground in a grinder in the kitchen. The tomato sauce is poured from a bottle and not prepared in a pot in the kitchen. Is this a homemade dinner? To most people it is.

Another example is a meal with sausages. Sausages were also prepared at home 100 years ago, but most people will consider sausages served with potatoes, greens, and sauce as a proper homemade meal. They may think otherwise if the sausages are served as hot dogs. In other words, what matters is not only the product per se but in which context the product is eaten.

The most striking example of a change from the homemade food is the baking of bread. When the stove was introduced and particularly after the invention of the electric stove, most people baked their own bread in the oven. A study from Sweden shows that while two-thirds of the breads were baked in private homes in the 1930s, only 2 percent are home-baked today.[12] Of the bought bread more and more come from the so-called bake-off departments in the supermarkets, where the consumer can pick up hot bread, just out of the oven. But in spite of this the consumer will hardly consider the bread a convenience food.

Cooking Methods

The increased availability of more- or less-prepared ingredients is certainly influencing the cooking and not least the time spent preparing a meal. When fish and meat stock may be poured from a pot or bottle, a soup or a casserole is much simpler to finish. A microwave reduces the time needed to make a piece of frozen meat or fish ready for cooking.

Most existing cooking methods in Western cuisine are used in Scandinavia: boiling, frying, roasting, baking, grilling, poaching, steaming, sautéing, deep-frying, stir-frying, and so on. The tendency over the last 150 years has been a reduction of the traditional boiling and an increase of frying and roasting, but other combinations also create new possibilities. Contemporary Scandinavian cooking includes dishes made with all conceivable methods, which means that one day a wok dish is served; the next day a meal consisting of baked fish, boiled potatoes, vegetables, and a sauce; and the third day a boiled one-pot dish. The choice of method is a result of available time, the importance of the occasion, the sort of fish or meat chosen, and the size and tenderness of the cuts.

Frying and Baking Meat

Roasts of pork and beef, legs and shoulder of lamb, chicken and other whole meat cuts are often fried or baked. Since nutritionists have warned against too much frying, a combination of frying and baking is often chosen. Fillets and steaks are made this way if they are not intended to be rare, while chops and cutlets usually are just fried and simmered in the pan.

Today a slow baking on low temperature is a method to obtain tender roasts. Meat may also be baked in a covered earthenware dish to avoid direct exposure to the heat.

Smaller cuts of tender meat may be deep-fried or stir-fried in a wok, but these methods are not as common as the others yet.

Boiling Meat

Several dishes are still boiled. This method goes back to the age before the stove, when chunks of salted or dried or smoked meat were boiled for hours in a pot over the fire, often with cabbage or roots. The liquid was served as a soup, for the elite with small meatballs. The meat was eaten as a separate dish with some garnish and a sauce, and from the nineteenth century on, also with potatoes.

Some dishes in this category are still highly appreciated traditional dishes, for example, brisket or chuck or shoulder of beef with the bone. These dishes are boiled for hours and served with a sweet-and-sour onion sauce in Norway, a horseradish sauce in Sweden, and with a cabbage stew in Denmark. The Danish dish is so much of a classic that it was chosen as the equivalent to corn beef and cabbage when the American comic strip *Bringing Up Father* about an Irish arriviste was translated into Danish. A similar dish in Iceland is *hangikjøt,* made from smoked lamb, but it is served somewhat differently.

Another classic, known since the Middle Ages and still made in all the countries, is pea soup with salt pork (salt lamb in Iceland). Yellow peas are boiled with the meat and the marrowbone. This heavy dish is considered a typical Thursday dish in Sweden, which probably means that the tradition goes back to Catholic times when Thursday was a meat day before the important fasting Friday.

Even if boiling primarily was applied to preserved meat, some fresh meat dishes are also boiled. One is a dish with alternating layers of cabbage and chunks of lamb shoulder, sprinkled with peppercorns. This *fårikål* (mutton-in-cabbage) is particularly popular in Norway in the autumn when the lambs are slaughtered, and it has been elected a national dish.

From the 1970s new boiled meat dishes became popular in different forms of casseroles. Small cuts of lamb or beef, even pork, were braised in a frying pan and then simmered in a meat broth or water with beef cubes dissolved. Vegetables such as onions, carrots, or red peppers, and tomatoes and other ingredients were added. New spices and garlic were used, and the dishes were often served with rice instead of potatoes.

These casseroles developed in two directions. The simple ones are made with ground meat and ready-made spice mixtures, the elaborate ones are made from scratch with the use of exclusive and exotic ingredients, and spices and wine added.

Cooking with Ground Meat

Much Scandinavian cooking is done with ground meat; in fact more and more dishes are based on this ingredient. The meat grinder, which became common from the last part of the nineteenth century, prepared the way for the success of meatballs, a cornerstone of Scandinavian cuisine and today regarded as national dishes: Danish *frikadeller*, Swedish *köttbullar*, and Norwegian *kjøttkaker*.

If compared to meatballs in other countries, the Scandinavian varieties are relatively similar, but people tend to regard their recipes almost with a sense of identity, something expressed in the name often given: *Mother's meatballs*. But even if every family has its own recipe, there are also certain national characteristics.

Grated onion, a little milk or water, and an egg are common ingredients, along with salt, pepper, and eventually nutmeg but no hot spices as found in Spanish and Turkish meatballs. Added to this is a little flour (mainly in Denmark), potato flour (mainly in Norway), or bread crumbs (mainly in Sweden).

The meat is pork, veal, or beef or a mixture. Pork holds the strongest position in Denmark, beef in the northern areas of Scandinavia.

The form is round as a golf ball in Sweden, more like a hen's egg in Norway, and flattened a little in Denmark to better serve as toppings on sandwiches.

The Danish and Swedish balls are fried in a pan; the Norwegian are first fried and then simmered in broth.

Ground meat is also fried as hamburgers or cooked in cabbage leaves. A nineteenth-century dish that has found new popularity is *boneless birds*. These are oblong meat rolls originally made with slices of veal, but now forcemeat is shaped to look like the torso of a bird. They were spiced the same way as grouse and other game birds, and this gave them their name, which also might be *mock birds* (as in *mock turtle soup*).

All these dishes are still possible to find in home cooking, but they belong to a traditional cuisine that does not always appeal to new generations. What is interesting these days is how ground meat has met with new types of dishes from abroad, many of them introduced through fast food culture. Ground meat is fried and used in taco shells, in pitas, on pizza crusts, and in moussaka, lasagna, and other dishes. These dishes are particularly popular with the younger generation and with children, partly because they represent something new and partly because they may be eaten without the traditional staples and garnishes of potatoes and vegetables, some of them also without knife and fork.

Cooking Fish

The cooking of fish differs according to the kind of fish, the size of the fish, the region, the season, and the day of the week. Whole fish poached or baked is particularly popular on Sundays. Chops of cod, halibut, salmon, and many other fish are also poached, as well as baked or steamed. Fat fish, such as mackerel and salmon, are often put in the fridge (in the stock) after poaching and served cold the next day, for instance, with cucumber salad, new potatoes, and sour cream.

Poaching is more common in Norway and Sweden than in Denmark, probably because more frozen fish is eaten in the two first countries. In Denmark people eat a lot of fresh plaice, dab, and flounder, small fish that may also be poached but are best when the fillets have been panfried in butter or margarine.

Chops of halibut, monkfish, and salmon are fried as beefsteaks. In Norway they have a *saithe steak* made from fillet of saithe, dredged in flour and fried and served with browned onion slices, just like the old-fashioned beefsteaks.

Eel, herring, and small mackerels are also dredged in flour or bread crumbs before frying. In Norway small mountain brook trout are fried in butter and then simmered in cream or rømme.

A lot of cakes, balls, and puddings are made from ground-up fish. They are particularly popular in Norway, where one-third of all fish dishes served on weekdays are based on ground-up fish. Even if more and more people prefer to buy these products canned or frozen in the supermarkets or fresh at the fish store, some enthusiasts continue the old tradition—people along the coast, in particular, who do a lot of sport fishing. The fish is ground up in a food processor or in a mortar if a coarser dough is preferred. Codfishes and monkfish make cakes of a light color; saithe, mackerel, and herring make darker and generally coarser cakes.

Grilling

The last 30 years have seen an explosion in the sales of barbecues, from the most simple ones to big yard installations. Even in a region with such unstable weather conditions, grilling has won a unique position in summer cooking. On sunny afternoons and evenings the aroma of grilled meat (and the stench of fuel) is floating in the air from yards, terraces, and balconies all over Scandinavia.

Fillets, chicken breasts and wings, chops, and sausages are the most popular grilling meats, and the supermarkets offer suitable cuts, spiced or marinated and ready to put on the grill. Lately salmon chops have become very popular.

Sauces

In *The Art of Scandinavian Cooking*, published in the United States in 1965, author Nika Hazelton, who had been to the Scandinavian countries, stated that "surprising to the visiting American is the lavish use Scandinavians make of sauces, both hot and cold. Most of them are excellent; all of them are devastatingly rich, since they are thickened with eggs and sweet and sour cream rather than with flour. . . . The Scandinavians love sauces, and cream sauces and gravies reign supreme."[13]

Many Scandinavian gourmets looking back at that time would probably represent a more critical attitude to the brown and white sauces that dominated so heavily. But gradually new methods and ingredients were introduced, such as red and white wine and spices of every variety. The sauces, made from reduced meat or fish stock, became lighter and more subtly seasoned.

But in contrast there has been a strong tendency to use industrially produced sauces, mayonnaise, and so forth, instead of making the sauces at home.

Cooking with Dairy Products

Sour milk or whey has often been used in the preparation of meat before the cooking proper. The *surstek* (sour roast, from German *sauerbraten*) was often made from horse meat marinated in vinegar in Denmark and in sour milk in the northern regions. Sea birds were also often marinated this way to remove the rank taste of fish oil.

In modern Western cooking various dairy products are used liberally as ingredients, notably butter, cream, *crème fraîche*, and yogurt. Such ingredients are fundamental in enriching many sauces and are increasing the taste in a lot of other dishes in Scandinavia. In the northern parts, where milk always has played such an important part in agriculture and diet, there are two examples that deserve to be mentioned: game dishes and fish soups.[14]

Tougher cuts of meat from deer, reindeer, and moose are often used in casseroles. Slices or cubes of meat are browned in butter with other ingredients, such as onions and mushrooms, particularly if chanterelles are available. Then cream or sour cream is added, often with crushed juniper berries to reinforce the taste of game.

Ptarmigan, so popular in Sweden, Norway, and Iceland, has traditionally been cleaned and trussed, browned in butter in an iron pot, and then boiled in a mixture of water and milk. Then sour cream is added, often also some slices of another milk and whey product, the brown cheese. In Iceland puffin is cooked more or less the same way.

The breast meat has a tendency to be rather dry and rough after this treatment, so lately a more common method is to remove the breasts of the birds before cooking and put them in the pot when the rest is ready, let them simmer for some minutes, and eat them while still pink inside.

Some European recipes for fish soups suggest the addition of an ingredient with an acidic edge, either vinegar or lemon juice. In North Scandinavian cooking, this acid is substituted by sour whey or sour cream. One example is the mackerel soup from the west coast of Sweden, consisting of boiled mackerel bits, potatoes, dill, and milk (or cream). Another example is the Bergen fish soup where milk and sour cream (*rømme*) is added.

Palesuppe (Bergen Young Saithe Soup)

- 3 pounds young saithe
- 3 pints of water
- 1 teaspoon salt
- 1/3 cup flour
- 1 1/3 cups milk
- 4 ounces carrots
- 3 ounces parsley root
- 3 ounces celeriac
- 1/2 cup rømme (sour cream)
- chives

Clean and wash the fish, remove the gills and the eyes. Cut the head in two and put it in a pot with the tail. Pour in cold water and salt and bring to a boil. Cut the rest of the fish in slices an inch thick and let them simmer for a few minutes, then put them aside. Strain the stock. Dice the vegetables to measure a half inch, and let them boil five minutes in the stock. Whisk flour smooth in cold milk and beat it into the boiling stock. Let it simmer for five minutes. Whisk in the sour cream, and sprinkle finely chopped chives if wanted. Serve the soup first, then the fish with boiled potatoes. Many Bergen citizens will insist that the stock has to be made from the entire fish, not only the trimmings, and that a little veal stock should be added to round out the flavor. Some will insist that the vegetables have to be cooked separately, and some that the soup is not complete without small fish balls. There are many ways to make a Bergen fish soup, but one common denominator is the *rømme*, the sour cream.

If saithe is not available, other fishes of the cod family may be used. Instead of or in addition to celeriac, parsnip or leeks may be used.

Potatoes and Vegetables

The most common preparation of potatoes is to boil them peeled or in their jackets. New potatoes in summer retain the skin and are a culinary delicacy served with gravlaks. Potatoes are also fried, in some cases with sugar, so they get caramelized. Big potatoes are oven baked, either oiled or wrapped in aluminum foil and served with garlic butter or a sauce, as a side dish to grilled meat. According to a survey,[15] boiled and baked potatoes were served on average between 14 and 20 times a month in Scandinavian meals, while mashed potatoes were served only two or three times, about as often as fried or French-fried potatoes were served.

A special dish of fried potatoes in Sweden is *råraka*. Grated raw potatoes are made into cakes and fried slowly in butter on both sides. To make
the *råraka* even better, grated onion and egg may be added. Another variety is the *raggmunk*, with egg, flour, and milk added to the grated potatoes.
Raggmunk is fried as a pancake on both sides and served with fried bacon
and lingonberry jam.

Mashed potatoes have been important, not least for children, and they
have also been mashed with fish leftovers into a *plukfisk*, an easier way to
get children to eat fish. Boiled potatoes in slices or cubes are stewed with
white sauce or served as a salad.

Potatoes have often been used as one of several ingredients in stews
and vegetable soups. Rutabaga was used the same way and also different
sorts of cabbage. In Denmark *grønlangkål* is still a popular dish even if not
served as often as before. The leaves of curly kale are boiled and mixed
with butter and cream into a stew.

Today many vegetables are boiled only briefly. Carrots have been a regular part of Scandinavian cuisine for more than 100 years and play an essential part in many stews and casseroles or boiled as a side dish. Tomatoes
are also used as an ingredient in a lot of fish and meat dishes. But the most
significant feature in the modern use of vegetables is to serve them raw.
Carrots are grated. Tomatoes and cucumbers are used to garnish different
dishes, as toppings on sandwiches and in salads, often with lettuce, spring
onions, and occasionally corn.

Dried, frozen, and canned beans are served with different meat dishes
in popular cuisine. One Swedish specialty is brown beans with fried pork.
The beans are boiled and a sweet-and-sour mixture of syrup and vinegar is

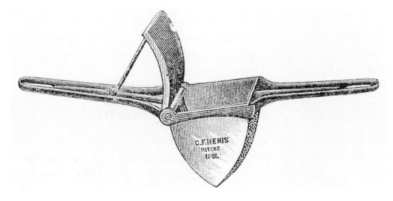

Device for mashing potatoes and other root vegetables. From Grethe
Haslund, Min Medhjælp, Kristiania, 1894.

added. Today, with all sorts of pulses available, many new bean and lentil dishes are made with recipes from Asia, Africa, and Latin America.

More recently shallots have been highly appreciated in dishes based on the traditions in French cuisine. Onion is also used in salads, and special salad onions with a milder flavor are on the market. Garlic is more and more considered a necessary ingredient in the kitchen, and little is heard of the jokes from a generation back about stinking garlic eaters.

Sweet peppers have become very popular in stews, soups, salads, and also as a garnish for cheese sandwiches and pizzas. They are also used with eggplant and squash/zucchini in Mediterranean dishes. A lot of other exotic vegetables, for example, sweet potatoes and yams, are now available, partly in the big supermarkets and partly in small shops run by immigrants.

Avocados, in earlier days used in appetizers with shrimp, are increasingly popular in salads and as guacamole.

Apples and Lingonberries

A lot of fruits and berries are used in jams and marmalades, cakes, and desserts or just served fresh with cream. But there are also examples of other uses. In the North, lingonberries are used as a substitute for the traditional jellies served with meat, red currant or rowanberry. In Sweden lingonberries are almost obligatory as a garnish with meatballs, and in Norway they are often served with roasts.

Apples are ingredients in various meat and fish dishes. The Danes are particularly good at inventing combinations. Best known is the apple (and prune) filling in geese and duck, but there is also æbleflæsk, slices of fried bacon or pork arranged on top of apples fried in the bacon fat and strewn with sugar. Another dish is æbletorsk, where codlings or cod steaks are dredged in flour and fried in butter. When they are almost cooked, apple wedges are added, and the dish is ready after a few minutes when the apple wedges are soft.[16]

REGIONAL COOKING

From about 1970 a strong tendency to emphasize local and regional culture has been seen in many fields. Groups and organizations, often backed by local museums, worked for a revitalization of traditional crafts, conservation or restoration of old buildings, collection of sources of local history, and recording of memories by old people. Particularly great was the interest in local food traditions, and this has resulted in a flood of books with examples of regional cooking. Festivals are also held to celebrate special products, for example, the singed lamb's head in Voss, western Norway.[17]

The reason behind this great interest is often a wish to give an identity to a village or a county at a time when national and international culture has become more uniform. The regional cooking emphasizes local products and cooking tradition in open contrast to mass-produced, anonymous food in the supermarkets. Some historians and ethnologists have warned against a certain naïveté in this movement, a danger of making stereotypes and creating certain emblematic dishes independent of the dynamics in food culture.[18] Revitalization often means that a particular dish is put in a new context that is completely different from the original one. It is also true that many of the so-called regional dishes were known over the whole of Scandinavia in earlier centuries, but developed certain regional characteristics that are now emphasized.

The revitalization is often supported by food producers in the local area, by tourist agencies, and by the national authorities. A Swedish ethnologist has shown how political this movement is. According to him, food product brands are created and shaped in marketing situations to match consumer ideas of place-related origin and "genuineness." They are based on stereotypes of preexisting food and meal culture.[19]

But whatever may be said against the genuineness of these dishes, they have often managed to establish themselves as regional in the consciousness of people within and outside the area.

The same is true for dishes in the autonomous areas under the Danish crown, Greenland and the Faroe Islands. Some of these dishes are presented here, even if they might be called *national* rather than *regional* by the inhabitants.

Potato Balls

One of these regional dishes is a ball or dumpling made from flour and potatoes—often with a piece of fat or meat inside—boiled in salt water. The tradition goes back to at least early modern time, but it has died out in many areas when a more modern cuisine has been introduced. In Sweden they are known as *palt* and *kroppkakor,* and the most famous are the *pitepalt,* named after the region around the northern city of Piteå, and the *öländska kroppkakor* from Öland, an island in the Baltic Sea off the east coast of Sweden. In Norway they have a particularly strong base in coastal towns where they belong to everyday dinners. They are called *raspeball* on the west coast around Bergen, *kumle* in the southwestern region around Stavanger, and *kompe* in the southern region around Kristiansand. Some of these dishes are made with boiled potatoes that give them a lighter color than the ones made from raw potatoes or a mixture of raw and boiled. The traditional flour is from barley, but in some of them wheat will be used today. A few of the more refined recipes add an egg to the dough.

Öland Kroppkakor (Potato Balls)

- 4 pounds raw potatoes, peeled
- 1 pound boiled, cold potatoes
- 1/2 cup flour
- 1 teaspoon salt
- 1 pound bacon
- 1 big onion

Cut the bacon in dices and chop the onion, fry the mixture in a pan, and add pepper generously. Shred the raw potatoes and mix with the crushed boiled potatoes. Add the flour and salt into this mixture and work it until it becomes a firm dough. Take a bit of dough with the hands and roll it into a ball almost as big as a tennis ball. Make a hole, put a tablespoon of the bacon-onion mixture into it, and tightly close the hole. Put the balls in boiling water one by one and stir carefully so the balls don't stick to each other. Boil for 45–60 minutes. Serve with melted butter and lingonberry jam.

Egg Cake

Regional dishes in the southern Swedish region of Skåne have many parallels in Denmark, the country Skåne belonged to until the seventeenth century. One example is the *Skånsk äggkaka* (Skåne egg cake), which is an omelette with flour.[20] Milk, eggs, and flour are mixed and fried slowly on both sides in a frying pan. It is served with fried bacon and lingonberry jam. In the Danish *æggekage* (egg cake), the fried bacon is put on top just before the omelette is completely solidified.

Brown Cabbage

Another dish Skåne shares with Denmark is *brunkål* (brown cabbage), where leaves or strips of white cabbage are browned in butter in a frying pan. In Denmark they mix the butter with sugar, in Skåne they drip syrup on top of the leaves. When brown, the cabbage simmers in water, or may be baked in an oven. In Skåne *brunkål* is served as a side dish to ham or other pork dishes, in Denmark pork cuts, minced pork, or even pig's trotters are boiled with the cabbage.

Brunkål Med Flæsk (Brown Cabbage with Pork)

- 1 cabbage, about 2 pounds
- 1 pound pork
- 3 ounces butter
- 2 tablespoons sugar
- 1 cup boiling water
- 1 teaspoon salt
- 1/2 teaspoon pepper

Melt butter and sugar in a pot. When the mixture is golden put in finely sliced cabbage and stir constantly until the leaves are brown. Make room in the middle of the pot for the pork and cover it with cabbage. Sprinkle salt and pepper and add boiling water. Simmer for one hour.

"Boiled" Bread

A very special regional dish is the *Upplandskubb* (Uppland log end) from the Swedish county of Uppland. It is a leavened bread "boiled" indirectly in water by using the bain-marie (water bath) technique. The dough is placed in a cylindrical container in which it is allowed to rise before the container is closed and placed in boiling water for several hours. The bread is brown and juicy and keeps well. The oldest formal recipe is from the mid-nineteenth century, but the name is fairly recent.[21] It has a parallel in the Icelandic *hverabrauð* (hot spring bread). This is also leavened rye bread, put in a tin or a metal bucket. It is covered tightly and left for 24 hours in a hole in the ground where a hot spring is coming up.[22]

Sami Cooking

In some regions in the northern parts of Scandinavia the Sami population had their own culinary traditions, based on the special conditions of a nomadic life. Today most Sami people live as other Scandinavians, in houses with all possible modern equipment and with access to all sorts of food and cooking methods. Many Sami, however, have continued some of the old culinary traditions, and even outside Sami circles several of the dishes are popular. When a sorrel soup was served as the starter in a Nobel Prize dinner in Stockholm, this may have been a reflection of the importance of sorrel in the Sami diet. The Sami based their food on three products: reindeer meat, reindeer milk, and fish from the rivers and lakes. But they added berries and certain wild plants and thereby got necessary vitamins. One dish was *juobmo* (common sorrel)[23] in reindeer milk. Another dish was *kombo*, or *gompa*. Garden angelica[24] was blanched, chopped, and mixed with reindeer milk. This mixture was warmed until it curdled and put away to be kept.[25]

Today reindeer is an exclusive foodstuff, and reindeer fillets are served in restaurants all over Scandinavia. *Renskav*, thin slices of meat, are bought frozen in most shops and are fried and served in a brown sauce. But reindeer meat is also eaten in other and more traditional preparations. The Sami never roasted their meat. They boiled most of it, often with the offal or other parts of the animal: heart, lungs, liver, tongue, udder, marrowbone, and even blood. Some of the most tender parts were dried or smoked and are considered delicacies today, for example, smoked leg of reindeer. Dried or smoked heart and boiled tongue were cut in fine slices and are still eaten this way, even served in restaurants.

Roe from freshwater fish was traditionally dried. When it was needed for a meal, it was crushed, mixed with water to expand, and then mixed with flour and salt. These *rompalt* (roe balls) were shaped with the hand and dropped in boiling water. This old tradition was adapted to modern times. A Sami housewife made a pancake of roe (3/4 cup), milk (2 pints), flour (2 1/4 cup), and salt. They were baked in the oven in a battered dish for about 20 minutes.[26]

Cooking in the Faroe Islands

The staple food in the Faroe Islands has always been fish. Because of the harsh climate, everything but rutabaga is difficult to grow, and most grain for bread is imported. Fish is eaten fresh, dried, or salted. Fresh fish is used for *knettir*, big balls of minced fish, onion, spices, and—particular for the Faroe Islands—lamb's tallow. The stock is used to make a sweet-and-sour soup containing carrots and prunes. *Knettir* and *knettasúpan* used to be a combination for festivals or Sunday dinners, but is daily fare today.[27]

Even if fish was eaten fresh, most of it was dried, as was meat from lamb, seabirds, seals, and whales. People still dry such products on the island. Fresh lamb is imported, because so much of the local production is dried for private consumption. Smoking and fermentation, so popular in Iceland, have not been practiced here. Salt used to be expensive and very scarce but is used today for the preservation of fish and meat.

Many dishes made with dried fish and meat are considered traditional today and are served for special occasions. But they are also beginning to appear on restaurant menus, and some of them are industrially produced and sold in the shops.

There are three types of dried products, the result of different stages in the drying process. The first stage, only used for fish, pilot whale, and some seabirds, comes after a couple of days and is called *visnadur* (withered), when a certain smell appears. The next stage, also used for lamb, comes after 3–4 weeks and is called *ræstur* (stored). The fish or meat is still soft but has matured and developed a strong smell and taste. In these two stages food has to be cooked, normally boiled, before it is eaten. The third stage is *turrur* (dry) and needs 9 months or more to be finished. The product is hard and dark and is eaten raw in thin slices like a Parma ham. Dried lamb is a popular dish, and so is dried pilot whale, eaten with salt blubber. Such blubber is also appreciated with dried fish.

Seabirds had to be preserved for storage during winter, but these birds are very tasty when eaten fresh, boiled or roasted. Among the many different birds, puffin has acquired a special position, and *filled puffin* is considered a national dish. The recipes are simple, once the birds have been properly cleaned. They are filled with a pancake batter, sewn up so nothing will leak, and boiled in lightly salted water.

Cooking in Greenland

The culinary heritage in Greenland is a mixture of traditions from the aboriginal population, the Icelandic settlers from the Middle Ages, the Danish colonial rulers, and even from American soldiers during World War II.[28] Today Greenland is influenced by a global food culture like every other part of Scandinavia, but there is a tendency to revitalize or strengthen traditional dishes, and many of them are now even served in restaurants.

The basic food in the aboriginal societies was meat from different animals, in particular seals, whales, and reindeer. At a later stage fishing became important, and the settlers brought with them domesticated animals, above all sheep.

The meat was so important for the native Greenlanders that the word for food was the same as the word for meat, *neqi*. Meat and offal were eaten raw, boiled, or dried. A simple soup of meat boiled in water with onion and rice, *suaassat*, is today considered a national dish. Seal meat is often suggested in the recipes, but also meat from whale, sheep, reindeer, and other animals may be used. This is a "use what is available" dish, and the rice is probably a new addition, because it was an expensive ingredient earlier. In the first Greenlandic cookbook from 1934, printed in Danish and Greenlandic, the *suaassat* is not made with rice, but with the cheaper barley grits.[29]

Fermentation of Greenland shark has been practiced in Greenland as in Iceland, but also fermentation of the hooded seal, *natsersuaq*. A recipe given by Greenlanders born in the early part of the twentieth century and referred to in a recent book, recommends tying the fresh head of a hooded seal up in a sealskin, placing it in a hole in the ground, and covering it with turf. The same method is used with front and hind flippers.[30]

Everything on the seal had to be used, and the nutritious blood was used in *puisip aava issortitaq* (seal black pudding) and *kukkarnaat* (dried seal blood). Products from whale were also well exploited. *Orsoq uutaq* is blubber from the lesser rorqual made into blubber cracklings. Bits of the blubber are boiled and dried on a stone so the oil is drained away. Another specialty is *mattak*, whale skin with some of the blubber left. It is eaten raw.

Fish is eaten boiled, dried, smoked, or fermented.

NOTES

1. Marianne Pipping Ekström: "Kvinnor, män och arbetet med maten," in *Nye og tradisjonelle trekk i nordisk matkultur*, ed. Eldbjørg Fossgard (Voss: Vestnorsk kulturakademi 2005), p. 24.

2. National Statistical Office, Norway: www.ssb.no.

3. Göran Ahrne and Christine Roman: *Hemmet, barnen och makten. Statens offentliga utredningar* (Government report) 1997:139 (Stockholm: Arbetsmarknadsdepartementet 1997), p. 27.

4. Marianne Pipping Ekström and Elisabeth L'Orange Fürst: "The gendered division of cooking," in *Eating patterns: A day in the lives of Nordic peoples*, ed. Unni Kjærnes (Lysaker, Norway: SIFO—National Institute of Consumer Research 2001).

5. Jan Krag Jacobsen: "Madkultur—et oplæg til en kulturpolitik på madområdet," in *Rapport om den danske madkultur* (Copenhagen: Kulturministeriet 1997).

6. *Mat, arbeid og kultur* (Lysaker, Norway: SIFO 1985).

7. HETUS—Harmonized European time use survey: www.testh2.scb.se/tus/tus.

8. Marianne Ekström: *Kost, klass och kön* (Umeå, Sweden: Umeå University 1990), p. 212.

9. Unni Kjærnes (ed.): *Eating patterns: A day in the lives of Nordic peoples* (Lysaker, Norway: SIFO 2001), p. 261.

10. See New Scandinavian Cooking: www.scandcook.com.

11. Sara Brinch: "Fjernsynskokken som mediefenomen," in *Tradisjon, opplysning og verkelegheit i norsk matkultur*, ed. Eldbjørg Fossgard (Voss: Vestnorsk kulturakademi 2002), pp. 162–64.

12. "Vem bakar brödet i Sverige?" Brödinstitutet: www.brodinstitutet.se (accessed May 23, 2008).

13. Nika Hazelton: *The art of Scandinavian cooking* (New York: Macmillan 1965), p. 2.

14. Recent archaeological research at the Viking site Borg in Lofoten, Norway, has documented mixture of fish and fermented milk in the crusts found in soapstone vessels. Egil Brodshaug and Brit Solli: "Kleber, mat og rom på Borg i middelalderen," in *Viking* (Oslo: Norsk arkeologisk selskap 2006), pp. 289–306.

15. *Consumption of vegetables, potatoes, fruit, bread and fish in the Nordic and Baltic countries*, The Norbagreen 2002 study, TemaNord 2003:556 (Nordic Council of Ministers 2003).

16. Alan Davidson, *North Atlantic seafood* (New York: Harper & Row 1989), p. 389.

17. Atle Wehn Hegnes: *Tradisjonsmatfestivalenes tvetydighet*, Fagrapport 3 (Oslo: SIFO 2003).

18. Ingrid Nordström: "Regionala matböcker—en etnologisk genre i tiden?" *Rig—Kulturhistorisk tidsskrift* (1994): 85.

19. Richard Tellström: "The construction of food and meal culture for political and commercial ends: EU-summits, rural businesses and world exhibitions" (summary, Örebro University, 2006), Available at www.oru.se/templates/oruExtNormal____41066.aspx (accessed August 21, 2008).

20. A detailed historical description in Kurt Genrup: *Mat som kultur* (Umeå, Sweden: Etnologiska institutionen, Umeå universitet 1988), pp. 121–31.

21. Charlotte Lagerberg Fogelberg, CUL—Centre for Sustainable Agriculture, Uppsala, Sweden: www.cul.slu.se/english.

22. Hallgerður Gísladóttir: *Íslensk matarhefð* (Reykjavik: Mál og menning 1999), pp. 217–19.

23. Common sorrel is *Rumex acetosa*.

24. Garden angelica is *Angelica archangelica*.

25. Phebe Fjällström: "Samisk mat i tradition och nutid," in *Gastronomisk kalender* (Stockholm: Prisma 2003), pp. 71–72.

26. Fjällström: "Samisk mat," pp. 74–75.

27. The information about food in the Faroe Islands is taken from Jóan Pauli Joensen: *Færøsk madkultur: En oversigt* (Faroese Research Council), Available at www.gransking.fo.(accessed May 15, 2008).

28. The information about food in Greenland is mainly based on Finn Larsen: *Food in southern Greenland for 1000 years* (Høybjerg: Hovedland c. 2000).

29. Meta Larsen-Imit: *Kalátdlit nunãne nerissagssiornermut Ilíniutigssat/Kogebog for husholdninger i Grønland* (Copenhagen: Bianco Luno 1934), p. 42.

30. Larsen: *Food*, p. 26.

4

Typical Meals

How the meals are organized, that is, where and when food is eaten, is part of the total organization of daily life in Scandinavia. On weekdays meals represent necessary breaks in the work routine, providing the body with food and rest. In agricultural societies people had to bring food with them when they had work to do in the forests and the fields, but on the farm they often worked near the home, so meals—even hot meals—were easy to eat at a chosen time. In today's urbanized society, work may be a long way from home, which has its effects on the meal structure.

In the early twenty-first century meal times, meal habits, meal structures, and the dishes eaten are all changing. The regional differences (between countryside and city, coast and inland, North and South) are waning, if not completely vanishing, and even national differences are gradually becoming less visible. This change is mainly a result of globalization, on the one hand, because multinational corporations offer more uniform products and, on the other hand, because new immigrants introduce ethnic products. Social differences based on income, education, and cultural background still have relevance, and age is a decisive factor, since the young tend to try out new trends with more openness and energy than older people. As shown in Chapter 3, Cooking, demographic changes are crucial to understanding changes in meal patterns and content, for example, the increased use of prepackaged meals.

DIFFERENT ASPECTS OF A MEAL

In a discussion of meals in a given society, many aspects of diet and lifestyle are relevant: what are the contents of the meal; which dishes are prepared; which ingredients are used; and how do time, taste, and nutrition influence all these factors? How is the meal eaten: seated at a nicely laid table or standing in the kitchen? Who is eating with whom? Is the meal eaten alone or with the whole family or with those in the family who happen to be present at the moment? How much does the social aspect of a meal mean? Is there a difference in the evaluation of different meals? Are hot meals considered better or of higher quality than cold meals, and are meals eaten in company with others better than individual meals?

A study made in the late 1990s of Scandinavian meal structures and eating habits answers many of these questions.[1] The description of typical meals in this chapter is primarily based on this study, which uses the same methods and interview techniques for all the countries and thereby is more reliable for comparison.

A general conclusion of this study is that the Swedish respondents were found to have more complex eating habits than those of the other countries, for example, more varied cold meals, more elements in hot meals, and a larger variety in beverages.

BREAKFAST

Some people limit their first morning meal to a drink: a cup of coffee or a glass of juice or milk, but breakfast generally is based on a combination of grain products and other components. The Scandinavian morning meal is generally more substantial than the breakfast in France and southern Europe but far from the famous full English breakfast.

A few people still stick to the traditional porridge. Oats porridge has had a certain revival on account of its positive health effects, but it is eaten only by a small minority. The Danish classic *øllebrød* (beer-and-bread), a soup of rye bread boiled in beer, is mostly eaten by the older generation.

The main grain product eaten at breakfast is bread, prepared as a so-called open sandwich. Adults and children—if they are not too young—help themselves to butter (or margarine) and various toppings and spreads. The meal being very informal, the different products are often kept in their packages and boxes, which are placed directly on the table. There is a broad choice of vegetable spreads and spreads made from animal products and toppings. Jams and marmalades are common, some of them imported, others homemade from berries collected in private gardens or in the woods, but this is a rapidly disappearing tradition. Cheese is a standard spread, for example, one of the hard yellow cheeses, and in Norway also one of the brown cheeses. There are pots with herrings in brine or in different spicy mixtures, or cans with mackerel in tomato sauce and sprat in olive oil. Cod roe and other caviar substitutes are also widely used. Cold cuts of salami and other cured sausages are popular besides boiled or cured ham and liver paste. The liver paste eaten at breakfast in Sweden and Norway will normally come out of a can, while the Danes prefer a homemade liver paste or one bought from their butcher, and they also serve it hot.

An increasing number of people eat packaged cereals with yogurt, more often in Sweden than in the other countries. Eggs are fairly rare on weekdays, but on Sundays a boiled egg or fried egg with bacon may be served. In Denmark a very special tradition at breakfast is the *wienerbrød* (Danish pastry). According to statistics, *wienerbrød* is eaten at 8 percent of the breakfasts on weekdays, and 25 percent of the Sunday morning breakfasts in Denmark, while the other Scandinavians consider *wienerbrød* a suitable accompaniment to coffee at other times of the day.[2]

Fruit is not common except in the form of canned orange juice. Juice is also served more often on Sundays than on weekdays. The preferred breakfast drink is a hot beverage. A few people drink tea, but tea never conquered the breakfast the way it did in Britain. Coffee stands out as the number-one morning drink. The traditional coffee boiled on the stove, with coffee grounds floating around, has been replaced by filtered coffee, taken black or white and most often without sugar. Some households have special coffee machines for espresso or percolating, but this is an exception, and in any case rarely used for breakfast.

Milk is also a breakfast drink, particularly among Norwegians. According to the Scandinavian survey, half of the Norwegian population had milk for breakfast, while only a quarter of the Danes and a third of the Swedes. This may be explained by the fact that Danes and Swedes had cereals with different milk products more often than Norwegians.

In Denmark a few may also have alcohol for breakfast, beer or a little shot of bitters, often called an Old Danish, after one of the brands.

The breakfast is eaten at home by more than 9 out of 10 Scandinavians but not always as a common family meal. Many family members will have breakfast on an individual basis because they leave at different times for work or school.

In the twentieth century coffee had become so important that substitutes were
made from peas in times of crisis. From an
advertisement in Tidsskrift for husstell-
lærerinner, Oslo, 1941.

Dansk Leverpostej (Danish Liver Paste)

- 1 pound pork liver
- 1/3 pound pork fat
- 2 or 3 anchovies (optional)
- 1 cup milk or cream
- 2 ounces butter
- 5 tablespoons flour
- 3 tablespoons bread crumbs
- 1 onion chopped
- 1 egg
- 1/2 teaspoon allspice
- 1/2 teaspoon pepper

When the liver has been properly cleaned, cut it into small bits. Put it through
the meat grinder with the fat, anchovy, bread crumbs, and onion. People have
different ideas about how fine or coarse a liver paste ought to be; the more times
the ingredients go through the grinder, the finer it becomes.

Melt the butter, add the flour, and let it simmer without getting colored. Add
milk slowly to this mixture, and let it simmer for 5–10 minutes. Add whipped egg
and spices to the mixture and finally the liver mixture.

Mix all well and put it in a fireproof dish. Bake in the oven for about an hour (375°F). The paste may be served warm with fried slices of bacon and fried mushrooms, or with pickles. In summer some people put a fresh cucumber salad on top, but it should be done immediately before serving, so the paste and the cucumber won't turn soggy.

LUNCH

While many Swedes have a hot meal for lunch, most Danes and Norwegians eat a cold lunch with bread as the basic component. To most people this still means an open sandwich, often more elaborate with many different trimmings in Denmark, and therefore eaten with knife and fork. But among the young, fast food lunches—hamburger, pizza, hot dog—are also popular. In Norway one survey found that among people between 15 and 24 years 10 percent ate a fast food type of meal at least once a week. This in contrast to the percentage for people between 40 and 60 years (2%) and people over 60 years (1%).[3]

About half of the Scandinavians eat their lunch at home, the other half at their place of work or study or in a café. Typical for the Danes and Norwegians have been their homemade lunch pack (*madpakke*), open sandwiches wrapped in wax paper or put in a lunch box.[4] The sandwich may also be bought in a café, but more and more cafés tend to serve bread in new forms that are easier to take away and consume without a knife and fork, as for example, the English sandwich, *ciabatta* or baguette with filling (cold meat cuts, shrimps, cheese and ham, mozzarella and tomato). The lunch is eaten with a hot beverage, mostly coffee, or with a soft drink, and in Denmark also with a beer.

Pytt-i-panna (Swedish Lunch Dish)

This is an old Swedish dish, which has won a new popularity, served in restaurants and available as prepackaged meal. It is also a popular night snack at parties. Beef is the preferred meat, but mixed with pork and sausages. The ideal composition is, according to the great chef Tore Wretman, twice as much potato as meat. Basically a dish with leftover meat, it is easy to cook.

- 4 cups sliced potatoes (leftovers)
- 2 cups sliced meat (leftovers)
- 2 cups sliced onions
- butter
- salt, pepper

Dice the potatoes and chop the onion. Fry in butter until golden. Increase the heat and add diced meat. Cook for a few minutes. Sprinkle with pepper and salt. Serve with pickled beets and pickles and a fried egg on top.

Sol over Gudhjem (Sun over Gudhjem, a Danish Lunch Sandwich)

Gudhjem is a village on the island Bornholm in the Baltic Sea, known for high-quality smoked herring. The recipe is for one sandwich.

- 1 smoked herring
- 1 buttered slice of rye bread
- 1 red onion
- 1 egg yolk
- chives
- salt, pepper

Remove head and tail. Open the herring and place it flat with the skin side up. Bank along the back of the herring with the broad side of a knife. Turn the herring and carefully remove the backbone so all the small bones follow. Put the fillets on the buttered bread. Peel the onion and cut two slices, and make sure you have a couple of entire rings that serve as a nest for the egg yolk. Sprinkle pepper and chopped chives on top.

Gravlaks

- 2 fillets of salmon with skin (the quantities given for spices are for 1 lb. fillets)
- 3 tablespoons of salt
- 2 tablespoons of sugar
- 2 teaspoons of ground pepper
- 1 bunch dill

Buy the salmon the day before and keep it in the freezer for 24 hours to kill parasites and bacteria. If you have a whole fish, clean, wash, and fillet. Do not remove the skin, but cut away fins and remove as many bones as possible. Dry the fillets with a paper towel and rub the flesh sides with a mixture of salt, sugar, and pepper. Place one fillet with the skin side down and strew coarsely chopped dill over it. Put the other fillet on top, skin side up, and head and tail side the opposite direction as the first fillet. Put in a plastic bag and keep in the refrigerator for two days. Some people place the fillets on a plate (glass, enamel, stainless steel, but not aluminum) and another plate or a board on top with some pressure.

Gravlaks Sauce

- 2–3 tablespoons mustard
- 2 tablespoons sugar

- 2 tablespoons wine vinegar
- 1/2–3/4 cup oil
- 3 tablespoons finely chopped dill
- salt and pepper

Mix mustard, vinegar, and sugar. Carefully add the oil drop by drop into the mustard mixture and stir constantly so the sauce becomes thick. Season with salt and pepper and add the dill. Serve cold.

Stegt Rødspætte (Fried Plaice)

For lunch fillets of plaice are used as toppings on open sandwiches and served with a remoulade sauce. For dinner they are eaten with potatoes and vegetables and served with parsley sauce. Both these combinations are Danish classics. Plaice is the most popular fish among the Danes after marinated herring.

- 4 plaice
- 1/2 cup bread crumbs
- 1 egg
- pepper, salt
- butter for frying

Clean and wash the plaice (and remove the skin, if wanted). Coat the fish with a whipped egg and the bread crumbs, seasoned with salt and pepper. Fry in browned butter 5–6 minutes on each side until done.

Remoulade

- 7 ounces mayonnaise
- 1 tablespoon French mustard
- 2 ounces chopped pickles
- 2 ounces chopped onion
- 1 ounce chopped capers
- 3 tablespoons parsley or chervil

Mix all the ingredients into the mayonnaise and serve cold with the cold fillets.

Persillesovs (Parsley Sauce)

- 2 tablespoons of flour
- 3 tablespoons of butter
- 1 1/2 cup of milk
- salt, pepper
- parsley

Melt the butter in a pan, stir in the flour, and add milk while constantly stirring. Let boil a few minutes. Add chopped parsley, and sprinkle a little salt and pepper over it.

SMALL MEALS AND SNACKS

Most Scandinavians eat between three and six meals a day; the average is four. But what is a meal? To draw a line between a meal and a snack is no easy task. A sandwich is considered a meal in Norway but only a snack in Sweden. Sandwiches may be served with hot meat patties and fried onions, and this is not very different from a Swedish meal with meat patties and fried onions and bread on the side. A hot dog, a pizza slice, and a portion of French fries may be considered a snack by some, a meal by others.

Mid-morning or afternoon is the time for a light snack, for example, a sweet pastry. Fruit, ice cream, chocolate, peanuts, or potato chips may also be eaten as a snack. For people constantly on the move, such as taxi drivers, truck drivers, messengers, and couriers, the gas stations offer more and more tempting combinations of coffee with hot or cold snacks.

Coffee is drunk at irregular intervals between meals and snacks. In many offices and other workplaces coffee makers continuously brew coffee that is either offered free or for a reduced price. At home, especially if someone is visiting, it is a norm to put the coffee kettle on. If there are buns in the freezer, or biscuits or cookies in the cupboard, they will accompany the coffee. A bun made of leavened dough and seasoned with sugar and cinnamon is very popular and is named after the cinnamon in Sweden, *kanelbulle* (cinnamon bun); after its shape in Denmark, *snegl* (snail); and after its old retail price in Norway, *skillingsbolle* (shilling bun).

Kanelbullar (Swedish Cinnamon Buns)

Buns

- 1 1/2 pound flour
- 4 ounces butter
- 4 ounces sugar
- 1 1/2 cup milk
- 1 1/2 ounces yeast
- 1 teaspoon salt
- 1 tablespoon cinnamon

Filling

- 2 ounces sugar
- 4 ounces butter
- 2 tablespoons cinnamon

Glaze

- 2 tablespoons of pearl sugar
- 1 egg

Stir crumbled yeast into a few tablespoons of lukewarm milk. Add the rest of the milk, melted butter, sugar, flour, and spices. Make a workable dough and let it rise at room temperature for about half an hour. Roll out the dough to a rectangle about 10–12 inches wide and 1/4 inch thick. Spread butter on top and sprinkle a mixture of sugar and cinnamon over it. Make a long roll of the rectangle and cut it in slices about 3/4 inch thick. Put the slices in paper molds on a baking sheet. Cover them with a towel and leave them for about an hour. Brush the buns with beaten egg and sprinkle with pearl sugar. Bake in the oven for 6–7 minutes (425°F).

Waffles and pancakes are also served at reunions with family or friends, particularly on the weekends. Pancakes are popular with adults and children alike and serve several functions. The method—to fry a flat cake made from a batter of flour, milk, and eggs—is not particularly Scandinavian but rather universal. In its simplest version this is the primitive flatbread made from flour and water and cooked in the embers, but gradually, more refined flours have been used and the dough enriched with fats (milk, cream, butter) and eggs or leavener. Even if they started out as ordinary breads for everyday use, they acquired a higher status with the more exclusive ingredients. They are eaten in many different ways and on different occasions, buttered or sprinkled with sugar or wrapped around a jam filling made from berries. Pancakes made with bacon constitute more of a main hot dish.

Waffles are the most popular treat made in irons. From Grethe Haslund, Min Medhjælp, Kristiania, 1894.

Icelanders also eat pancakes as a starter with a filling of shrimp or mush-rooms. Waffles are made in a waffle iron instead of in a frying pan but are based on the same type of dough and served and eaten like the pancakes. In other words, there are a lot of intermediate stages between the snack and what some people call a *proper meal.*

Svele (Pancakes from Sunnmøre, Norway)

This pancake variety is typical of northwestern Norway, where it is served with coffee on the ferries crossing the numerous fjords.

- 3 eggs
- 4 1/2 cups flour
- 3/4 cup sugar
- 4 1/2 cups sour milk
- 1 teaspoon baking powder
- 1 teaspoon baking soda

Beat egg and sugar well. Whisk baking soda and powder into the milk, and add this to the egg and sugar. Stir in the flour little by little. The sveles were normally fried on a griddle, but today a frying pan with a little butter is fine. They are eaten with a little sugar or syrup, or with *rømme* and jam, or with brown cheese.

If the hot meal is not served too late in the afternoon, the evening meal will consist of bread and different spreads. The ubiquitous evening porridge from earlier centuries has completely disappeared. An increasing number of Scandinavians—if still a definite minority—have a can of beer or a glass of wine in the evening, even if they don't eat or only have some chips to go with it. Normally they have drunk water or another nonalco-holic beverage for the main hot meal in the late afternoon and use the wine as a nightcap.

Hot Meals

There is a fundamental difference between Denmark, Norway, and Iceland, where one hot meal per day is typical, and Sweden, where two hot meals a day are fairly normal. According to the Scandinavian survey, four out of five Danes and Norwegians eat one hot meal a day, normally served in the late afternoon or early evening. Only 6 percent in Norway and 12 percent in Denmark eat two hot meals, compared to 40 percent of the Swedes. In Sweden a hot meal may be served both for lunch and in the afternoon, but the pattern seems to be changing. For lunch more and more people prefer a cold salad instead of a heavy dish with meat and gravy. Authorities have recommended white meat over red, and this has helped the consumption of chicken through salads with cold chicken cuts and vegetables. So even if the Swedish lunch differs from the Danish and Norwegian sandwich meal, it is not necessarily a hot meal any longer. On the other hand, many Swedes who eat a hot meal for lunch now prefer a simpler and less labor-intensive meal preparation in the evening.

Few hot meals include more than one course, according to the Scandinavian survey. Starters of any kind appear very rarely, while two out of three meals always are without a dessert.

There also seems to be interesting differences between different age groups and different household categories. In Norway, where ground meat dishes are served at least once a week among 50 percent of the households, the proportion in households with children is 65 percent.[5] In a Danish survey about the most popular hot dinner dishes, pizza is among the top 10 until people are 45 years old, and then it drops in popularity. Burgers reach the climax among young people (19–24 years), where it is number 8 on the list. These two dishes are not even among the top 20 for people of 55 years and more. In this older age group whole cuts of meat are on top, and they eat fish more often than the young.[6]

With hot meals most people drink water or soft drinks and, to a lesser degree, milk and hot beverages. Alcoholic beverages are drunk by only 12 percent of the Norwegians on Sundays, and 7 percent on weekdays, and this is less than half of what is consumed in Sweden and less than a third of the Danish consumption. It seems, however, that this pattern is changing with the strong increase in the consumption of wine in all countries.

Lúða í Sítrónusósu (Halibut in Lemon Sauce, Iceland)

- 1 1/2 pounds halibut (washed cleaned and skin removed)
- 1 onion
- 1 pound mushrooms
- 1 cup whey (or white wine)
- 3/4 cup water
- juice of one lemon
- 1 1/2 tablespoons flour
- 2 egg yolks
- 2 teaspoons salt
- 2 ounces butter
- parsley

Chop onions and mushrooms and fry them gently in one tablespoon of butter. Put this in an ovenproof dish and place slices of fish on top. Mix whey, water, and lemon juice and pour it over the fish. Cover the dish with a lid and bake in the oven for 25 minutes (400°F). Carefully pour out all the liquid, strain it, and have it in a pot. Stir in the flour and enough water to make a sauce. Beat egg yolks with salt and butter and mix with the sauce. Pour the sauce over the fish and sprinkle chopped parsley on top. Put the ovenproof dish back into the oven and bake until golden brown. Serve with boiled potatoes and a salad of raw vegetables.

Kåldolmar (Swedish Cabbage Rolls)

This is ground meat wrapped up in cabbage leaves and braised (and served with the gravy) or boiled (and served with white sauce). They are called *kålruletter* (cabbage rolls), except in Sweden, where the name is *kåldolmar*, as in the Turkish rolls made with grape leaves. Swedish cabbage dolma is different from the others. It contains rice in addition to the meat. The traditional explanation given for this difference is that the dish was brought home after king Charles XII's stay in Turkey, but more probable is an influence from a group of Turkish financiers who lived in Stockholm with their families at the beginning of the eighteenth century.

- 1 head of white cabbage
- 1 cup of milk
- 11 ounces pork or pork/beef forcemeat
- 3/4 cup of boiled rice
- 1 teaspoon salt
- white pepper, thyme
- 2 tablespoons butter or margarine for frying
- a little syrup to taste

Cut out the core and put the cabbage in a pot with boiling water. After about five minutes the leaves are slightly soft and easy to peal off one by one. Trim the coarse vein of each leaf and let the leaves drain.

Mix the ground meat, boiled rice, and spices; then add milk carefully until the mixture is like a soft porridge. Put two tablespoons of filling on a leaf, fold the leaf around the filling to make a packet and secure it with a toothpick or a sewing thread.

Brown the butter in a frying pan and fry the roll on all sides. Don't put too many rolls in the pan at the same time. Transfer them one by one to a pot, where they continue to cook. Some people want them extra brown and drip a little syrup upon them. They are ready when the cabbage is soft. They are served with boiled potatoes, lingonberry jam, and the gravy.

Fiskegrateng (Norwegian Fish au gratin)

- 1 pound fish (leftovers of any fish)
- 2 tablespoons of butter
- 3 tablespoons of flour
- 1 1/2 cups of milk
- 3–4 eggs
- 2–3 tablespoons of ground dried bread crumbs
- salt, pepper

Melt the butter in a pan, and add flour and milk to make a thick white sauce. Stir in the egg yolks and the fish, broken in small pieces. Season with salt and pepper. Beat egg whites stiff and fold them into the sauce. Pour the whole mixture into a buttered ovenproof dish and sprinkle with bread crumbs. Some people like to sprinkle with grated cheese on top (about a half cup). Bake on the bottom rack until golden brown, about 45 minutes (375°F).

A Proper Meal

Investigations about attitudes to cooking and meals reveal that many people (and more women than men) have very firm convictions about what a real meal is. Such a meal is often referred to in studies as a "proper meal," even if this is not an expression used by the women themselves. The proper meal concept was developed in Great Britain after studies of working class food habits in the 1970s, and this type of meal was generally defined as consisting of meat, potatoes, one or more vegetable side dishes and a sauce.[7]

In the study of Scandinavian eating patterns from the late 1990s, the proper meal concept was investigated by a systematic comparison of the different components of the hot meal.

Given the apparent differences between Scandinavian and British traditions, the researchers listed five components particular to the Scandinavian pattern:

1. A main dish (called center in the study) consisting of meat, fish, or vegetables
2. A staple consisting of potatoes, rice, pasta, or pulses
3. A side dish of vegetables, raw or cooked
4. Accompaniments, for example, hot and cold sauces, preserves, condiments
5. Bread

Ten percent of the meals consisted of only one component, for example, a vegetable soup, a porridge, or a pizza, but some of the meals with one component were one-pot dishes where different ingredients were mixed (meat, staples, vegetables).

About one-third of the meals consisted of two components, most of them a main dish with a staple, for example, sausages and mashed potatoes or stir-fried vegetables with rice. Less common were combinations where the main dish was mixed with bread (hot dog) or accompaniment (pasta with a sauce).

The most typical meal was a combination of three components. In all countries, but in Norway more than in the others, the preferred combination was a center with staple and vegetables. This might be meatballs with boiled potatoes and cabbage stew or grilled chicken with French fries and a salad, or fried fish cakes with mashed potatoes and grated raw carrots.

Another common combination was made by substituting the vegetables with a trimming, for example, gravy, ketchup, or melted butter. Less frequent was a main dish without staple.

About one in five meals consisted of four components, and here the preferred combination was a main dish with staple, vegetables, and trimmings, for example, a roast with baked potatoes, salad, and gravy or an oven-baked fish with boiled potatoes, steamed sugar peas, and a remoulade sauce.

Sweden was the country where a dish with more than three components was the most common. There was a clear tendency in all countries to serve a larger number of components on Sundays than during the week.

Main Dish

Meat was the most common main dish (center) in all types of hot meals. On average meat was an ingredient in two-thirds of all hot meals, more often on Sundays than during the week. Meat is also considered most important in a so-called proper meal, except in Norway, where fish is about as popular as meat. Norwegians had fish as the main dish in their meals 27 percent of all weekdays, far above the Swedes (15%) and Danes (9%). Vegetarian dishes, omelettes, pizzas, and pasta dishes were less common but eaten as hot meals in Sweden more often than in the other countries.

Staples and Bread

Almost half of the meals were served with potatoes as staple. Rice and pasta contributed about 10 percent each. More than two-thirds of hot meals had only one staple. The only place where a second staple was of any importance was in Sweden, where about 10 percent of hot meals had bread as a component besides potatoes, rice, or pasta. One explanation for this is that the Swedes do not eat sandwiches as often as do Norwegians and Danes. Bread might also be used as a second staple when other staples were used as ingredients in the dish itself, for example, one-pot dishes with rice or potatoes.

Vegetables

Vegetables of different kinds are included in about half of the Scandinavian meals. But there is a clear difference in the way vegetables are eaten. According to the survey, Swedes eat fresh vegetables (for instance, tomatoes, cucumber, or lettuce) 28 times a month in average, whereas the other Scandinavians limit such consumption to 16–18 times a month. Norwegians eat boiled vegetables 13 times a month compared to 8 times in Sweden. Fried or stir-fried vegetables are only used three or four times a month in all countries. There was a certain homogeneity in the choice of vegetables, because the variety in each country was quite limited. In Norway, which represents an extreme case, about one-third of all hot meals included carrots.

From Scratch

The preferred proper meal is prepared from scratch, which means with fresh ingredients. Even women who work outside their homes feel that making such meals is an obligation. But because of all the time involved in shopping and preparation of such dishes, these ambitions are not easy to realize. The size of the Scandinavian households is also a factor to consider. The number of children is down, and many children live with one single parent. To spend a lot of time every day on a hot meal with several ingredients is not always thought to be worthwhile. Therefore convenience foods are often a necessary resort.

Köttbullar (Swedish Meatballs)

Köttbullar, often called *Mother's meatballs*, are served for dinner with a thick brown gravy or a thin meat juice, or without juice at *smörgåsbord*. They are generally served with potatoes, mashed or boiled, and lingonberry jam or just crushed fresh lingonberries.

- 1 pound ground meat (for example, a mixture of pork and beef)
- 1 egg

- 1 onion
- 1 cup milk
- 2/3 cup white bread crumbs
- salt, pepper, and allspice

First put the bread crumbs in the milk and let them soak. Heat butter and sauté finely chopped onion gently. Blend the ground meat with the onion, egg, spices, and the mixture of milk and bread crumbs. If the mixture is too firm, add a little water. Form small balls with clean hands, heat butter in a frying pan, and brown the meatballs on all sides, shaking the pan continuously to prevent sticking. Test one ball first to ensure that the taste and the consistency are right.

Lingonsylt (Lingonberry Jam)

- 2 pounds fresh lingonberries
- 3/4 cup water
- 2 cups white sugar (or more if wanted)

Rinse and wash the lingonberries. Place them in a pot with the water and boil carefully 10 to 15 minutes. Put the pot aside and stir in sugar until all of it is dissolved in the lingonberries. If you want the jam a little darker, let the sugar cook with the berries. Ladle jam into sterile jars (not quite to the top) and cover with lids immediately.

Combined fresh lingonberries and sugar may just be put in a plastic container and kept in the freezer.

Fish Cakes from Northwestern Norway

- 3/4 pound fish fillets
- 1 cup milk
- 1 1/2 teaspoons salt
- 1/4 teaspoon nutmeg
- 1/2 onion
- 1 topped tablespoon potato starch (or corn starch)

The best fish is haddock and pollack, but also saithe (pollock) may be used. The saithe gives a darker color to the cakes, and will need a little less milk than the other fish.

Cut the fish and onion in bits and put all the ingredients in the food processor. Let it run on full speed for 30–40 seconds. Divide the dough into about 12 portions and shape them into flat round cakes, a bit smaller than hamburgers. Fry them in butter or margarine on both sides in a frying pan and put them in an ovenproof dish. Bake them in the oven for 15 minutes (400° F). Serve them with boiled or mashed potatoes and grated carrots.

The same ground-up meat may be used for fish balls, small and oblong about the size of golf balls, poached in hot water or a stock (made from the trimmings of the filleted fish). Reduce the stock and use it in a white sauce to be served with the balls.

Kjötsúpa (Icelandic Meat Soup)

- 3 pounds shoulder or rack of lamb
- 10 cups water
- 2 teaspoons salt
- 2–3 tablespoons rice
- 1 big onion
- 1 pound rutabaga
- 1 pound carrots

Cut the meat in pieces and put pieces in a pot with boiling water and salt. Bring to a boil, skim, and sprinkle rice over it. Simmer on low heat for about an hour. Clean the vegetables and cut them into pieces. Boil them with the meat for 10 to 20 minutes. The meat and vegetables are served separately with boiled potatoes.

Rotmos (Swedish Mashed Rutabagas)

- 1 rutabaga (about 1 1/2 pound)
- 8 medium-sized potatoes
- 2 carrots
- 3 cups of water
- salt, pepper
- a little sugar to taste ("as grandma always did")

Peel the rutabaga and dice it and add to boiling water. When the rutabaga is beginning to get soft, put in the potato cubes and finally the carrots. When everything is soft, pour off the water and mash the root vegetables well. Use the stock to give the mash the wanted consistency. Salt and pepper to taste. Serve with boiled pork, sausages, or corned beef.

Social and Cultural Frameworks for Hot Meals

When it comes to the practice of preparing a hot meal, distinguishing between proper meals and meals that fall outside this category is not enough. The different dishes that constitute a dinner pattern can be seen as a result of the possibilities and even more of the limitations that unfold within the dinner culture.[8] The choice of different recipes for different occasions can be seen in the light of a social and cultural code. An example of one study of Norwegian hot meals involved ground meat, eaten at least once a week by half the population. Three different dinners with ground meat were served at different times in the home.

1. Everyday dinner, served in the kitchen around 5 P.M. from Monday through Thursday. This meal consists of minced meat patties, meatballs, meat casserole, or sauce bolognese, served with boiled potatoes, pasta, or rice.

2. Weekend evening meal, served in the cozy corner of the living room around 8 P.M. on Fridays and Saturdays. The dishes are tacos, enchiladas, hamburger, pizza, risotto, lasagna, or something similar.

3. Sunday dinner, served late afternoon in the dining room. Dishes are homemade meatballs or cabbage rolls with boiled potatoes and boiled root vegetables.

The different dishes with ground meat carry different meanings. A dish that can be served on Mondays is often not an alternative on Saturday night. What can be eaten at the kitchen table is not a good alternative at the dining room table. To further illustrate the point, there is a fourth hot meal alternative, "the problematic ground meat dish": hamburgers and kebabs served with French fries and ketchup or dressing. The women who participated in the study objected to this dinner, called it "junk food," based on a whole range of moral considerations and principles.

Take-Away and Delivered Hot Meals

One special form of hot meals eaten at home is the dish delivered to the door or picked up at a take-away outlet. According to a recent Norwegian study 9 percent of the population eat such hot meals delivered to the door (Chinese, Indian, pizza, etc.) at least once a month. A little more, 13 percent, eat food bought at a take-away outlet. There are slight differences in gender; men eat such food more often than women. But the striking contrast is between the generations. About three-quarters of the population over 60 years never eat this kind of food, compared to 28 percent of the young between 16 and 24 years. In this youngest age group 23 percent had food delivered to the door and 26 percent bought take-away food once a month or more often. The percentage for the 40- to 60-year-olds was 5 percent and 10 percent, respectively, and for people over 60 years, 1 percent and 3 percent.[9]

A Family Meal

The idea of a proper meal is not only linked to what is eaten and how it is prepared, but also to a broader social context, the family meal. The ideal of the family meal around a table is strongly implanted. A family meal is a hot meal eaten in the home in the company of all the other family members. In Scandinavia this type of meal is still part of ordinary everyday eating habits, whether or not there are children in the household.

Most Scandinavians eat most of their meals in their own home; approximately half of the entire population eat *all* their meals at home. Eating at home is even more common during weekends than during the week, and except for breakfast, most meals at weekends were eaten in common. The house is, in other words, the dominant location for Scandinavian meals, a different situation from that in the United States, where far less eating takes place in the home.

The meal around the kitchen or dining room table is the ideal and the usual, but a relatively high percentage of the meals, between 19 and 30 percent, were eaten at a coffee table, seated on a sofa, or in a comfortable armchair.

Eating with friends is not very common; it is barely perceptible in the statistics. There are occasions when friends are invited to coffee or dinner, but friends as a social framework for meals come third after eating at home and eating with colleagues at work. The young are, not surprisingly, eating more often with friends than are older people.

Several studies in Scandinavia indicate a high regard for family meals. Many women see it as an important element in building a family unit and in maintaining the cohesiveness of this unit, and consequently they try to organize the day in a way that makes a family meal possible. But at the same time a majority admits that it is difficult, particularly during the week, to realize their ideal. The different members of a household tend to spend parts of the day in separate social spheres. Parents may have different working hours, and sometimes they must drive their children to sports and other obligations.

On this background a discussion around the concept "grazing" has come up. Are traditional meals with a hot dinner and the whole family present disappearing and being substituted by irregular eating patterns, where people eat as they move from one place to another and where the social aspect is absent? Is eating becoming an individualized activity that lacks any social significance insofar as it becomes an isolated and mechanical activity?[10]

Danish family with fish dishes. Courtesy of
Art Directors and Trip/John Garrett.

This concern has been expressed by both individuals and official institutions. There are without doubt important changes going on, but they
may be explained by changing family structures. More and more households consist of only one person, and the studies show that living with
someone is the only factor that increases the probability of eating a hot
meal in the afternoon. It seems, in fact, that a majority of multiperson
households have meals with a structure. Thus, there do not seem to be
major arguments supporting the idea of increasingly unstructured eating
habits in Scandinavian families.[11]

One special aspect is the Sunday lunch or dinner. This is still important
in many families, but it seems that there is a tendency to give more and
more culinary priority to the Saturday (and even Friday) dinner.

On the weekends almost one out of three families has a dessert with
their meal, while this happens in less than one-fourth of the weekday
meals.

Hakkebøf (Danish Minced Beefsteaks)

- 1 pound minced beef
- 2 big or 3 small onions
- 2 ounces butter
- 3/4 cup bouillon
- flour
- salt
- pepper

Divide the meat into four portions, form them into flat patties, round or oval. Dredge them in flour mixed with salt and pepper.

Peel the onions and cut them into thin rings. Fry the onions in butter in a pan until they are golden brown. Remove them from the pan and fry the patties in the rest of the butter, 3–4 minutes on each side. Remove them and pour the bouillon into the pan (with a little cream if wanted). Let the gravy boil and thicken with some flour (1–2 tablespoons). The steaks are served with the onion rings on top, gravy, and, for example, pickled beets, cucumber salad, capers, or with a more modern attitude, tomato slices and basil leaves.

Fårikål (Mutton-in-Cabbage)

- 2 pounds lamb or mutton, preferably from shoulder or breast
- 2–3 pounds cabbage
- 2 tablespoons whole black peppercorns
- 2 teaspoons salt
- 2 cups water

Cut the meat into pieces 2–3 inches square, trimming off the fat. Rinse the cabbage and cut into small chunks. Put the fattest pieces of meat in the bottom of the cooking pot, then cabbage above, and so on in alternate layers. Sprinkle salt and pepper between the layers. Pour in boiling water. Bring to a boil and let simmer in 1 1/2 to 2 hours or until the meat is tender. Serve with boiled potatoes.

Some people keep the peppercorns in a perforated metal container or in a cloth, but much of the charm is to pick the peppercorns out of the cabbage.

Västkustsallad (Swedish West Coast Salad)

This is a popular summer dish. The ingredients are not always available in areas far from the coast. It is possible to substitute the lobster with canned crabmeat, and the mussels, mushrooms, and asparagus with canned products.

- 1/2 pound boiled and shelled shrimps
- 30–40 boiled mussels
- 1 lobster
- 1/2 pound white mushrooms (button mushrooms)
- 1/2 pound green asparagus, blanched and chilled
- 2 heads of lettuce

Garnish

- 1 bunch of dill
- 2 medium-sized ripe tomatoes
- 1 lemon

Dressing

- vinaigrette

Serve the salad on a big platter, in a bowl, or on individual plates. Begin with the lettuce leaves—they should cover the plate. Arrange the different ingredients on top. Cut the tomatoes and the lemon in wedges and decorate the plate with them. Put a sprig of dill on each plate. Drizzle the vinaigrette over the salad just before serving it, or put it in the fridge for a while to cool.

Rødgrød Med Fløde (Red Pudding with Cream)

This is a Danish specialty, considered a national dish, with the red and white representing *Dannebrog* (the Danish flag).

- 2 pounds of red berries
- 3 cups water
- 1 1/2 cups sugar
- 1 teaspoon vanilla sugar
- 5 tablespoons potato starch (or cornstarch)

Rinse berries and place them in a pot with cold water. Add sugar and vanilla and boil for about 10 minutes. Mix cornstarch with a little water and add it, stirring constantly for a couple of minutes. Remove the kettle from the stove, so it won't be sticky.

This is one way to prepare the famous dish, but there are two schools, and supporters of the second school do not want any berries in the pudding. Then the berries and the juice must be put in a sieve. The juice, now free of the berries, is put in a clean kettle and brought to a boil.

The starch is added as above, and the pudding is ready. In both schools it is recommended to find a personal balance between the ingredients, so the pudding gets the right sweetness and the right thickness. When the pudding is cold, some will sprinkle sugar on it and even decorate it with almonds. The cream (or milk for the weight conscious) is absolutely necessary.

Tilslørte Bondepiker ("Veiled Farm Girls," Norwegian Apple Dessert)

The name may refer to veils used with the traditional costumes in rural areas, but the expression is not from Norwegian dialects, rather from Danish. Nothing is known of the origin of this dish.

- 1 1/2 pounds apples
- 1/2 cup water
- 7 ounces sugar
- 1 1/2 cups dried bread crumbs (of white bread)
- 2 tablespoons of butter
- 1 1/2 cups heavy cream

Make the applesauce first. Peel and core the apples. Cut them in wedges and boil them in the water until soft. Stir in half of the sugar and cook until the consistency is like a thick sauce.

Melt butter in a frying pan. Add the bread crumbs and the rest of the sugar. Mix everything well and stir constantly over medium heat. (Some of the bread crumbs may be substituted by a little bit of finely chopped almonds.) When the mixture becomes light caramel in color, put aside to cool.

Put layers of bread crumbs and applesauce on a platter or a big bowl, and put whipped cream on top. The dessert may also be made on individual plates or glass dessert bowls.

Rabarbaragrautur (Icelandic Stewed Rhubarb)

Rhubarb has played an important part in Scandinavian horticultural history. In Iceland and the Faroe Islands, where the summers may be relatively cold, it has been a good substitute for other fruits and is used for porridges, stews, soups, jams, compotes, chutneys, and of course, wine.

- 1/2 pound rhubarb
- 3 cups water
- 3/4 cup sugar
- 3 tablespoons potato starch (dissolved in a little cold water)

Wash the rhubarb well and cut it into small pieces. Boil in water for about 20 minutes, until the rhubarb pieces fall apart. Stir in sugar and the potato starch, dissolved in a little cold water. Pour into a glass bowl and sprinkle a little sugar over the mixture. Serve cold with sugar and milk or cream. It is also possible to make a cold rhubarb soup this way, only with less starch (2 teaspoons).

NOTES

1. Unni Kjærnes (ed): *Eating patterns: A day in the lives of Nordic peoples* (Lysaker, Norway: SIFO—National Institute of Consumer Research 2001). This is a study of diet in Denmark, Norway, Sweden, and Finland; Iceland is not included.

2. Johanna Mäkelä, Unni Kjærnes, and Marianne Pipping Ekström: "What did they eat?" in *Eating patterns,* ed. Unni Kjærnes, p. 70.

3. Annechen Bugge and Randi Lavik: *Å spise ute* (Oslo: SIFO 2007), p. 78.

4. René Bühlmann and Stig Püschl: *Madpakken* (Copenhagen: Fremad 1991).

5. Annechen Bugge: "Middag—et betydningsfullt hverdagsrituale," in *Den kultiverte maten,* ed. Virgilie Amelien and Erling Krohg (Oslo: fagbokforlaget 2007), p. 97.

6. Sisse Fagt and Anja Biltoft-Jensen: *Populære middagsretter* (Copenhagen: The Danish Institute for Food and Veterinary Research 2006).

7. Laura Mason: *Food culture in Great Britain* (Westport, CT: Greenwood Press, 2004), p. 131.

8. All references in this section from Bugge: "Middag," pp. 101–3.

9. Bugge and Lavik: *Å spise ute,* pp. 73–76.

10. Lotte Holm: "Family Meals," *Eating patterns,* ed. Unni Kjærnes, p. 200.

11. Bugge: "Middag," p. 113.

5

Eating Out

Eating out is not an important part of Scandinavian food consumption or social life. This may partly be explained by historical factors. Scandinavia never had the broad restaurant tradition, as in many European countries from the early nineteenth century, with a strong urban culture and a wealthy bourgeoisie. Apart from a few big cities, Scandinavia was for a long time dominated by a sparsely populated countryside, villages, and small provincial towns, where the clientele for a restaurant was too small. The elite in these places rather arranged dinner parties for each other in their homes.

The people who had to travel through the countries had inns at their disposal along the roads, and later hotels grew up in urban centers along the ever-expanding railways. There were also a lot of beer cellars and wine cellars and other watering holes of varying quality and social status, mainly for men, later also cafés and bars, but most of the important *eating* was done in the homes, as it still is.

As late as in the 1960s an American visitor observed the following about Scandinavian restaurant culture: "Generally speaking, the Scandinavians don't eat out the way we so often do—to avoid cooking, or because it is quicker. When they eat out, they do so for a treat, and they expect their restaurants to be tops. Consequently there are few plain eating places, compared to the many in America, but there are a good number of superb restaurants that rank along the finest of Europe."[1]

Since this was written, important changes have taken place in Scandinavian societies. To most people a meal in a fine restaurant is still something special, but more and more are eating out, and a greater proportion of the disposable income is spent in cafés and restaurants than ever before.[2] There is a wide choice of alternatives, top gourmet restaurants, cafeterias, hamburger restaurants, and so on. There is, however, a difference in the purpose of eating that also decides the choice of place. In most cases people eat out for practical reasons, out of necessity, because they have to be away from home, and not out of a wish to enjoy food.

Eating away from home does not necessarily mean eating in a restaurant, where food is ordered according to choice and paid for by the customer. A very common tradition is to eat as guests in the home of friends. It may be an afternoon coffee with a bun, a child's birthday party, a garden barbecue, or a more formal dinner. In many residential areas people get together after doing voluntary work in their common area, and they bring along food and drink. Picnicking has not completely died out; in Norway the *tur* is still popular, hikes in forests and mountains, where simple meals are prepared over the fire.

A different form of eating away from home is eating in institutions. Men doing military service eat in the army canteens or on board their ships. Hospitals and other social institutions, part of the welfare state, also serve meals, and some old people are day guests in such institutions.

Most young people eat their meals in school, either brought with them from home or provided in the school cafeteria. These meals have been the focus of attention among nutritionists for more than 100 years and are discussed in Chapter 7, Diet and Health.

To most people these forms of eating away from home are rarely considered examples of "eating out."

LUNCHING OUT

Most professionals eat lunch away from home, and they constitute an important segment of the eating-out population. There is a significant difference between professionals and retired people who rarely eat out.

Statistics show that more men than women are professionally active on a full-time basis, and more men than women are consequently eating out. But compared to the situation only a few decades ago, the proportion of women eating out is very high, a result of their increasing importance in the labor market.

According to a Scandinavian study from 1999, most people who ate their meals at work or school did so in a cafeteria or in smaller spaces such as a lunchroom or a break room.[3] Only in Sweden, where lunch is more substantial than in the other countries, and normally hot, visits to cafés or restaurants at lunchtime were fairly common. The percentage of Swedes who visited a café or restaurant on a weekly basis was twice as high as for Norwegians and three times as high as for Danes. In Denmark and Norway they have had an alternative to the restaurant and the hot meal, as a Danish restaurant historian states: "*Madpakken* (the lunch pack) has taken care of us, when we did not have enough time to go home for lunch."[4] In a Norwegian study from 2007 only 4 percent said they were eating lunch in a café or restaurant once a week or more. When people were asked what type of meal they had last time they were eating out, only 20 percent answered lunch.[5] The restaurant lunch was more common in the capital than elsewhere in the country and more common among young than among older people.

Even if the lunch pack is still important in Denmark and Norway, it is often substituted by a simple snack, a sandwich or hot dog bought at a kiosk, a gasoline station, or another fast food outlet. Whether this is the beginning of the end of the *matpakke* culture is too early to predict.

THE SWEDISH RESTAURANT LUNCH

An important segment of the Swedish population eats lunch in a restaurant on a regular basis. A study of Swedish lunch habits was made among restaurant guests in Stockholm and the provincial town Jönköping in 2001.[6] About two-thirds of the guests who were interviewed said they were eating their lunch in a restaurant almost every day during the week.

They were also asked about their choice of dishes and the reasons for these choices. Half of the dishes eaten by the people who participated in the study had meat, less than a fifth had fish, and pizza or pie was only chosen by 1 percent. The most important group of meat dishes consisted of whole meat cuts, representing 24 percent of the total. These were steaks, fillets, chops, schnitzel, pork rack, and so on. Fourteen percent of the dishes were with minced meat, meatballs, meat patties, pasta dishes, and Mexican or other exotic dishes with minced beef or mutton. Nine percent chose stews or casseroles with meat, and 3 percent sausages. The fish was herring, flounder, pollock, cod, and salmon, and it was poached or fried, often battered, or oven baked. Most restaurant guests had salad or bread and butter with their food. In other words, they were eating what has been called a *proper meal* (see Chapter 4, Typical Meals).

The reasons for choosing a special dish are varied. Most important is a wish for something that look appetizing and tastes good. One-third said that the health aspect was important. Price in itself was not so important, but the value related to the price.

Variation was important; one would not like to have the same thing two days in row. Some restaurants are specializing in *husmannskost*, or peasant fare, that is, traditional dishes that take time and effort to prepare and therefore are rarely eaten at home. Many Swedes, who eat such a hot meal at lunch, do not prepare a proper meal when they come home in the evening.

DINING OUT

Eating out in the evenings may also be related to work, dining with business associates or visitors from abroad, but to most people an evening dinner in a restaurant with family or friends is a "treat" as the American observer said, often a celebration of an important event. One reason for this is that restaurants are expensive, with a combination of high-price

Outdoor dining in Copenhagen, Denmark. Courtesy of Art Directors and Trip/Robert Belbin.

ingredients, good wages to staff, and high taxes and the service tips that are included in the total amount on the bill. This is particularly true of the finer and more exclusive restaurants. Young people, couples without children, and single men and women, who eat out often as part of their leisure time and who have been instrumental in prolonging the night life, chose also among the more inexpensive bars and cafés that have sprung up in cities and towns in recent years.

The younger population is among the most frequent visitors to restaurants, when all types of eating out establishments are considered. A study from Denmark in 2006 shows that the age group with most visits to a restaurant (of any kind) was between 20 and 29 years old.[7] A Norwegian survey from 2007 found that a very high number of people under 25 years eat in pizza restaurants or buy snacks in kiosks, but in the finer restaurants they represent a smaller portion of the customers, whereas in the latter people 40 years old and up represent well over the average, and their part is increasing.[8]

CLASSIFICATION OF EATING PLACES

Gourmet restaurants and other exclusive restaurants are easy enough to distinguish from the rest. They have a well-planned concept with design and décor, professional waiters and sommeliers, a representative wine list, and top or near-the-top cuisine.

Fast food venues, hamburger restaurants, and pizza restaurants also have typical identification marks and are conceived as informal places with a menu of well-known standardized dishes, made after certain established rules and therefore predictable.

Between these two groups are many different concepts of eating places with food of varying quality, and it is difficult to put them into distinct categories. They don't normally pretend to serve food of high gastronomic value, but some of them have decent food at reasonable prices. In many smaller towns they represent the only alternative for people who want an evening out without paying too much. The food they offer is a mixture of traditional home cooking (sausages, meatballs, meat patties, fried battered fish), traditional restaurant dishes (steaks, wiener schnitzel, cutlets, poached fish) and more recently integrated dishes in Scandinavian food culture (pasta, pizza, hamburgers). Most of the traditional dishes are served with mashed potatoes or fries. More and more of these restaurants are owned by chains and have standardized menus.

A difficulty in classification is that the total restaurant picture is changing, because new types of eating (and drinking) places are springing up,

Outdoor restaurant in Bergen, Norway. Courtesy of Art Directors and Trip/Tibor Bognar.

some traditional ones are losing influence, and others are playing a new part in the modern restaurant business. Many of the simple roadside cafés, earlier known for local food and traditional dishes, have gotten a global image, with dishes from the fast food culture. Yet many of the urban cafés and restaurants, originally created around an international conception of eating out, today emphasize local ingredients and local recipes.[9]

Instead of a classification based on objective characteristics of the restaurants, it is possible to work out a typology based on people's perception of different restaurants and the parts they play in their lives.[10] When people have the *basic* biological need to eat and they don't have too much time, they use fast food restaurants and kiosks. Another situation is described as the *social* frame, when it is important to meet and spend time with friends. The different chains of cafés, pizza restaurants, and ethnic restaurants meet this need. To some people in some situations the social is not enough, they want something *innovative*, surprising, untraditional, for example, organic food, vegetarian dishes, or new and unknown dishes from abroad or from the local area. Finally it is the *unique* eating venue, the gourmet restaurant, where a complete break with everyday life and food is expected, and price is subordinated to the desire of an extraordinary experience.

ETHNIC RESTAURANTS

Scandinavia has no Chinatowns, but Chinese immigrants set up restaurants around the 1950s, not only in the big cities, but also in small localities. This started a new foreign restaurant tradition in the culturally and ethnically homogeneous Scandinavian societies. The foreign influences from the North Sea countries and from France were already well integrated in the national food cultures.

In the 1960s tourism to southern Europe brought thousands and thousands of Scandinavians into contact with Mediterranean food, and in the following years Italian and Greek restaurants were established in many cities. With the great influx of immigrants from Asia followed Turkish, Indian, and Pakistani restaurants, often combining table service with take-away possibilities.

Today there are more than 50 different culinary cultures represented among the ethnic restaurants: Mexican, Caribbean, North African, Japanese, Lebanese, and Thai, for example. Some of them are part of big chains with standardized menus; others aspire to a higher gastronomic level. In Copenhagen, a Danish cook with five years' experience from Thailand created a Thai cuisine restaurant that now has been awarded a Michelin star.

Ethnic cuisines have been an inspiration for many Scandinavian cooks, who have experimented with different influences in a fusion, or crossover, cooking.

FAST FOOD RESTAURANTS

In the 1999 survey of Scandinavian eating patterns a very small percentage said they were eating at fast food venues. They were asked if they had eaten out the day before the interview was given, and only 1 percent of the Danes, 2 percent of the Norwegians, and 3 percent of the Swedes said that they had been to a fast food establishment.

Many different categories of restaurants may be classified as *fast food* outlets or *street kitchens*. The oldest ones are the hot dog stands, followed by grill bars or snack bars in the 1950s and 1960s, and then by shopping center cafés, hamburger restaurants, and pizza restaurants. Today gasoline stations are increasingly important in the distribution of hot dogs and other hot and cold snacks.

The hot dog has played an important part, not only as a quick snack during working hours, but also for fairs, in sports arenas, and for children's birthday parties. The simplest form of hot dog sales were by people who carried boxes suspended from their necks. The sausages were kept in hot water in the boxes. More permanent were the kiosks (stands) or wagons (carts). The first sausage wagons with simple heating arrangements were introduced to Scandinavia from Germany around World War I. The wagons and the stands have small windows facing the street, and the customer is handed the hot dog through this window, usually with mustard and ketchup as toppings, and wrapped in a little bun. Today the selection of toppings is wide and includes roasted or raw onion, pickles, shrimp salad, remoulade sauce, and in Sweden even lingonberry jam. There are certain national differences. The Danes have the special red sausages, *røde pølser*, which are served on a little rectangular paper plate, with a bun and sauce. The sausage and the bread are alternately dipped in the sauce and eaten. In Norway and Sweden the bun may be substituted by a wrap of soft thin bread.

More recently many exotic sausages have been made available in addition to the traditional national *Vienna sausages* and *grill sausages*. But there also seems to be a movement away from the old kiosk to the gasoline stations and other big kiosks, which are becoming more and more important as fast food outlets.

Among the foreign fast food restaurant chains McDonald's is without comparison the biggest in Scandinavia. The first restaurant was opened in Sweden in 1973, and there are now almost 400 in the area. In addition to the well-known international menus (Big Mac with fries, etc.), the different countries have introduced special national campaigns with dishes for the local customers: in Norway *LakseWrap* (salmon wrap), in Denmark *Frikadelleburger* (meatball burger), and in Sweden *Frukostmackan* (breakfast sandwich), with cheese or cheese and ham, tomato, and salad.

Recent surveys show a lower interest in fast food restaurants than earlier. In Denmark burger bars and grill bars are less visited than only a few years ago.[11] In Norway the percentage of the population visiting a hamburger restaurant twice a month or more went down from 18 to 13 between 1999 and 2005.[12] In both Denmark and Norway the most dramatic reduction is found among the young. For the group between 15 and 24 years in Norway only 28 percent said they visited a hamburger restaurant once a month or more often. Six years ago 42 percent did this.

The same surveys show that the young now visit pizza restaurants more often than before. The pizza restaurants, often simple and informal, are becoming increasingly important, and—even if products and concepts are more American than Italian—this corresponds with a strong interest in Italian cuisine.

BARS, PUBS, AND CAFÉS

Places for drinks, alcoholic or nonalcoholic, hot or cold, are also changing. Beer is not only drunk in the traditional dark cafés, where men assemble to discuss football and other masculine subjects. A new type of pub and beer café offers many special brands, both foreign and local from the new Scandinavian microbreweries. There are also more possibilities for drinking out of doors, when the weather permits it. In many urban centers streets and squares have been closed to traffic, and in these pedestrian zones small tables and chairs are put out in a similar way to what people have been used to in southern Europe.

Wine bars are also new, offering a wide selection of wines from all over the world, sold by the glass for those who want to try out different grapes and producers.

Coffee has been served in many different settings. One of them, now in danger of extinction, is the *konditori*. It was originally a sort of patisserie, selling cakes and cookies of all kinds, but often with a small room where people could sit down with a cup of coffee and a sample of the baked products. This was a classic meeting place for ladies of the leisured classes, but in the later part of the twentieth century, when women started to work outside the home, it lost its former importance. The new cafés and cafeterias in the supermarkets were more efficient for a short lunch or afternoon break. Today there is a rapid growth in coffee bars with professional *barristas* serving top-quality, new-ground coffee in a variety of forms, particularly Italian espresso, cappuccino, latte, and so on.

OLD RESTAURANTS BECOMING NEW

The traditional inn, called *kro* in Denmark and *krog* in Sweden, has been used the last decades by professional cooks who wanted to try out new ideas. These inns have very long traditions, often back to the early modern period.

The first rules about inns were written into the laws during the Middle Ages, and from the seventeenth century a network of inns with royal privileges began to grow up in the kingdoms. They are hotel and restaurant for the traveler, but also a local pub, and in Denmark, where there are several hundreds of them, they have been the place where local weddings and other special occasions are celebrated. A common marketing strategy has attracted many tourists in recent years, both Danish and foreign, but one of the most interesting developments is how some of the inns have reached the top gastronomic level among Scandinavian restaurants. One of the first was Falsled Kro in Fyn (Funen), where gourmets from the EU elite in Brussels flew in to taste the delicacies. In Sweden, the only two-star restaurant is situated just outside the capital, in such an inn from the seventeenth century, Edsbacka Krog.

In Denmark and Sweden a lot of castles, palaces, and manors have been made into hotels with first-class restaurants and facilities for conferences and seminars. Such conferences are also held in many of the old seaside hotels along the Scandinavian coasts, and in the fjord hotels and mountain hotels of Norway, where the former kings and emperors of Europe no longer come to visit. Many of these restaurants have tried to make their reputation through an excellent cuisine, but they know that quality is not enough; they have to offer something special, a combination of international and local cuisine. In one such hotel in Norway, the cook Arne Brimi in the 1980s developed a *nature's cuisine*, inspired by French cooking techniques but using Norwegian ingredients, often ignored in classic urban restaurant gastronomy.

GOURMET RESTAURANTS

Gourmet restaurant is an expression from the last decades, when Scandinavian cooks have won prizes and awards in Europe. Top restaurants in the biggest centers were not a new phenomenon, as the American visitor from the 1960s observed. They often had cooks with their education from France or from French and French-educated chefs working in the Scandinavian cities. In the 1960s the cuisine practiced in these restaurants was in the classic French tradition, with few exceptions rather rich and heavy. New cooking trends had already emerged in France but were made internationally known from the 1970s under the name *nouvelle cuisine*, marketed by a group of cooks who advocated lighter dishes, where the taste of the raw materials was emphasized. In the 1970s and 1980s many Scandinavian cooks picked up the new trends, working as apprentices in French restaurants, and from the 1990s they began to dominate elite cuisines in their respective countries.

Scandinavian cooks have made a success in the competition initiated by French star chef Paul Bocuse, Bocuse d'Or, where they have 13 medals (4 gold, 6 silver, 3 bronze).[13] President in the European Bocuse d'Or, Norwegian chef Eyvind Hellstrøm, who represents the French cuisine par excellence and has received the French Legion of Honor, was the first Scandinavian with two Michelin stars. The Michelin Red Guide inspectors only visit two cities in Sweden, one in Denmark and one in Norway, so they miss a lot of what is happening in the exclusive countryside inns. In 2008 they awarded one star to 5 restaurants in Gothenburg, 6 in Stockholm, 10 in Copenhagen, and 6 in Oslo. Only two restaurants got two stars, Edsbacka Krog near Stockholm and Noma in Copenhagen. Noma is also ranked as number 10 in the San Pellegrino World's 50 Best Restaurants list.[14]

The basic concepts in Noma are *genuine* and *Nordic* (i.e., Scandinavian). Genuine refers to wild products from nature, not grown artificially. The chef René Redzepi refers to the Danish *Dogma* movie ideas, refusing artificial light, added sound, and optic filters. The Nordic refers to the products, which all come from the Scandinavian area. Musk ox,[15] a mammal related to the goat, is imported from Greenland, sea urchin[16] from the Faroe Islands, and wild herbs and mushrooms from the forests around Copenhagen. Potato chips with salt and algae from Iceland are used as appetizers. Another dish is razor clams rolled in parsley gel and covered with a "snow" of horseradish and frozen buttermilk. Traditional flatbreads are buttered with smoked pork fat, and oil is made from rapeseed or pumpkin seed.

SPECIAL RESTAURANT MENUS

Many people use restaurants for a wedding dinner or a reunion with coffee and sandwiches after a funeral. The *Þorrablót* in Iceland, with all its meticulously prepared dishes, is often celebrated among friends, acquaintances, or other associates in a restaurant. In Norway friends often choose to eat lutefisk together in November and December, and there are restaurants with special offers for lutefisk lovers.

When colleagues and friends from work meet socially over a lunch or dinner in the weeks before Christmas, this may be arranged in a cafeteria or hall at the workplace, but often a restaurant is preferred.

A special restaurant offer is the lunch buffet. The Swedish *smørgåsbord* and the Danish sandwich lunch have been turned into traditional or even national meals. They may be prepared in the homes, but this is mainly for big parties or special occasions, for instance, Christmas. Such meals demand a lot of work and ingredients and are not easy to put together in today's small families. It is easier to visit a restaurant—alone or in company with others—and pick favorite dishes from the table.

THE SWEDISH *SMÖRGÅSBORD*

The *smörgåsbord* is known all over the world. It was introduced to the United States before World War II, and the world exhibitions in New York in 1939 and 1964 did much to familiarize people with it.

The *smörgåsbord* has its roots in the *brännvinsbord* (spirits table) used as introductions to the banquets in the houses of wealthy people.[17] In the seventeenth century bread and butter with beer used to be served before the main meal. In the eighteenth century, when *akevitt* had become an important part of Swedish drinking habits, the tradition developed. A glass of *akevitt* was served with bread, butter, salted and cured fish and meat, and cheese. The similarity with the Russian *zakuski* is apparent, but it has not been proven whether the custom was imported from Russia, or if it was the other way round. From the nineteenth century the tradition was called *smörgåsbord,* and it was increasingly varied and refined, promoted by the new restaurant and food industries.

Restaurants, not least the railway station cafés and the steamboat restaurants, started to offer this kind of meal. In the 1880s and 1890s the canning industries grew enormously and offered cheap herring dishes and other necessary ingredients. This way the *smörgåsbord* reached a far broader public and was consequently considered a vulgar form of meal among representatives of the elite.

The great variety of the *smörgåsbord* made it soon difficult to eat a proper dinner after it was finished. At the Olympic Games in Stockholm in 1912 many restaurateurs saw that guests from abroad finished the *smörgåsbord* and dropped the main meal. Restaurateurs from about this time started to offer a separate *smörgåsbord* at a higher price.

Even if the *smörgåsbord* consists of a long series of different dishes, for the connoisseurs there is no danger of chaos as long as certain rules about the sequence of these dishes are observed. One of the great masters of Swedish cuisine in the last part of the twentieth century, Tore Wretman, royal cook and chef at the Opera Cellar restaurant in Stockholm, put up a model menu of five stages the guests ought to follow when they helped themselves to the food.

The first stage consists of salted fish, foremost among them the herring, either in a spicy sauce, in mustard, or with chives and sour cream or as part of a herring salad. In this first stage Wretman also put the cheeses, but many people today would rather have the cheese toward the end of the meal.

The second stage consists of other types of fish, first of all salmon, that may be boiled whole and served with mayonnaise, or cured and served with mustard sauce, or smoked, or served in a jelly. In this sequence it

Akevitt is found in many different varieties. Photo by Atle Koren.

is also possible to serve seafood, for example, West Coast Salad or hard-boiled eggs with shrimp.

In the third stage are cold cuts of ham, tongue, brawns and collars, pies, sausages, and liver paste (mousse), with pickled gherkins and beetroots, tomatoes, and salads of white and red cabbage.

The fourth stage consists of hot dishes, meatballs, asparagus omelettes, stewed kidney, small *prinskorv* (prince sausages), Jansson's temptation, *pytt-i-panna*, and Biff à la Lindström (ground beef patty).

The fifth stage is for desserts and other sweets.

The guests will take care to change their plates for every new stage, so the different tastes won't be mixed. It is interesting to observe the development of this five-stage meal because it has a logic that corresponds to the normal sequence of dishes in a menu, from fish to meat, from cold to hot.

As the *smörgåsbord* has developed through the years, new additions will always be made. But is the *smörgåsbord* able to incorporate all sorts of new dishes without losing its identity? This is a Swedish discussion, particularly important after the tradition has been declared as national.[18]

Then it became necessary to define what *genuine* Swedish *smörgåsbord* really means. Wretman was especially against preserved fruits in fruit salads and as decorations (tangerine quarters and maraschino cherries). He also banned Italian and French blue cheeses as well as brie and camembert. But even if Wretman still has a lot of prestige in Sweden, things are changing. One recent tendency, based on an awareness of how diet is important for health, is to use more green and lean products instead of fat.

The drinks for a *smörgåsbord* are beer and *akevitt,* and there are a lot of different breads to go with all the fish and meat.

The expression *smörgåsbord* may be a bit confusing, because it is not a table with *smörgås.* The word *smörgås* (or *macka* in more modern language) is an open sandwich, a slice of bread with a topping. At a *smörgåsbord,* guests are free to make their own *smörgås* with the ingredients from the table, but they may just as well eat the bread on the side.

THE DANISH *FROKOST*

In Denmark and Norway a tradition similar to the *smörgåsbord* is the lunch buffet, served in restaurants and particularly in many hotel restaurants. This tradition goes back to what was called the *cold table* in the nineteenth century and consisted of many different fish, meat, and vegetable dishes, and of course fruits, cakes, and desserts. The word *cold* does not give a correct description because many of the dishes are hot.

Parallel to this cold table tradition, another Scandinavian tradition was refined in the late nineteenth century, that of the open sandwich. In Denmark such *smørrebrød* (bread and butter) first served as a supper, often with leftovers from the midday meal as toppings. In Norway, where thin flatbread was the daily fare among the majority of the people in the nineteenth century, the *smørrebrød* tradition developed mainly within the middle classes, also first as an evening meal.

In the 1880s Danish restaurateurs began to elaborate the sandwiches into veritable dishes. In restaurants and cafés professional *smørrebrød maids* piled the most exclusive ingredients onto the thin rye bread slices. An example of how this *sandwich art* works as adornment on the table is given in a description that itself is a little piece of art:

We have the best possibility to let the complimentary colors work in harmony with each other, in the glowing red of the tomato and the fresh green of the lettuce, we have the pure yellow of egg yolks, crowned by rings of white against the silvery glimmer of the anchovy, and the deep violet of the red beet, against the light delicate colour of the pork. The brilliant variations of red in the lobster meat, as a contrast to the yellow and green, is a feast for the eye and the palate, and the shiny green olives are firm and solid points in a pale salad of vegetables. We see the pink of prawn and crawfish through a transparent jelly, or reposing on a mayonnaise in pale yellow, sprinkled with the virginal green of spring.[19]

In Norway, where the cold table is found in a lot of tourist hotels, the open sandwiches play a minor part today, even if they still exist. In Denmark they have been the basis and the trademark for the classic restaurant lunch.

The word *frokost* was originally used for the first meal of the day, as it still is in Norway and Sweden, but in Denmark it has come to stand for a meal at lunchtime. In many inns and cafés the open sandwiches have been replaced with single hot dishes, pastas, pizzas, and the similar items, but it is still possible to find places offering the classic variants of *smørrebrød*.

A sandwich menu in a restaurant may be an enormously long list of different ingredients, but many establishments offer selections of three to five sandwiches as a set menu. The sequence is taken into consideration, so the guest will taste all the different groups.

At the bottom of the sandwich—quite literally—is a slice of dark rye bread, with a few exceptions, for example, shrimp may be served on a *franskbrød* (white wheat bread), and smoked salmon often on a *surbrød* (based on buttermilk). The slices of bread are buttered generously, but other fats may also be used, predominantly pork fat.

The first sandwich in the meal ought to be with herring; to skip herring is almost sacrilegious. The herring may be prepared in a spiced marinade or in a karri sauce (a special mixture of Indian spices). There are also special varieties where fresh herring is dredged in flour and fried and then marinated in a sweet-and-sour brine.

The next stage in the *frokost* may be smoked eel with scrambled eggs, shrimp, and smoked salmon.

The hot dishes consist of fish and meat. In the case of fish the most usual is fried fillet of plaice, served either with remoulade or with shrimps and asparagus. A more luxurious variety is the *stjerneskudd* (shooting star) with one steamed and one fried, battered fillet of fish.

The most common hot meat spreads are slices of pork roast, rib of pork, sirloin steak, meatballs, and liver paste, served with pickled gherkins, beetroot, cucumber, or fried onion.

After the hot dishes one may chose roast beef, cold cuts, chicken salad, or tartare. And finally comes the cheese, either a blue French or Italian (served with, for instance, chopped raw onion and raw egg yolks) or an aged yellow Danish cheese with a distinct and strong taste (served with gravy, onion, and pork fat).

THE NEW NORDIC FOOD

In 2004 a group of cooks and gastronomes signed a document called "The New Nordic Food Manifest." One of the ideas was to take advantage of all the different ingredients in the Scandinavian area; another was to strengthen the competitive edge in the international food market through an emphasis on Nordic cultural identity. Key words are *simplicity, purity, freshness,* and *ethical standards* in the production of food and preparation of dishes.

The New Nordic Food program has since 2007 official support from the Nordic Council and has representatives from the authorities, from farmers and fishermen, from nutritionists, and from the tourist and food industry and business. The New Nordic Food is not a description of actual Scandinavian cuisine; rather it is a vision or, as the president of the Danish Gastronomic Academy has formulated it, a utopia.

MEAL HOUSE

An encouragement for many cooks is the gastronomic center built in an old Swedish mining town, Grythyttan, with a university college for culinary students and a restaurant business curriculum, a large library, and a book museum with classic works from the Renaissance until today. The building itself, the spectacular Swedish pavilion from the World Exhibition in Seville, Spain, in 1992, stands out in a striking contrast to the serene and tall dark spruces around it. But most important is the innovative spirit in this growing research center, initiated by Carl-Jan Granqvist, who has managed to impart a professional attitude to concepts such as gastronomy, taste, and the meal as a social and gustatory meeting place. The center is called Måltidens Hus, which means "Meal House."

NOTES

1. Nika Hazelton: *The art of Scandinavian cooking* (New York: Macmillan 1965), p. 17.

2. Based on data from the national statistical institutes.

3. Unni Kjærnes (ed.): *Eating patterns. A day in the lives of Nordic peoples* (Lysaker, Norway: SIFO—National Institute of Consumer Research 2001).

4. Jan Ulrik Grathwohl: "På restaurant og værtshus," in Georg Nellemann et al.: *Dagligliv i Danmark i vor tid,* vol. 2 (Copenhagen: Nyt Nordisk Forlag 1989), p. 284.

5. Annechen Bugge and Randi Lavik: *Å spise ute* (Oslo: SIFO 2007), pp. 64–65, 120.

6. Clara Westman and Marie Skans: *Val av lunchrätt* (Stockholm: Livsmedelsverket 2001).

7. "Danskene går mere ud og spiser," *Tendens* (Copenhagen: Horesta 2006).

8. Bugge and Lavik: *Å spise ute*.

9. Virginie Amelien: "The rise of restaurants in Norway in the twentieth century," in Peter Scholliers and Mark Jacobs, *Eating out in Europe* (Oxford: Berg 2003), p. 190.

10. This typology is taken from Bugge and Lavik: *Å spise ute*, p. 29.

11. "Danskene går mere," *Tendens* (Copenhagen: Horesta July 2006): www.horesta.dk/Service/Om%20Horesta/Medier/~/media/migration%20folder/upload/filer/medier/tendens/tendensrestauranter06.pdf.ashx (accessed August 21, 2008).

12. Bugge and Lavik: *Å spise ute*, p. 99.

13. Bocuse d'Or: http://www.bocusedor.com/2009/concours/palmares.php.

14. S. Pellegrino World's 50 Best Restaurants: www.theworlds50best.com/2008_list.html.

15. The musk ox is *Ovibos moschatus*.

16. The sea urchin is *Echinus esculentus*.

17. Gösta Berg: "Det svenska smörgåsbordet," *Fataburen* (Stockholm: Nordiska museet 1989), pp. 54–61.

18. Metzger, Jonathan: *I köttbullslande: Konstruktionen av svenskt och utländskt på kulinariska fältet* (Stockholm: University of Stockholm 2005).

19. Mimi Krag: *Smørbrødboken* (Oslo: Tanum 1933).

6

Special Occasions

Food has always played a prominent part in the celebrations of the rites of passage in the family as well as in the annual festivals based on the secular or the religious calendar in these predominantly Lutheran countries. Christmastime is the most significant food season. Never is so much emphasis put on food and on old habits and customs from the nineteenth century and earlier. Wedding food may be even more prestigious and luxurious, as well as modern and surprising, but old traditions and childhood memories dictate the choice of Christmas foods. A natural consequence is a greater diversity between the different regions in Scandinavia at the Christmas table than for other types of festivals and celebrations.

CHRISTMAS FOODS

The Christmas season is characterized by two kinds of food: meat and sweet breads and cakes. The slaughtering season and the baking season, which used to last for days, were among the most important preparations for Christmas. Two other types of dishes traditionally have been very important in the meals of this period: fish and porridge. But they have changed their place and function in significant ways and are less important in the total picture today.

Meat

A wide range of different dishes is produced from the slaughtered pig, both fresh and salted. A very spectacular way of using a pig's head was to serve it boiled on the table, eventually with an apple in its mouth. This is less common now. Pig's trotters are less popular now too, even if some people still insist on them for Christmas.

The meat of the pig's head, however, is absolutely saved. It is used in the traditional *sylte*. All the meat is removed, cubed and boiled with the rind in water spiced with pepper and cloves. When ready, the meat is put in a cloth and made into the form of a cheese, which was actually called *head cheese* in some places. It is then put under heavy pressure, to make it firm enough to cut in thin slices when it is cold. Today *sylte* is normally purchased in shops, but some people still buy a pig's head and make the dish themselves. A great variety of sausages are made from the liver, blood, fat, and meat of the pig, and these sausages belong to the Christmas table. In Iceland and parts of Norway similar products are made from lamb, in Sweden and Denmark also from veal.

Several of these traditions show similarities among the Scandinavian countries, but there are still significant differences in the choice of main dishes for Christmas dinners, partly as a result of which livestock is the dominant one, which sort of preservation method is the most common, and when the slaughtering season takes place. In Iceland and western Norway dried, salted, or smoked lamb is eaten, duck is preferred in Denmark, and pork in Sweden and the eastern parts of Norway. Until well into the twentieth century, the quality and amount of meat depended on social status and economic means, but such social differences have more or less disappeared today. This does not mean that everybody can afford to buy the most exclusive foods, but some dishes are considered necessary on the tables of both rich and poor, at least on Christmas Eve.

Breads and Cookies

The weeks immediately before Christmas are filled with baking activity; sweet breads, buns, cakes, and cookies have to be ready when the Christmas bells toll. Most Scandinavians believe that some of the baking ought to be done in the kitchen at home with the whole family participating, even if this ideal is not always realized. Particularly difficult to fulfill is the ambition of baking the *seven sorts* (of Christmas cookies), a tradition that goes back at least 100 years.

Many of the products have much longer traditions, something that clearly shows in some of the shapes or decorations. There are cookies shaped as animals, such as a calf, pig, ox, hen, or ram. Other cookies are in the shape of a cross or decorated with other Christian symbols or pre-Christian sun symbols.

The Icelandic leaf breads are decorated in many different ways.

One very old cookie that is still popular is the *pepper nut,* a name translated from the German *Pfeffernüsse*. The name reflects the size and the texture of these small, hard cookies made from unleavened dough of rye flour, honey, and strong spices.

Other old-time cookies are baked with special irons, the same way as waffles, but they are thin and crisp. The irons have geometrical patterns or religious illustrations on the interior, and these imprints are left on the cookies. Some are rectangular such as the *good fortune* (Swedish *gorån,* Danish *gode raad,* Icelandic *góð ráð,* Norwegian *goro*). Others are round and often rolled up on a stick as a scroll or made into a cornet and filled with whipped cream.

Another old method that is still popular is to fry dough in hot liquid fat. Some of these cookies are simple rings such as doughnuts, but others are in different forms. Best known is a small crullerlike cookie that is called *klejne* in Danish and Icelandic and *klenät* in Sweden, a word that has to do with *klenodium* (a small valuable object). The word *klenät* has a special meaning, a poor and weak fellow, and this may have been the reason that the cookie in Norway became known as *fattigmann* (poor man).

Fattigmann

- 1 cup flour
- 4 tablespoons sugar
- 4 tablespoons whipped cream
- 1 egg

- 4 egg yolks
- 1 tablespoon brandy
- 1/2 teaspoon ground cardamom

Beat the egg and the egg yolks with the sugar. Whip in the cream carefully and add flour, brandy, and cardamom. Handle the dough as little as possible and put it in a cool place overnight. Roll out the dough with a rolling pin and cut it in diamond shapes. Make a slit in the center of each diamond and pull one corner through the slit. Fry in hot lard until lightly browned (375°F).

Many cakes and cookies were baked in the big ovens of the manors or in the town bakeries. Most people did not have such ovens and had to buy the cookies at the baker's if they wanted them for special occasion such as Christmas or weddings. Outside such rare situations only the elite had the means to bake them and the necessary money to purchase the expensive ingredients. The cakes were often served with jam and sweet wine after a meal.

A change occurred during the last part of the nineteenth century, when the stove became the norm in most homes. Then the cookies were baked in the oven. At about the same time the prices of sugar and wheat flour went down. The cookies were now eaten with coffee, which had become a general drink in all homes around 1900.

Cookies in the form of men, women, and animals are still baked today. Photo by Atle Koren.

Norwegian mother and child baking Christmas cookies. Courtesy of Art Directors and Trip/GV Press.

Among the many Scandinavian cookies, some are considered typical Christmas cookies and only eaten on this occasion. Some of them are thin as flatbread, but with more exclusive products in the dough, for example, sour cream. In Denmark where *jødekager* (Jew cakes) had been bought in Jewish bakeries since the eighteenth century, these now became homemade cakes.

Popular today are Norwegian and Danish *sandkaker* and Swedish *mandelmusslor*, baked in shell-like tins. Danish vanilla wreaths and Norwegian Berlin wreaths and serina cookies are shaped as rings or wreaths. A lot of flat cookies containing honey or syrup are made in fascinating shapes: *brunkager*, *pepperkaker*, *sirupssnipper*, and *spekulasjer*.

Brunkager (Danish Brown Cookies)

- 1 pound flour
- 1 cup sugar
- 1 cup syrup

- 5 ounces butter
- blanched almonds
- 1 teaspoon baking powder
- 1 teaspoon ground cardamom
- 1 teaspoon ground cloves
- 1 teaspoon ground cinnamon
- grated lemon peel

Mix sugar and butter into a soft paste and add syrup. Heat it so everything melts. Mix the dry ingredients and add them to the melted mixture. Cover the dough with plastic wrap, so it is completely sealed and leave it in the fridge overnight. Roll the dough thin and cut out cookies with a cookie cutter. You can also make the dough into a roll about two inches thick and cut thin slices from the roll. Put the cookies on a buttered baking sheet and put half an almond in the middle of each. Bake five to seven minutes until they are dark golden brown (375°F). Use whatever spices you prefer; ginger, mace, and allspice are options as well.

Berlinerkranser (Norwegian Berlin Wreaths)

- 2 raw egg yolks
- 2 boiled egg yolks (8 minutes)
- 1 1/2 cups flour
- 1/2 cup sugar
- 9 ounces butter

Glaze

- 2 egg whites
- pearl sugar

Crush the boiled egg yolks, mix them with the raw, and blend to a smooth paste. Beat in the sugar. Work in flour and soft butter, but handle the dough carefully. Let cool. Make the dough into rolls about 1/3 inch thick and five inches long. Shape them into wreaths. Brush with lightly whipped egg whites and sprinkle with pearl sugar (coarse sugar). Put them on a baking sheet and bake in oven for about 10 minutes (350°F).

Mandelmusslor (Swedish Almond Shells)

- 2 cups flour
- 1/2 cup sugar

- 7 ounces butter
- 1 egg
- 1 cup almonds

Mix butter, flour, minced almonds, and sugar. Add the eggs and make into a dough. Let it cool for an hour or overnight. Butter the special tart shell tins and press the dough thinly and evenly into sides and bottom. Place the tins on a baking sheet and bake 10–12 minutes until they are golden (375°F). When cool, turn the tins upside down and tap gently on the bottom. The tarts will then drop out, but be careful because they are very fragile. The cakes may be served as they are, but are particularly delightful with whipped cream and strawberry or raspberry preserves.

Fish

Not many Scandinavians eat fish as their main dish on Christmas Eve, but a few eat *lutefisk* or fresh cod. *Lutefisk* plays, however, an important part in the pre-Christmas season in Norway and Sweden and is now served in restaurants and homes from late October onward. This dish has since the nineteenth century been more and more identified with Christmas in the two countries, and both Swedes and Norwegians conceive it as a national dish. The preparation is more or less the same, but with different sauces and accompaniments. In Sweden white sauce is common, but some regions use mustard (Skåne) or horseradish (Mälar area). In Norway bacon fat is the norm, and pea stew is added to the potatoes. Some still follow old traditions with syrup or brown cheese.

It is possible that *lutefisk* has been eaten in Denmark, but from the end of the seventeenth and beginning of the eighteenth century, when the *klippfisk* entered the market, the Danes preferred this to the stockfish. It had to be soaked in water as other dried fish, and lye or other chemical solutions might be added to help the softening process.[1] In later years *klippfisk* dishes have often been postponed to New Year's Eve or New Year's Day or just dropped.

To understand the tradition of fish dishes eaten in November and December, it is necessary to keep in mind certain aspects of Scandinavian history. In Catholic times, fish was extremely important in the fasting period before Christmas, and as this period lasted until midnight, December 24, fish was a natural choice for the Christmas Eve dinner. Many different species were eaten, including cod, halibut, pike, and eel. They were either eaten preserved or fresh in coastal regions and along rivers and lakes and by those who had the means to acquire such luxury.

Fish is so important that special plates are designed for fish dishes. Photo by Atle Koren.

After the Lutheran Reformation in the early sixteenth century, fasting traditions waned and meat dishes were included in the Christmas Eve menu. Many people, however, continued to serve fish, either as one of several dishes in the evening or earlier in the day. Some cold fish dishes are very popular, for instance, herring, smoked salmon and cured salmon (gravlaks).

Porridge

The other traditional dish, porridge, has also changed in form and function throughout history. Containing no meat, it was a fasting dish and therefore constituted an important part of the food on Christmas Eve. Since Christmas was a special feast, the grain should be of better quality than the daily barley or oats flour, but in many areas it was made from barley grits. In the northern region where milk was more available than grain, it was often made as a gruel with whole milk.

Rice was very exclusive but became the norm among the elite in the eighteenth century, and around 1900 the price of rice was so low that rice porridge became a common festive dish among most people, particularly on Christmas Eve. It used to be sprinkled with ground cinnamon and sugar, and a lump of butter was put in the middle. Originally this *butter eye*, as it was called, is said to have been in the form of a cross and may have been thought of as a form of ritual protection against evil forces.

Porridge gradually lost its importance as a main dish but found new outlets. It was eaten in the morning or during the day or it was served as an appetizer to the main meal in the evening or as a dessert. The elite developed more sophisticated dessert varieties and mixed the porridge with cream, sugar, vanilla, and almonds. In Denmark it is called *risalamande*, but in spite of the name, originally *riz à l'amande*, it has nothing to do with French gastronomy.

The Swedes have a *ris à la Malta*, which has nothing to do with the island of Malta. The name is just a distortion of the Danish name, but this dish contains no almonds. Instead, it may be mixed with orange juice or small bits of orange.

The Norwegian dish is simply *rice cream*, and it is generally made without almonds, except perhaps for Christmas. In all countries this pudding is served with a red sauce made from sour cherries or other red berries.

The tradition with an almond hidden in the porridge is probably from the nineteenth century. The one who found the almond in the porridge on his plate was either seen as destined to be married before next Christmas or was given a little prize, for example, a small marzipan pig.

Risalamande (Danish Rice Dessert)

- 1 1/2 cup water
- 1 cup rice
- 4 1/2 cups milk
- 3 1/2 ounces minced almonds
- 2 vanilla pods
- 4 tablespoons sugar
- 1 cup cream
- red cherry sauce

Make a rice porridge. Heat water and rice in a pan and boil for two minutes. Add milk and boil for 10 minutes while stirring. Put a lid on the pan and boil for 30 minutes, stirring occasionally. Cover and chill. Mix minced almonds, crushed vanilla, and sugar with the porridge. Whip the cream and fold it carefully into the mixture. Chill in the fridge for two hours. Serve with red cherry sauce.

CHRISTMAS SEASON MEALS

The Christmas season begins earlier and earlier, also in culinary terms. This has partly to do with an increasing commercialization. The supermarkets sell typical Christmas foods, either fresh or ready to eat, from the end of November at least. Firms arrange lunches or dinners for their employees, with traditional fare, but where drinking often is just as important as eating. In homes, kindergartens, and schools gingerbread houses are built and gifts prepared. In the dark and cold evenings before Christmas people are offering visiting friends gingersnaps, in Denmark also apple fritters. The drink to follow it is *gløg/glögg*, a mulled and spiced wine with raisins and almonds (or nonalcoholic alternatives).

Æbleskiver (Danish Apple Fritters)

- 2 cups flour
- 1 cup milk
- 2 eggs
- 1 tablespoon sugar
- 2 ounces butter
- 2 ounces yeast
- 1/2 teaspoon cardamom

Separate the eggs in yolks and whites. Whip the whites until stiff peaks form and set aside. Put the yeast in lukewarm milk and add the sugar, egg yolks, cardamom, and flour and stir. Fold the stiff whites into the mixture. Let the dough rise for about 30 minutes. Warm the æbleskive pan (a special pan with round deep holes). Have some melted butter in each of the holes. Put in dough so it fills about two-thirds or three-fourths of the hole. When the outside is golden after two to three minutes, put in a bit of boiled apple and flip the fritter upside down so the other side also becomes golden. Stick a toothpick in to see whether it is ready; if done it will come out clean. Remove from pan and sprinkle with sugar.

Many Danes prefer to use baking powder (1 teaspoon) instead of yeast. Many will also forgo the filling and serve the cake with jam and sugar.

Pepparkakor (Swedish Gingersnaps)

- 10 ounces sugar
- 1 cup syrup
- 3/4 cup milk
- 2 pounds flour

- 7 ounces butter
- 2 teaspoons ground ginger
- 2 teaspoons ground cloves
- 2 teaspoons ground cinnamon
- 2 teaspoons baking soda

Beat sugar and syrup in a pot until the sugar melts. Add milk, butter, and spices and stir until the butter melts. Cool slightly and add and stir flour mixed with the baking soda until the dough has got a smooth consistency. Let the dough rest in a cool place overnight. Knead the dough smooth and thin and cut it into different shapes with cookie cutters. Put the cookies on a baking sheet and bake in oven six to eight minutes (400°F).

Lucíadagen

One festival that has long traditions in Sweden, but is also getting increasingly popular in the other Scandinavian countries, is *Lucíadagen* (Lucia's Day). This is a festival of light held on December 13, which was the day of winter solstice in the old Julian calendar. The light is evident in the name of Lucia, who is generally thought to be an early Christian martyr and saint, celebrated in legends and folk songs as, for example, the Neopolitan ballad "Santa Lucia." In the early hours of the morning a Lucia bride (*lussebrud*) appears, wearing a long white gown and a crown with blazing lights and lingonberry twigs. It is popular in homes with children, particularly with a girl who can play the Lucia bride and serve the golden saffron buns to the rest of the family. These buns are called *lussekatter* (Lucia cats) and are, according to some stories, the devil's cats subdued by the virgin saint. Buns will also be served in schools this day, after a procession with a Lucia bride accompanied by *stjärngossar* (star boys) holding a stick with a golden star in their hands.

Lussekatter (Swedish Saffron Buns)

- 5–6 ounces butter
- 1 1/2 cups milk
- 2 ounces yeast
- 1/8 ounce saffron threads
- 1 cube of sugar
- 1 3/4 pounds flour
- 1 egg

- 1 teaspoon salt
- 3/4 cup sugar
- 3 ounces raisins

Glaze

- 1 egg
- 2 tablespoons water

Melt the butter and add lukewarm milk. Crumble the yeast in a little of the liquid and add it to the rest. Crush the saffron threads and the cube of sugar and mix in together with flour, egg, sugar, and salt. Work the dough well and mix in the raisins (but leave about 50 for decorations). Let the covered dough rise at room temperature for about 30 minutes until the size is doubled. Divide the dough in 25 pieces and make oblong rolls, about 1 inch in diameter and 6–8 inches long. Form each roll into the shape of an S or an 8. Put a raisin in each of the halves of the buns. Place the buns on a greased baking sheet and let rise for one hour and a half. Bake them in the oven on 420°F. Make a mixture of one egg and two tablespoons of water and glaze the buns with this to make them shiny.

Þorláksmessa

Þorlákur's Day, or St. Thorlak's mass, is a special Icelandic feast, celebrated on December 23, the day before Christmas Eve. Bishop Þorlák, patron saint of Iceland, died December 23, 1193. He was canonized by pope John Paul II in 1985.

The food eaten this day is fish, possibly a remnant from the old Catholic fast. The fish dish is made from cured salted skate, recognizable by a pungent aroma of ammonia, and served with potatoes and *hamsatólg* (melted sheep's tallow with cracklings) or *hnoðmör* (sheep's tallow that is kneaded and dried before it is melted).[2]

Christmas Eve

December 25 and 26 are public holidays, and many Scandinavians take a vacation between Christmas and New Year's Eve. But it is the December 24, Christmas Eve, that represents the real climax of the season. The social element is still considered to be the most important part of the celebration. The extended family gets together, and with several generations present, they distribute Christmas gifts and enjoy the typical Christmas food.

The day develops in different ways in the different countries, in different regions, even in different families. The feeling of family is very strong.

Many adults look back at the Christmases of their own childhood and want to bring to their own children the traditions they remember from the time when their grandparents still lived. Even if there are changes over time, and there undoubtedly are, they are not felt as such because certain basic elements are always kept from one year to the next.

Some people will start the day with a relatively normal breakfast, but perhaps with some of the special Christmas foods, for example, the *sylte*. Later in the day at some stage many will eat a rice porridge if they don't have it as a dessert for the main meal. Coffee may be served with a selection of the homemade Christmas cookies.

In Sweden this day is called *dopparedan* (the dip day). Some people still gather in the kitchen around the large pot where the ham is boiled and they take a bit of bread and dip it into the broth so it is soaked with fat liquid. It is called *doppet i grytan* (the dip in the cauldron) and is a tradition that seems to have been common in many areas of Scandinavia on one of the last days before Christmas, when meat was boiled. In Norway the broth was often poured out on deep plates and the bread was added as in the jumble dish described in Chapter 1, Historical Overview.

In Norway and Denmark the main Christmas meal is served in the afternoon, after people have visited the graveyard and put flowers or candles on the tombs of deceased family members, or have been to church, or just watched one of the popular TV programs.

Danish Roast Duck

In Denmark roast duck is almost a national Christmas dish, even if many people will serve roast pork, particularly the rack. Some people still eat the traditional roast goose, probably known to people around the world through the moving tale by Hans Christian Andersen, "The Little Match Girl." There the goose was served at the table, where it "steamed gloriously, stuffed with apples and prunes." The goose was, however, not a dish for most Danes but a privilege for rich farmers and the urban upper classes.

The roast duck is stuffed the same way as the Andersen goose, and it is eaten with white and *brunede* (brown, caramelized) potatoes and with red cabbage. Some will add apple halves boiled in sugared water, and when they are cold a little red currant jelly is added.

Norwegian Roast of Lamb and Pork

Between half and two-thirds of the Norwegians, mainly in the eastern part of the country, eat roast rib of pork. The rind is cut up in a pattern

Roast goose the Danish way. From Fru Nimbs Kogebog, Copenhagen, 1900.

of one-inch squares with a sharp knife that cuts through the rind without going into the fat underneath. The big issue is to make the rind crackling crisp and golden. In addition to the rib, sausages and patties made from ground pork and fat are served with boiled potatoes and sour cabbage, and often accompanied by pickles and lingonberry jam.

In the communities along the western coast of Norway dried and salted (and some places smoked) rib of lamb is eaten, and in recent decades this Christmas dish has been taken up in other parts of the country, either for Christmas Eve or for one of the other Christmas dinners. The rib is cut into single pieces that must be soaked in water for about 24 hours to soften the meat and drain it of salt. The ribs used to be roasted on the embers, but today they are steamed over a rack of wooden sticks, preferably from birch to give a special flavor. The sticks or twigs are about as long as the diameter of the kettle, and they are piled up to make a platform about one or two inches above the bottom of the kettle. Cold water is filled to just below the top of the platform. The ribs are placed on top, and the kettle is covered with a tight lid. The meat is ready after about two and one half hours of steaming, depending on the age of the animal. Some people attribute the name of this dish, *pinnekjøtt* (stick meat) to the use of birch sticks, while others think the sticks refer to the long thin ribs. The ribs are often served with sausages, for example, the lamb sausage from Voss (*Vossakorv*), and with boiled potatoes and mashed rutabaga, where the fat-enriched water in the bottom of the lamb cauldron is added together with cream and spiced with mace and a little pepper. Desserts may vary, but whipped cream with cloudberries is a good choice.

Iceland: Lamb and Leaf Bread

In Iceland on Christmas Eve or Christmas Day people eat the traditional *hangikjöt*,[3] smoked leg of lamb, served with potatoes and a white sauce or mashed potatoes and green peas and occasionally red cabbage. A mutton soup with roots and cabbage may be served Christmas Eve and meat dishes as *rjúpa*, rock ptarmigan, or *hamborgarhryggur*, smoked rack or loin of pork, with brown caramelized potatoes. All Christmas meals in Iceland are accompanied by *laufabrauð*, the thin circular leaf bread or lace bread, perforated with small holes to give different geometrical patterns. The tradition has its roots in the northern part of the country but has spread to all regions. It is now possible to buy it in the bakeries; one can also buy the dough there for baking at home.

Laufabrauð (Icelandic Leaf Bread)

- 1 pound flour
- 1 cup milk
- 1 tablespoon butter
- 1 tablespoon sugar
- 1 teaspoon salt
- 1 teaspoon baking powder

Boil the milk and let the butter melt in it. Mix flour, sugar, salt, and baking powder well. Pour in the hot milk and knead into a smooth dough. Make the dough into a cylinder, cover with a damp cloth and let cool. Cut the dough into 25 pieces and cover them with the cloth to keep them from drying out. Flatten the pieces with a rolling pin until they are almost paper-thin and cut out circular shapes and cover them with the cloth. When all the cakes are made, heat a pan for deep-frying. The Icelanders use sheep's tallow, but other fats may be used. Decorate the cakes with patterns using a sharp knife or a special iron. Prick the cakes with fork to avoid blistering and put them into the fat. They will sink to the bottom but soon resurface. Then they are turned over, and when they are golden in color, they are ready to be picked up and placed on a baking paper to drain. Put a tray on top so they stay flat.

The Swedish Christmas Table

The main Christmas meal in Sweden is now something called the *Christmas table*. Some Swedes still serve a traditional dinner in the evening, often consisting of porridge and lutefisk, but these are mainly the older generation. According to statistics, the lutefisk is rapidly losing its place as a Christmas Eve dish.

The Christmas table is a specially adapted *smörgåsbord*, served either as a late lunch or as an early dinner in late afternoon. It contains a great variety of fish and meat, greens, sweets, fruits, and nuts. Some of the dishes belong to a Swedish dinner table throughout the year—smoked or cured salmon (gravlaks), herring, and meatballs—but it is the special combinations that make this into a particular Christmas table.

The jewel in the crown is the baked Christmas ham. The ham is first boiled, then the rind is taken away without removing the fat, and it is covered with a mixture of egg yolks and mustard that is then covered with bread crumbs. This is put in the oven and grilled on high temperature until the crust becomes golden brown. This delicacy is mentioned as early as 1689, but for a long time it was just served on manors. During the twentieth century it has become more and more common and is now served in 83 percent of Swedish households on this particular day.

On the table are small sausages, for example, *prinskorv*, where a little cross is cut in each end to make them look like small piglets when they are fried. Another prominent feature is the Christmas paste made in a mold (terrine) from minced veal liver and butter mixed with salt, pepper, allspice, egg, milk or cream, and a little brandy. There are also ribs of pork, pig's feet (less and less common), porridge, lutefisk, *sylte,* and a special Christmas cheese. Originally this cheese was as big as possible, but today it is sold in family-sized packets.

And there are, of course, a lot of herring preparations. *Glasmästarsill* consists of *matjes* herring fillets marinated in a tightly closed glass jar with vinegar, sugar, horseradish, carrots, onions, gingerroot, and other spices. After a couple of days in the refrigerator it is ready to be served. *Senapssill* is salted herring marinated with onions and dill in a marinade of vinegar, sugar, and spices. After 24 hours the marinade is removed and the rest is mixed with a mustard sauce made from mustard, oil, sugar, vinegar, salt, and chopped dill. Another herring dish is *Janssons frestelse* (Jansson's temptation), originally the name of a 1928 movie. The dish has also been explained as an invention by a famous opera singer and gourmet of the nineteenth century, Pelle Janzon, but this is less probable. The recipe was first published in 1940 and has become extremely popular. The Swedish *ansjovis* is not the anchovy, but sprat, which is pickled in salt, sugar, and spices and sold in small boxes, particularly for Christmas.

Janssons Frestelse (Swedish Sprat and Potato Dish)

- 2 1/2 pounds potatoes
- 3 small onions

- 10 ounces anchovies
- 1 cup cream
- 2 ounces butter
- bread crumbs

Cut peeled potatoes in thin strips. Chop the onions in thin slices and sauté them gently over medium-low heat until they are soft but not brown. Grease a baking or gratin dish and put in layers of potatoes, onions, and herring, repeat layers, and finish with potatoes on top. Sprinkle freshly ground pepper and salt, pour in the cream and put thin slices of butter on top. Sprinkle with bread crumbs and bake in the oven (450–475°F) for about an hour until the potatoes are done and the crust is golden.

Christmas Week

In Denmark Christmas Day is the time for the big Christmas lunch, a variety of the *Danish frokost* with various herring dishes, smoked salmon, homemade liver paste with bacon and mushrooms, tartlets with chicken and asparagus, roast pork with red cabbage, different cheeses and *æble-flæsk*, slices of fried bacon or pork arranged on top of apples fried in the bacon fat and strewn with sugar.

In Norway and Sweden there is no set menu for this day. Some will have a variety of the Christmas dishes, some will eat cold cuts and sausages, and others will eat turkey or other meat dishes.

During the rest of the Christmas week many families visit relatives or friends. Typical Christmas foods or more exclusive dishes are served. Fish is also well received after so many days with fat and heavy food.

New Year's Eve has no set menu. In Denmark, where *klippfisk* or boiled cod was the rule, it is now more common to serve beef dishes such as roasts and steaks. In Norway turkey has become one of the most popular dishes this evening. In all the countries lobster and seafood in general are increasingly popular, either as an appetizer or a main dish. Special festival cakes built as pyramids or towers are also served this evening, as they are during other big events. In Sweden it is *spettkaka*, and in Denmark and Norway it is *kransekage*.

Layer cakes with many different ingredients are baked at Christmas and other special events. In Iceland, one of the traditional festival cakes, probably one of the first to be introduced after the stove became common in homes, is *vínartarta*. The word means originally Viennese tart, a cake known in many countries. But in Icelandic the word can also mean "friend's tart." Other names for the same cake are *randabraud* (striped bread) and *randalin* (striped lady).

Vínartarta (Icelandic Layer Cake)

- 4 cups flour
- 1 cup butter
- 1 cup sugar
- 1/4 cup milk
- 2 eggs
- 1 teaspoon vanilla
- 1 1/2 teaspoons baking powder

Filling

- 2 pound prunes
- 1 cup sugar
- 1 teaspoon vanilla
- 1/2 teaspoon ground cardamom

Make the filling first. Boil and pit the prunes and put them through a food processor to be chopped. Add sugar, vanilla, and cardamom and 1/2 cup of the liquid where the prunes were boiled. Bring to a boil and keep warm.

Mix sugar and butter to a paste. Beat in eggs and vanilla and add milk, flour, and baking powder but do not knead too much. Divide the dough into equal parts, as many as you want layers (three to six). Roll out the dough with a rolling pin until it is about 1/2 inch thick. Make a circular cake with 9-inch diameter (for example, by using a baking tin). Bake the cakes until golden brown (375°F). When cool, spread the filling on top of each layer except the last one. Put something a little heavy on top to keep the layers together.

This cake can be frozen and it thaws easily, so it may be stored for unexpected guests.

Drink

The old Scandinavian festival drink is beer, and a strong beer was expected for such an important feast as Christmas. An old expression for celebrating this period was to "drink yule." Beer is so well suited to the fat foods and even more to the salted or in other ways preserved foods, lutefisk, dried mutton, and pickled herring. Beer is often followed by a shot or two of *akevitt*, which is also thought to help digest the fat. The temperance movements, particularly those in Sweden and Norway, gained a strong position in the last part of the nineteenth century, and this led many families to abstain from all alcoholic drinks. They were substituted by bottled carbonated soft drinks and fruit juices. Today beer is again more common, and many brands of Christmas beers are offered by the breweries. In Sweden a mixture of dark beer (porter) and strong wines, spirits, or champagne is called *mumma*. Wine is also drunk in increasing quantities at Christmas, and for New Year's Eve the favorite drink is champagne or other sparkling wines.

One hot drink has been mentioned as a tradition in the pre-Christmas period: the glogg (in Swedish *glögg*, in Danish *gløg*). It is now commonly drunk in all the Scandinavian countries, but it originated in Sweden where it has been known since the seventeenth century. The name is an abbreviated form of "glowing wine," related to the German *glühwein*. There are lots of slightly different recipes in all countries, but the base is a red wine, often fortified with half a cup of neutral eau-de-vie or vodka. Some will also add madeira or port wine. The dish is spiced with ginger, cinnamon, cardamom. and cloves. Other ingredients are sugar, bitter orange peel, raisins, and almonds. A simpler way is to buy a bottle of *glögg* extract in the supermarket, mix it with wine, and add the raisins and almonds. It is also possible to make a *glögg* without alcohol, by using hot water instead.

The Swedes also have a refreshing soft drink for Christmas, *julmust*, which is a black, sweet drink, somewhat similar to Coca-Cola. The recipe is secret, but among the ingredients are malt and hops. This is drunk with the typical Christmas foods, particularly by the children.

Homemade?

The ideal is to prepare as much as possible of the Christmas food at home, but more and more products are offered in shops and catering firms. The time when stockfish was soaked in lye in the homes to become lutefisk is long gone, and very few people today prepare their own dry mutton rib. It is also possible to buy *kransekake* and many other cakes and cookies in the bakeries. Red cabbage and sour cabbage are sold in small pots or jars. The Swedish ham can be obtained boiled and ready to bake. Many of the sauces and trimmings are available in bottles and cans. Ready-to-eat herring dishes are sold in cans and jars. But the roasting and baking and steaming processes are still done in the home, so the aromas can spread through the house and give the right associations with Christmases of years past.

Table Setting

The laying of the table is very important during the Christmas week. The whole house is full of small and large Christmas decorations in addition to the Christmas tree. On the table is a cloth and candlesticks that are only brought out for Christmas; these are items remembered from childhood, very often family heirlooms from earlier generations. Some families have special plates decorated with Christmas motives, not religious ones, but bells, spruce twigs, holly, reindeer, Father Christmas, or the Scandinavian Yule goblins. In a family the husband and wife may bring with them different traditions, for example, from different regions. This calls for compromises, and it is easy to see how every family will develop their own traditions.

OTHER ANNUAL FESTIVALS

To many people Easter, Whitsuntide, and most saints' days have lost their original connections with the Christian religion. Even if the majority of the Scandinavians are nominally Christians—belonging to Lutheran state or folk churches—attendance at church ceremonies is low except on Christmas Eve. This means that elements other than the religious ones, for example, leisure, entertainment, and food, acquire an even more important part in the celebrations. The extended family, so important at Christmas, is far less prominent in the other festivals, when many people just celebrate with friends. There are very few traditional foods, perhaps except the Easter eggs, in some cases real eggs painted for the Easter Day breakfast, but mainly big chocolate eggs filled with candy. Roast leg of lamb is a dinner tradition in Iceland and Norway that is rapidly spreading to Sweden and Denmark.

Among the non-European immigrants, Muslims, Jews, Buddhists, Sikhs, Hindus, and others follow their own religious calendar with festivals where food plays a central part.

Þorrablót

In Iceland the long and cold winter is shortened through the festival Þorrablót, a demonstration of traditional foods in this country's culture, based on mutton, sea mammals, shark, stockfish, whey, and grains.[4] The name refers to the month Þorri in the medieval Icelandic calendar, running from the last part of January to the end of February. Þorri was probably a nature spirit in the local religious cult in which a blót was a sacrificial event.

Very little is known about this festival in ancient times, and the present form dates back to the late nineteenth century and the struggle for independence. It is typical that the first modern Þorrablót was held in Copenhagen in 1873 by nationalist Icelandic students, and the tradition as it is known today—the public eating of Þorramatur—is mainly a result of revitalization during the last 50 years. The food eaten is preserved and in the last phase an extra emphasis is on food preserved in whey, soured or fermented.

The most important meat is mutton, and *hangikjöt* is the pièce de resistance of Þorrablót. But there are also many other dishes made from sheep and lamb. The ram's testicles (*hrutpungar*) are boiled and molded into flat cakes and soured in whey. When served the cakes are cut up in thick slices. *Lundabaggar* are rolls made from mutton or lamb. Originally, when the dish was prepared on the farms, they took meat from the sirloin or neck, wrapped it in the colon and suet, and sewed the whole thing up in the diaphragm, boiled it, pressed it, and soured it for a couple of weeks. The singed head, split in two, boiled and served whole is another delicacy, but the salted and soured sheep's feet has more or less been dropped at Þorrablót.

Sea mammals played an important part earlier when blubber from whales and flippers from seals were eaten, but today many species are protected and hunting is forbidden. On the other hand, shark is still an obligatory part of the festival table. The huge Greenland shark, *hákarl*[5] has a flesh that cannot be eaten without a certain preparation. It contains cyanic acid, but if it goes through fermentation, the poison is leached out. This was done earlier by burying pieces of flesh in the sand on the beach, but today the process is controlled in big plastic vessels. When the process is finished the flesh is hung for some time, and when it is ready to be served, it is cut up in small dices. It has a very strong ammonia smell and goes down with the help of a drink called *svartadaudir* (Black Death), an *akevitt* made from potatoes and spiced with caraway seeds. Other drinks are beer, which was legal to sell in Iceland only since 1989, and whey.

The bread eaten with this meat may be flatbread, dark rye bread, or the very thin *laufabrauð* (leaf breads).

Some of the dishes may be interpreted as not only traditional, but also popular in contrast to bourgeois. It is easy to see part of the old festivity, for example, the *hnutukast* (bone throwing), in the light of this interpretation. When the *hangikjöt* had been eaten there were lots of bones around, and a competition in precise throwing was often held, but it seems to have developed into chaos and violence too often and is not seen today. The Þorrablót is also normally celebrated in restaurants and not in homes.

Shrovetide Buns

The Shrovetide bun (*fastlagsbulle, fastelavnsbolle*) is the only important culinary remnant of the *carnival* in Scandinavia. It is a wheat bun filled with whipped cream and with different other ingredients, such as marzipan and—in Norway—raspberry jam. Confectioners' sugar is sprinkled on the top.

The Scandinavian names for Shrovetide go back to a word in Low German, *vastel avend*, meaning the evening before Lent. This Tuesday was also called Fat Tuesday, but sometimes the ritual was moved to Monday or even to Sunday.

This is one of the few traditions kept after the Reformation had abolished the fasting days, and it is a very timid and modest ritual compared to the burlesque and exuberant festivals in countries with a carnival culture.

Today's buns are too fat according to general dietary measures, but they are very simple and healthy compared to the earlier *hedvig/hetvägg/heitevegg*, a name taken from the German *heisse Wecken* (hot wedges). They were dunked in hot milk or cream and butter and often eaten with a spoon from a plate.

The fat is an aspect in this tradition so important that anecdotes about it live on. The most famous is one about the Swedish king Adolf Frederik who died in 1771. It is said that he died because he ate too many Shrovetide buns, but a closer study of the sources reveal that he had already finished a copious meal with fish and meat, caviar and lobsters, and lots of champagne.

Some people still bake their own Shrovetide buns, but all bakers provide them.

Semlor (Swedish Shrove Tuesday Buns)

- 2 ounces yeast
- 1 pound flour
- 1/2 cup sugar
- 1/2 cup butter
- 1 1/4 cup milk
- 1 egg
- 1/2 teaspoon salt
- 1/2 teaspoon cardamom (optional)
- powdered sugar

Dissolve the yeast in lukewarm milk and add melted butter, half of the egg slightly beaten, and sugar. Mix the salt (and cardamom) with the flour and add as much flower as is necessary to make a workable dough. Cover the dough with a cloth and let it rise for almost an hour. Divide the dough in between 12 and 20 parts (depending of how big buns you want) and form the parts into round buns with your hands. Put the buns on a baking paper on a sheet, cover with a cloth, and let them rise for 30–45 minutes until they have almost doubled in size. Brush them with the rest of the slightly beaten egg and put them in the oven (425°F) for about 10 minutes until they are golden. Let them cool, cut the top off with a sharp knife, remove some of the interior of the bun to make room for a filling, either almond paste, made from ground almonds and powdered sugar or from ground almonds mixed with sugar and warm milk.

Sun Coffee

Solarkaffi is a celebration in Iceland of the day the sun comes back after the period of arctic winter darkness. Many of the narrow valleys and fjords are completely without sun for some time, and when they have the first minutes of sunshine in early spring, people meet for coffee and cakes, eventually pancakes. These parties in small remote communities are often attended by people who grew up in the area but later have moved to the capital or other towns.

Midsummer

June is a very particular month in Scandinavia with the long, so-called blond nights. In the northernmost areas the midnight sun shines for shorter or longer time depending on the latitude, but even in the south the night lasts no more than a couple of hours.

In Denmark and Norway the midsummer celebration is a continuation of a saint's feast, that of St. John the Baptist, who according to tradition was born six months before Jesus, on June 24. The feast takes place in the evening of the June 23 with dancing, and along the coasts, with enormous bonfires. In Norway traditional fare at this time is cold cuts of cured meat and *rømmegrøt*, the sour cream porridge. In Denmark no traditional food is common to this day, but it is the time when the new potatoes are first harvested, it is the last days of the asparagus season, the fjord shrimp are particularly tasty, and the strawberries are ready to be eaten—so putting together a tempting menu is easy.

In Sweden it is June 21, the longest day of the year, that has tradition-ally been celebrated. Today Midsummer Day is officially defined as the Friday in the week that goes from June 19 until June 25, which means that it may fall on another day than the very shortest. There are many special traditions linked to Midsummer. Best known are the dances and games around the Maistång, a pole decorated with birch leaves and flowers and with a flower wreath in the top. Women and children and some men

Swedish Midsummer family meal of pickled herring, greens, Schnapps, and beer. Courtesy of Art Directors and Trip/Mike Feeney.

wear flower wreaths in the hair. The food consists of treasures from the *smörgåsbord*, herrings of different sorts, served with boiled new potatoes and cream, sausages, and meatballs. Recently, grilled meats and salads have been more common. The food is served outside, if possible, on long tables. After the main dishes have been eaten, it is time for coffee and a dessert, often a form of strawberry dish, for example, the strawberry tart. A *nubbe* (schnapps) or two is common.

August Crayfish Parties

August is the time for crayfish parties. This was the time when the crayfish season started. In the nineteenth century crayfish became so popular among the elite that the authorities understood they had to introduce restrictions to protect the species. They limited the catching season (and selling season) to a period between the middle of August and the end of

October. Then Sweden was hit by a crayfish plague that extinguished the animal in rivers and lakes, and today most of the crayfish is imported from other countries. The restrictions on sale were therefore abolished in 1990, and crayfish may be sold all year round. However, the Swedes still celebrate the opening of the catching season in August, when they consume 95 percent of the crayfish.

Crayfish, being an exclusive delicacy in the nineteenth and early twentieth centuries, was met with prejudice by the lower classes, but it has since 1945 reached all layers of society. Crayfish is eaten at special parties. These parties are still held in homes, where friends are invited, or they are arranged as small festivals where local people get together. The ideal place for a crayfish party is outdoors, if it does not rain. August is still a warm month, even if the sun sets earlier. Colored lanterns are hung in the trees, tablecloths, napkins, and plates are decorated with crayfish motifs, and the guests wear funny paper hats in many colors.

Family and friends having a traditional crayfish party on a veranda in the Stockholm archipelago, 2005. AP photo/Pressens bild/ Hasse Holmberg.

Crayfish is boiled in salt water with dill. Before serving, they are drained and put on a platter decorated with dill sprigs. When crayfish is eaten, the head is removed, and all the heads are put side by side in a circle along the outer edge of the plate.

Drinking is an important part of a crayfish party; beer and *akevitt* are accompanied by traditional drinking songs during the entire meal.

Mortensgås (Martin's Goose)

The evening before November 11, Martinmas, is celebrated with goose, even if many Danes choose duck as they also do for Christmas. A filling of prunes and apples is documented in Denmark as early as 1616. A traditional dish that accompanies the eating of roast goose is the so-called black soup based on giblets and blood, originally from the goose, but pig's blood is now a preferred ingredient.

The saint in question is Martin of Tours, beatified in 650. The population of Tours wanted the modest cleric as their bishop, but he ran away and was only found thanks to the geese, who divulged his hiding place by their intense cackling. In France the day marks the end of the wine season and the start of the slaughtering season. In Northern Europe the day came to be associated with the slaughtering of geese, which were now well-enough fed to be consumed or to be preserved for Christmas. In the Protestant countries, where the saints were not revered, the name Martin was later associated with the reformer Martin Luther, called Morten by most Scandinavians.

The tradition seems to go back to the Middle Ages, at least in Denmark and southern Sweden (Skåne), but the dish is documented early in other parts of Scandinavia, at the court, in aristocratic houses, and among crown officials. But the modern celebration of Mortensgås is a more recent phenomenon, developed with the help of the restaurant industry during the last 100 years or so.[6]

RITES OF PASSAGE

Initiation rituals to important new stages in a person's life have been marked with different ceremonies in all societies: birth, coming of age, wedding, and death. These changes in a person's social or sexual status have been celebrated in different ways in Scandinavia, both in style and content. Women relatives or neighbors used to visit with gifts the first week after a child was born (see Chapter 1, Historical Overview). Today there are meals to celebrate name giving or christening, but they are generally much more low key than, for example, a wedding feast, even when it is a formal sit-down dinner for godmother, godfather, and other close relations.

Through the centuries the religious Confirmation marked the coming of age, and a majority of the young still follow this tradition, but today there are also alternative nonreligious ceremonies. A meal is common after the ritual is finished, either a buffet dinner or a sit-down dinner, where the menu may be chosen from the favorite dishes of the young person.

Funerals used to be major events, with people visiting from far away and staying for several days, consuming lots of food and ales. Today it has been replaced by a far simpler get-together after the funeral has taken place. The family invites mourners to a simple meal with coffee, sandwiches, and cakes in the banqueting rooms of a café or in the home of the deceased. On this occasion friends and relatives give speeches where they reminisce about episodes in the life of the deceased.

Weddings

In the past, the wedding was of particularly great importance, especially in higher social circles and among wealthy farmers, because the marriage meant that two families were united and bound to plan their future as a common enterprise.

Today this is not an important aspect, except among certain immigrant groups that still practice arranged marriages. The most important change in late twentieth-century Scandinavia was the tendency to live together without being formally married. About half of all children are now born out of wedlock, something that was considered a shame, or even a sin, less than 100 years ago. Some of the couples who live together marry later, for example, when they have children. Another factor that has changed the attitude toward weddings is that many people marry for a second or a third time.

A wedding may be a very simple event, a civil ceremony followed by a lunch for the closest friends, the maid of honor and the best man. But traditional, "romantic" weddings on Saturday afternoon are still extremely popular with brides in white in the church or the city hall, followed by a big banquet in a restaurant or a hotel, eventually at home if there is enough room, but then with food served by a catering firm.

The dinner normally follows certain established rules. There is a toastmaster who announces the speakers, of whom the most important traditionally are the father of the bride who "gives" his daughter to the bridegroom, and the bridegroom who thanks his in-laws for their daughter. It is common that printed texts are placed at every plate, songs written by friends and relatives as a tribute to the couple, but often with humorous or satiric contents.

The food is not based on old traditions, as is the case for Christmas. It rather consists of new and fancy dishes or prestigious dishes such as roasts. The British type of wedding cake is becoming increasingly popular and threatens the old position of the Scandinavian showpieces, the *kransekake* in Denmark and Norway and the *spettkaka* in Sweden. They are both towerlike cakes, the *kransekake* built with graduated almond paste rings, rising from the largest ring at the bottom to the smallest on top.

Spettkaka was known in seventeenth-century German recipe collections as *Baumkuchen*. It was introduced to Sweden early on and became a fashionable dish at the Swedish court, but during the nineteenth century it established a reputation as a regional cake in the southern part of the country, Skåne. Today it is officially recognized as a regional culinary specialty by the relevant institutions in the European Union.[7]

The cake is primarily eaten by people in Skåne or Skåne-born Swedes living in other parts of the country. They order the cake from a Skåne bakery for special occasions, and the bakery will send it by courier or post. Very few bake the cake themselves; they purchase it from one of the many *spettkaka* bakers, because the baking process is difficult and time-consuming. A fluffy mixture is made out of eggs, potato flour, and sugar. This mixture is piped onto rotating cone-shaped metal skewers that are heated. When the mixture is dry, the next layer is added. Up to nine or ten layers are applied and dried.

When the baking is finished and the cake has been removed from the skewer, it is decorated with pastel-colored icing, usually in pink and white. The cake can only be cut with a serrated knife—which can be bought from the baker with the cake—and there are certain established rules for how to cut and how to interpret the shapes of the pieces.

Kransekake

- 18 ounces almonds
- 18 ounces powdered sugar
- 3 tablespoons flour
- 3 egg whites

Frosting

- 1 cup powdered sugar
- 1 egg white

Mix the peeled and minced almonds with the flour and powdered sugar and add lightly whipped egg whites. Work the dough well so it is firm, but not too hard to roll. In Norway and Denmark most people just put dough into special (buttered) molds in the shape of rings in different sizes. But it is also possible to make the rings without molds. Roll out the dough in cylinders about 1/2 inch thick in diameter. Cut off 5–6 inches to make the smallest ring. The next ring should be 3/4–1 inch longer and so on until 12 or 18 rings are made. Put them on a baking sheet and bake in oven until golden, about 10–12 minutes (350°F). Make a frosting of the egg white and powdered sugar and put some of it on a platter. Put the largest ring on this, so it sticks. Put small dots of frosting on the ring. The frosting will serve as a form of glue, so the next largest ring will be kept in place. Continue until all the rings are fastened, one smaller than the other all the way to the top. Put frosting in a little plastic bag, cut a small hole in the corner, and spray frosting through the hole onto the rings in a pattern. The cake is garnished with lots of decorations, candy, party favors, and flags. For a wedding, a figurine couple made of chocolate (or more often simply of plastic) will be put on top.

OTHER FAMILY EVENTS

Birthdays, graduations, and different forms of anniversaries are also celebrated with meals, but very few are based on traditional foods or dishes. Birthdays for small children have their rituals, but these are also changing with better economy and more possibilities. Favorite foods are sweets and ice creams and colored sweet fruit jellies (made from flavored gelatin dissolved in water and then cooled). Today some families will celebrate a birthday with a visit to a McDonald's. Birthdays for adults are more or less made as other parties with buffets or sit-down dinners and good food and drink.

NOTES

1.   Edith Mandrup Rønn: *Klipfisk, spegesild og ansjoser* (Roskilde, Denmark: Roskilde Museums Forlag 1986), p. 19.

2.   Nanna Rögnvaldardóttir: *Icelandic food and cookery* (New York: Hippocrene Books 2000).

3.   Hallgerður Gísladóttir: "Islandske madtraditioner før og nu," *Bol og by* (Copenhagen: Landbohistorisk Selskab 2002: 76).

4.   Arni Bjørnsson: *Icelandic feasts and holidays* (Reykjavik: Iceland Review 1980), pp. 14–17.

5.   *Hákarl* is classified as *Somniosus microcephalus*.

6.   Sigfrid Svensson: "Mortensgås," in Nils-Arvid Bringéus: *Mat och miljö* (Lund: Gleerup 1970), p. 112.

7.   Annelie Mannertorn: "Spettkaka, a culinary specialty from Skåne": www.skane.com.

7

Diet and Health

Scandinavians are increasingly aware of how important a healthy diet is to prevent serious diseases, for instance, cardiovascular diseases and cancer, which account for most deaths in both men and women. Public campaigns, encouraging reductions in the intake of fat foods and recommending a more substantial consumption of vegetables have made some progress. In general the diet has improved over the last 20 years, but Scandinavians still eat too few greens, fish, and whole meal bread, and too much fat and sugar.[1] A more nutritionally correct consumption of these foods is recommended by the World Health Organization (WHO) as well as by the national health institutions in Scandinavia.[2]

Even with the relatively high level of information about nutrition, a discrepancy may exist between what some people consider healthy and what nutritionists recommend. A survey among Norwegians in 2007 showed that 9 out of 10 were satisfied with their diet and characterized it as "healthy" or "very healthy," a result that is not easy to reconcile with the data about actual consumption.[3] The explanation may be that people have fragmented views of what good nutrition standards really are. For some people the absence of fat is the most important aspect, but to others this factor is not so crucial compared to how the food is produced and conserved. Many people demand organic food; they want food without any additives, food that has not been subject to genetic modification, in their own words, food that has not been "tampered with." To many people healthy food is defined by the fact that the dishes are homemade and not industrially produced. There are also some who still refuse to believe in the official health advice and maintain that a diet is good if one appreciates and enjoys what one eats.

The increased media coverage of food and nutrition is also ambiguous, sometimes repeating public recommendations, sometimes reflecting attitudes in the food industry, and sometimes bringing forth spectacular or sectarian attitudes and ideas with no scientific foundation.

When diet is evaluated, it is necessary to consider the total picture, for example, the relationship between food consumption and physical exercise, that is, between how much energy is taken in and how much is used.

There is also a growing awareness among many nutritionists that the restaurant sector and food industry have more and more power in deciding people's choice of food.

OFFICIAL FOOD POLICY

Health authorities in the Scandinavian societies recognized the basic problems in diet and nutrition early (before World War II) and seem to have perceived them in similar terms. They also have made efforts to influence food consumption and eating patterns in accordance with the scientifically elaborated norms about healthy diet.

Before World War II there were recommendations, both national and within the League of Nations, about how to compose meals with the correct nutritional contents, and a Scandinavian specialist participated in the 12-man nutrition committee of the league.[4]

For several decades, the Scandinavian countries have collaborated in setting guidelines for dietary composition and recommended intakes of nutrients. Similarities in dietary habits as well as in the prevalence of diet-related diseases, such as cardiovascular disease, osteoporosis, obesity, and diabetes, warranted a focus on the gross composition of the diet.[5] Already in 1968 medical societies in Denmark, Finland, Norway, and Sweden published a joint official statement on medical aspects of the diet in the Scandinavian countries. These countries started to develop a national policy for nutrition very early; Norway was one of the first in the world with an official nutrition policy in 1975. The first official *Nordic Nutrition Recommendations* (NNR) were issued in 1980 and have been revised four times, with the last edition in 2004. The Nordic Council of Ministers released a plan in 2006 that includes a number of common positions on issues that are currently being discussed in the European Union and WHO, as well as in specific Scandinavian initiatives.

Early on, many nutritionists were conscious of the relationship between poverty and diet, and improving the diet was seen as part of the welfare state that these nations were building after World War II.

In Sweden, a practical result of this consciousness was the development of certain nutrition-related social services, for instance, the free school lunches. In Norway the policy measures were associated with agricultural policy and directed toward market regulation, whereas the Danes did not see nutrition as a task for public policy, except in the field of education.[6]

Educational campaigns were seen as important in all the countries and were stepped up from the 1960s. Health service in Scandinavia is public with well-established systems of primary health care. Official information and recommendations about nutrition are the responsibility of public institutions, under the ministries of either health or agriculture in the various countries.

National recommendations for food intake by public health authorities may lead to conflicts of interest with other sectors of the society. When a lower intake of animal fats was recommended, this immediately created strong resistance from the agricultural sector and particularly from the dairy industry.[7] Consequently, agricultural policies had to be redefined and adapted to new market regulations.

Today the rapid growth in the food processing industry has led to an increased demand for legal measures to guarantee certain nutritional standards. The technological development within food production has created new processes and made new additives necessary. One consequence is problems with hygiene and the presence of certain toxic bacteria, for instance, salmonella.[8] One important measure is to ensure sufficient access to product information. Regulatory measures in this field have been more necessary with liberalization and structural changes in the international food market, and they are harmonized with the rules developed within the framework of the European Union.

Fats

Over the last 50 years health authorities have worked systematically to reduce the intake of fat, and more particularly, to reduce the percentage of fat in the total energy intake. According to the *Nordic Nutrition Recommendations*, 10–20 percent of the total energy intake should come from proteins, 50–60 percent from carbohydrates, and 25–35 percent from fat. For planning purposes the *NNR* has set up population goals of 15 percent protein, 55 percent carbohydrates, and a maximum of 30 percent fat of the total energy intake.[9] These proportions are in accordance with the recommendations from the World Health Organization.

There has, in fact, been a reduction in fat intake over the last quarter century, from about 40 percent (in Denmark 44%) and down to about 35 percent, or a little less. Since 2000 however, no further reduction has occurred. Thus there is still a long way to go before the ideal goal of 30 percent is reached.

The most important sources of fat in the food consumed by the Scandinavians are milk and milk products; meat and meat products; and various sorts of fats, margarine in particular. On the one hand, an increase in the consumption of meat has occurred over the last decades; on the other hand, a reduction has taken place in the consumption of margarine and in the use of lard and tallow in the cooking. The fat intake from milk products has been relatively stable. Fats from milk and butter play a far less important part than before, but the consumption of cream and cheese is up. A significant trend has been the increased portion of more-fat-rich cheeses of the French and Italian type.

In 1955, the Danes, big exporters of agricultural products, each consumed yearly an average of 28 kilos (62 pounds) of butter and margarine and fats from pigs and cows; in 2001 the amount was only 17 kilos (37 pounds).[10] This reduction in the consumption of butter and margarine may perhaps be explained by the fact that the quantity of fat applied to bread has been dramatically reduced, and that fewer and fewer are applying it at all. In Denmark, where the open sandwiches have such a prominent position, 93 percent spread butter on rye bread and 96 percent on white bread in 1985, but only 68 percent and 83 percent in 2001.[11] But gender differences may be at play here. A Swedish study of people who ate their lunch at restaurants showed that twice as many men as women used butter or margarine with their meals.[12] The reduction in fat from milk is the result of a swing away from whole milk to low-fat milks.

To understand how these changes in food consumption influence health, a widening of perspective is necessary. The total percentage of fat must be broken down into the different groups of fatty acids. The *Nordic Nutrition Recommendations* stipulate a maximum percentage of 10 for saturated fat and trans fatty acids, 10–15 for monounsaturated fatty acids, and 5–10 of polyunsaturated fatty acids.

Trans fatty acids, even if they are unsaturated, have a structure that gives them effects similar to those of saturated fatty acids. Among other things, they increase the level of (the negative) LDL cholesterol in the blood and lower correspondingly the level of (the positive) HDL. Naturally produced trans fatty acids are made by ruminants and are found in milk, mutton, and beef. Industrially produced trans fatty acids come from hardened plant and fish oils, notably used in margarine and similar products. The industry has, however, recently reduced the content of trans fatty acids in many products, not only in margarine, but in cookies, biscuits and popcorn.

The consequence of these changes is that the consumption of trans fatty acids is about as low as recommended by the WHO, about 1 percent. The real problem today is evidently not trans fatty acids, but saturated acids. The recommended 10 percent is far away from what the Scandinavians actually consume, 12–15 percent. Therefore, a further reduction in fat milk products, and fat cheeses in particular, is absolutely necessary. Danes still top the statistics of per-capita daily calorie intake from butter and raw animal fats.[13]

A reduction of fatty meats is also necessary, and nutrition campaigns have greatly pushed for white meat, chicken in particular, consumption over red meat. But the consumption in fast food restaurants of hamburgers and pizzas is a negative factor because these foods include high quantities of red meat or cheese containing saturated fat.

High intake of saturated fat is one of the factors behind coronary heart disease. In Denmark it is estimated that the number of cardiac deaths would be reduced with 22 percent if the population kept their consumption of saturated fats to the recommended level.[14] In Norway sudden cardiac deaths have been reduced to less than the half among men between 40 and 69 years. Part of this development may be explained by a reduced consumption of saturated fat and trans fatty acids and by an increased use of fruit and vegetables.[15]

Sugar

According to the *Nordic Nutrition Recommendations*, people should not get more than 10 percent of their total energy from sugar. The actual percentage is as high as 14 percent, but it is necessary to observe a fundamental change in how sugar is consumed in Scandinavian families. The use of syrup and refined sugar in cooking and in meals is reduced, but this is compensated by an extraordinary strong increase in the consumption of sweet carbonated drinks, fruit juices, and candy. In Sweden 3 out of 10 said they consumed such foods or drinks at least once a day.

Consumption surveys from Norway show that an increased part of the household expenses goes to sweet products. Almost one-fifth of the total budget for food and drink (alcohol excluded) is spent on carbonated drinks, candy, and similar items. This group takes a bigger part of the budget now than fruit, vegetables, bread, and dairy products. The money spent on sweet foods and drinks is three times as much as is spent on fish. Only meat represents a bigger part of the budget.[16]

In general men consume more sugar than women; although women eat more sweets, men drink more soft drinks. People with a low level of education consume more sweet products than people with a high level of education, but the significant difference is between the generations. Children and young people eat substantially more sweets and drink more soft drinks than does the older generation. Of Danish children, 30 percent eat chocolates and sweets almost every day. Four-fifths of the children in Denmark are eating too much sugar (more than 10 percent of the total energy intake), and the proportion of children eating twice the recommended quantity is up from 8 percent in 1995 to 12 percent in 2001.[17] In a survey from 2005, among Norwegian men between 15 and 24 years, about 50 percent said they drank soft drinks or juice with sugar daily.[18]

The intake of sweets seems to be the bigger problem. There may be a change going on in the attitude toward sweet carbonated drinks. Even if the young still drink too much of these, there is an increase in the consumption of water and sugar-free or so-called light carbonated drinks. In Norway the percentage of young people drinking Coca Cola at least once a week dropped from 54 to 35 between 1997 and 2005.[19] In Denmark there was a substantial reduction in the consumption of sweet carbonated drinks from 2003 to 2007, but the consumption of sugar-free carbonated drinks almost doubled in the same period.[20]

OBESITY AND WEIGHT ISSUES

Obesity and being overweight are partly a result of increased energy intake and partly a result of reduced physical activity. The authorities have encouraged physical exercise for all age groups, since it is considered essential to health in general and in particular to the problems of obesity.

An increase in people being overweight, that is, where the body mass index (BMI) is 25–30, or in being obese, where the BMI is 30 plus, has been characteristic of Scandinavians since the 1960s. The MONICA project, sponsored by the WHO, studied obesity in a number of countries, among them Sweden, Denmark, and Norway. They picked a region they considered representative of the country and selected the age group 35–64 years. They found that about 10 percent of the Scandinavians suffered from obesity. But there were certain gender differences. In Denmark the percentage was 11 for men and 8 for women, in Norway 8 for men and 13 for women.[21] But a Norwegian survey from 2000 to 2003 showed obesity among 14–22 percent of men between 40 and 45 years, and 13–20 percent of women in the same age group.[22]

These numbers are still low compared to the situation in the United States and in certain East European countries where the percentage of obese people is more than 25. But it is enough to cause alarm among nutrition specialists in the Scandinavian countries. They are particularly concerned about the increase in overweight children and young people. In Sweden 25 percent of the children are overweight and 3 percent are obese.[23] In Norway, between 1993 and 2000, the proportion of overweight 13-year-olds increased with about 50 percent, more among the girls than among the boys. Overweight children are particularly worrisome because experience reveals great difficulties in losing weight once one is overweight or obesity is established. Recently more emphasis has been put on the form of obesity than on the BMI alone. Fat is much more dangerous in some places on the body than in others, and weight associated with fat is different from weight associated with muscle.

Obesity increases the risk for a long series of diseases, chronic pain in muscles and joints and gallstones and kidney stones. Coronary heart disease, stroke, cancer, and type 2 diabetes are all linked to a lifestyle with little physical activity and high BMI.[24] In Denmark more than three out of four people diagnosed with type 2 diabetes were overweight.

VEGETABLES AND FRUITS

Today clear evidence supports the hypothesis that consumption of fruits and vegetables has a protective effect against diseases such as cancer,[25] coronary heart disease, stroke, and diabetes. Fruits and vegetables have a high content of vitamins, minerals, antioxidants, and dietary fiber. A doubling of the consumption of vegetables is assumed to reduce the risk of cancer and cardiovascular diseases substantially.[26] Increased intake of fruits and vegetables may also have an extra effect in replacing less favorable foods in the dietary pattern.

In Scandinavia in the last quarter of the nineteenth century, the consumption of fruits and vegetables increased. The highest consumption is in Sweden, the lowest in Iceland.[27] Vegetables were eaten on average 39 times a month in Sweden, which is 50 percent more than in the other countries. The difference is even more striking when daily consumption is studied. One-third of the Swedes eat vegetables twice a day or more. This is four times as often as in Norway, three times as often as in Iceland, and twice as often as in Denmark. The highest increase in vegetables was for tomatoes and cucumber, both vegetables with high water content. Authorities recommend more fiber-rich vegetables and darker vegetables.

Fruit was eaten on average 37 times a month in Sweden, 25–30 percent more than in the other countries. Three out of 10 Swedes eat fruit or berries twice a day or more, and this is four times as often as in Iceland and twice as often as in Denmark and in Norway. The increase in fruit consumption is primarily due to an increase in the intake of fruit juices.

The high consumption of vegetables in Sweden may have to do with the meal pattern. The hot lunches in Sweden are often accompanied by salads, while vegetables don't go so well with the sandwiches used for lunch in the other countries. But Sweden is also the country with the highest number of vegetarians. Less than 2 percent of Scandinavians are pure vegetarians who eat neither meat nor fish. Between 2–3 percent of Danes, Icelanders, and Norwegians eat fish but not meat. The percentage in Sweden is, by contrast, 7 percent.

But even if consumption is up, the goals set by the health authorities are still higher. Compared to the vegetable and fruit minimum of 400 grams (14 ounces) per day recommended by FAO and WHO, the dietary guidelines in Sweden and Iceland propose 500 grams (17.5 ounces) per day, in Denmark 600 grams (21 ounces), and in Norway 750 grams (26 ounces). In the Norwegian and Icelandic guidelines potatoes are included. In Denmark and Sweden only about 1 in 10 follow the official recommendations.

Consumption differs within populations. Women eat more vegetables, fruits, and berries than men do. In Norway only 6 percent of the men and 16 percent of the women ate fruits and vegetables four times a day. The consumption is higher in the older age groups than in the younger age groups. Men and women with a higher level of education eat more fruits and vegetable than people with a lower level of education. This difference has to be taken seriously both in the way educational campaigns are run and politically in the way price policies are structured. The increase in the price of fruits and vegetables is high enough to discourage certain low-income groups.

POTATOES

The consumption of potatoes has declined during the last decades. The highest consumption is in Iceland where potatoes are eaten on average 23 times per month, and the lowest is in Denmark where potatoes are eaten 17 times a month. In general men eat more potatoes than do women, and people with less education more than people with more education.

The health authorities are not so much concerned with the total amount of potato consumption as with the way potatoes are consumed. Today an increasing part of potatoes are sold as French fries, chips, and other processed potato products. In Norway only half of the potato consumption is of fresh potatoes. The processed products have high contents of unhealthy saturated fat. The official recommendations are directed against this trend and encourage a swing back to baked and boiled potatoes.

FISH

Campaigns for increased consumption of fish have been going on for several decades in the Scandinavian countries. Evidence clearly supports that high consumption of fish has beneficial effects on health. The main reason is the presence in fish of omega-3 fatty acids, even though the iodine, selenium, and vitamin D also are considered important. Omega-3 fatty acids from fish reduce the risk of fatal coronary disease (sudden cardiac death).

The highest consumption of fish is in Iceland and Norway. Fish as the main dish was eaten eight times a month in Iceland, seven times in Norway, six times in Sweden, and four times in Denmark. But the difference becomes much more significant if observations are made of how many people ate fish three times a week or more. Here the percentage in Iceland and Norway is 30 and 21, but only eight and six in Sweden and Denmark. In Denmark almost 60 percent of the population ate fish as their main meal less than once a week. Consumption is lowest among the younger age groups. Fish used as a topping on sandwiches (herring, mackerel, sprat) was most common in Norway and Denmark. But even in Norway the consumption of fish is lower than that of meat and far below the recommended quantity. The value of the high consumption is also to some extent reduced because fish is often eaten with saturated fats (margarine, butter).

A lot of fish is still very expensive, but fish farming has made salmon or trout more available to new population groups. Packets with frozen fillets of trout and salmon are sold in supermarkets of reasonable prices.

There has been some discussion about the level of mercury and other contaminants in fish, but it is not considered a big problem by most people. These concerns are more important regarding fish (especially fatty fish) from very polluted waters.

WHOLE-GRAIN PRODUCTS

An increase in the intake of carbohydrate is recommended, but it should come primarily from whole-grain foods. In addition to vitamins and minerals whole-grain cereals provide natural dietary fiber and resistant starch.

A high consumption of such cereals seems to have a beneficial role in reducing the risk of coronary heart disease and a protective effect against the development of hypertension and diabetes.

The average consumption of bread a day is 4.6 slices in Norway, 3.6–3.7 slices in Denmark and Sweden, and only 2.6 slices in Iceland. Cereals are the most important source of dietary fiber. Even if more than half of the intake of cereals consists of whole-grain products (except in Iceland where it is less than one-third), the intake is below the recommendations from health authorities.

In Denmark, where the consumption of white bread is highest, health authorities have expressed concern over the reduction in consumption of the traditional rye bread, which is thought to give a slower and lower increase of blood sugar than white bread. In Sweden a minimum of three slices of whole-grain bread is recommended per day, but only 40 percent of the population fills this quota. Even in Norway, with the highest consumption of bread and the lowest consumption of white bread, the recommended dietary fiber content (25 to 35 grams [about one ounce per person per day]) is not satisfied.

Breakfast cereals contain whole-grain products, but they are often mixed with too much sugar to have a total nutritional value.

VITAMINS AND MINERALS

Awareness is very high in Scandinavia of the importance of adequate intake of vitamins and minerals, and in some foodstuffs vitamins and minerals are added, to make sure the population gets the necessary amount. In general, a varied diet will cover the necessary intake, and the increased consumption of fruits and vegetables has helped for the last few years. But the reduced consumption of fish and increased sugar intake work in the opposite direction. The NNR recommends more vitamin D among all age groups, because there is too little vitamin D in the average diet. Vitamin D and calcium are important for the bone structure, particularly in Norway with a very high occurrence of fractures in wrists and the neck of the femur. Many women get too little of the vitamin B12 (cobalamin), especially during pregnancies, when this vitamin is crucial.

SALT AND ALCOHOL

Most Scandinavians eat too much salt, about 10 grams (1/3 ounce) a day. Too much salt increases the blood pressure and may be a contributing factor in heart disease and stroke. The NNR recommends lowering the intake to 6 grams (1/5 ounce) for women and 7 (1/4 ounce) grams for men, and acknowledges that a further reduction to 5 grams (1/6 ounce) will give even better results. Children should be given as little salt as possible so that they will not become used to a high salt content in food.

Whereas consumption of meat and fat is partly dependent on individual choice, this is not the case with consumption of salt. How much salt is added during cooking or at the table is not so important when the major part of the salt intake comes from industrially produced foods, in Norway as much as 75 percent. This means that the higher the consumption of convenience foods, the higher the intake of salt; thus a reduction of salt involves far more drastic changes in food habits than merely eliminating salt at the table.

High consumption of alcohol also is causing serious health problems. Even if the Scandinavian countries consume less than other European countries, there has been a strong increase in wine consumption the last decades. But the drinking of alcohol is not evenly distributed among different groups of the society. In Norway it has been estimated that 50 percent of the total alcohol consumption is made by the 10 percent of the population who drink most.

RECOMMENDATIONS

Increased consumption of

- vegetables, fruits, berries
- whole-meal bread
- fish
- boiled or baked potatoes

Reduced consumption of

- fatty meat products
- fatty dairy products
- fatty potato products
- cooking fats
- sugar and salt

A Norwegian nutritionist has published the following list of what is needed to change in the diet for an average inhabitant if he or she wants to reach the wanted goals.[28] The suggested changes will not be very different for the other Scandinavian countries.

- A reduction of 1/3 ounce per day in fat intake, corresponding to a glass and a half of whole milk (9 ounces)
- A reduction of 1/3 ounce per day in the intake of saturated fats, corresponding to a portion of sausages (4 1/2 ounces) or fat cheese for three slices of bread (2 ounces)
- A reduction of 1 ounce per day in sugar intake, corresponding to one and a half glasses of a soft drink (9 ounces)
- A reduction in the salt intake from 1/3 to 1/6 ounce a day, corresponding to a bag of chips (11 ounces)
- An increase in dietary fiber of 1/2 ounce per day, corresponding to four slices of whole-meal bread or six carrots
- An increase of 12 ounces per day in the intake of fruits, greens, and potatoes, corresponding to an orange, a potato, a tomato, and a portion of cooked vegetables

HOW TO CHANGE A DIET

If Scandinavians want to eat in a healthier way, a substantial part of the population has to make important changes in their dietary habits. But such changes do not come easily, and they are rarely the product of information and knowledge only. Many people have a pretty good idea of what is good for their health; they know that they ought to eat more vegetables and less meat, but this does not immediately lead to changes. The public authorities responsible for national health cannot scare people into new habits by publishing lists with so-called forbidden products. Many Scandinavians felt a moral pang in much of the early initiatives to promote healthier eating. Competition with the massive and appealing publicity from the food industry does not make nutritional advice easier to deliver. To remedy this situation nutritionists have realized that improving the diet is not a question of warning against certain nutrients and cooking techniques and recommending others. It is necessary to consider the meal situation as a cultural event, where traditional attitudes and prejudices are involved. The various components and ingredients in a dish relate to each other, and if one ingredient is dropped, the whole dish may change character.

Ida Husby, a Danish scholar, has been involved with official nutritional policies in her country since the 1990s. She explains that it was important in the work she and her colleagues did, to maintain a food cultural point of view.[29] The intention was to respect traditional and popular dishes, those eaten by most Danes, while trying to improve the nutritional value. The first priority was reduction of saturated fat, and they discovered that in hot meals most of the fat was consumed through sauces; 50 percent of the sauces contained frying fat, and 20 percent contained crème fraîche. They soon realized that dropping the sauce altogether was no solution to the problem. They were supported in this conclusion by a survey in 1993, showing that 70 percent of the Danes ate sauce with their hot meal very day. To most Danes the sauce was one of the necessary ingredients in a proper meal.

As an example, Husby uses the traditional Danish dish meatballs with brown sauce. To drop the brown sauce would have created a risk for a confrontation in the family between those who wanted the traditional dish, for instance, husband and small children, and the others who wanted to modernize with a wider use of vegetables. But in many cases when the brown sauce was dropped, other and even fatter alternatives crept in. To eat potatoes or pasta alone is difficult, and therefore garlic butter and cheese might be added. A better solution would have been to elaborate a recipe for a brown sauce with less fat, so the health could be improved without destroying the family harmony. Use of sauce is also an encouragement to a higher consumption of potatoes, and thereby a better balance between starch and meat in the meal.

A similar dilemma was apparent when salads were recommended for lunch in Norway instead of open sandwiches with butter and toppings. Women, particularly those who wanted to lose weight, chose salads mainly consisting of vegetables and small pieces of chicken. But the salad did not taste like much, so they added dressings or mayonnaise, often richer in fat than the sandwiches they were running away from.

Another example is the consumption of highly recommended boiled fish. In Mediterranean societies such fish is eaten with a little olive oil, lemon juice, and vegetables. In Scandinavia butter or margarine has been used and thereby reduced the positive health effect of a fish meal. This shows how important it is to consider the nutrients and foodstuffs in a wider perspective. In Norway the nutrition council hired the most famous TV cook as a consultant in their information service.

FOOD IN SCHOOLS

Young people's health is one of the primary concerns of the authorities, and many initiatives are directed toward schools. Nutrition has always been an important element in the teaching of household science, but much emphasis has also been given to the daily diet during school hours.

In Sweden free hot meals were given to pupils from poor families when primary schools became compulsory in 1845, in Denmark and

Norway from the 1880s. This was generally a form of private charity, but it developed differently in the Scandinavian countries during the twentieth century. Among the Scandinavian countries only Sweden has a system with free hot meals served at the lunch break.[30] In Denmark and Norway a system of voluntary subscription to milk and fruit has been developed.

Sweden

The present system goes back to 1946 and started as a means to help raise dietetic standards of children from poor families, but it soon became the norm and covered in 1973–1974 all pupils in the whole country. In a law from 1997 the municipalities were given the responsibility of serving free food to all children in the primary schools. The school lunch is stipulated to provide 30 percent of the total energy intake per day. The meals have not always been of a desired quality, and there has been criticism from nutritionists and pupils. An average of 15 percent of the children drop the free meal and buy something in the cafeteria or outside the school, often less healthy snacks. Dropping the lunch is something that increases with age. In a survey the children were asked if they ate the school lunch every day (five days a week), and the answer was yes among 91 percent of the eight-year-olds, but only 77 percent among the 11-year-olds. Among the 15-year-olds, 52 percent of the boys ate the school lunch every day and 49 percent of the girls.[31]

The Swedish parliament has therefore commissioned the national institute of food, known as Livsmedelsverket,[32] to elaborate guidelines for healthy and tasty food in schools. These guidelines are based on the recommendations for a dietarily correct composition of meals. The schools are recommended to offer two different dishes so the pupils have a real choice.

The organizations and enterprises of Swedish farmers (food producers) have created a movement to encourage the work with school lunches and to improve the quality. It is called Skolmatens Venner (Friends of the School Meals).

Norway

In Norway the municipal authorities gradually took over the responsibility for the free meals in schools in the first part of the twentieth century, and a breakthrough in the meal pattern took place in the 1930s. A prominent nutritionist and city school doctor, Carl Schiøtz, made a study of school children in Oslo and found that the hot meals were not an ideal diet.[33] Influenced by the new discoveries of vitamins, he developed a school breakfast consisting of coarse dark bread with a topping (cheese, liver paste, slices of sausages, etc.) and fruit or vegetables (a carrot, an apple, or an orange).[34] This *Oslo breakfast* was adapted to local conditions around the country, and a modified system developed, in which the children were asked to prepare a nutritionally correct breakfast pack at home and bring it with them to school. This *matpakke* (food pack) had an enormous long-term impact on food habits in Norwegian homes.

The present system with milk delivery in schools started in Norway in 1971. Today more than 90 percent of the milk delivered has a low-fat content. The pupils have to pay a certain amount on a regular basis and receive the milk during the lunch break. Almost all schools participate in this system and about 60 percent of all pupils subscribe. The older pupils are least receptive of this arrangement. According to a recent survey, only 15 percent of the young between 15 and 17 years participate, and only 3 percent of the young between 17 and 19 years.[35]

Fruits and vegetables were introduced in schools through a similar system in the 1990s, when the national health directorate cooperated with the promotion center for fruit and vegetable distributors. They established a subscription system, subsidized by the state, and from 2004 it covered the whole country; 90,000 pupils participated. From 2007 some municipalities offered free fruit and vegetables to schoolchildren. Among the older pupils, 15 years and more, who in general express an interest in fruits and vegetables, very few seem to take advantage of this system.[36]

Denmark

The Oslo breakfast system was picked up by nutritionists in Denmark— where the lunch pack had a long tradition—and introduced in Danish schools from 1937. The breakfast packs were partly made in cafeterias and partly by private firms and given to underprivileged children. This system peaked around 1950 and lasted until the 1980s. Pupils from more well-situated families brought their own packs with them to school, and as in Norway, the school *madpakke* became an institution and a part of national identity.[37]

Today several local initiatives have introduced subscription systems for fruits and vegetables to pupils, and about 20 percent of the schools participate. An evaluation of this system showed a higher consumption of fruit and vegetables in these schools than in schools without the system, and the consumption was not only higher for the pupils who subscribed but also for other pupils in these schools. There is also a similar system for milk delivery, subsidized by the European Union.

The quality of food and meals in schools has been taken up as a responsibility by the official organs for food, health, and nutrition research.[38]
The government has initiated a Web site where all available information
about these subjects are published. Groups or teams of specialists also go
to schools around the country, put up guidelines for nutrition policies,
and help to establish healthy and tasty meals.

In Denmark similar initiatives have been tried in workplaces, either with
free fruits and vegetables or with subsidized. The general impression is that
the more available these products are, the higher the consumption.

NOTES

1. I am greatly indebted to Lars Johansson at the Norwegian Directorate of
Health in Oslo for much of the information about diet and health in this chapter.

2. *Diet, nutrition and the prevention of chronic diseases*. Technical report series
916 (Geneva: WHO 2003).

3. *Mat og måltider* (Oslo: Norsk landbrukssamvirke 2007).

4. Inger Johanne Lyngø: *Vitaminer! Kultur og vitenskap i mellomkrigstidens
kostholdspropaganda* (Oslo: Universitetet i Oslo 2003), p. 39.

5. W. Becker, N. Lyhne, A. N. Pedersen, A. Aro, M. Fogelholm, I. Þórsdottír, J. Alexander, S. A. Anderssen, H. M. Meltzer, and J. L. Pedersen: *Nordic
nutrition recommendations 2004: Integrating nutrition and physical activity* (Copenhagen: Nordic Council of Ministers 2004), p. 9.

6. Unni Kjærnes (ed.): *Eating patterns. A day in the lives of Nordic peoples*
(Lysaker, Norway: SIFO—National Institute of Consumer Research 2001), pp.
60–62.

7. Inger Johanne Lyngø: "The National Nutrition Exhibition," in *Food,
drink and identity*, ed. Peter Scholliers (Oxford: Berg 2001), pp. 150–51.

8. Jan Krag Jacobsen: "Madkultur—et oplæg til en kulturpolitik på madområdet," in *Rapport om den danske madkultur*: www.kum.dk.

9. Becker et al.: *Nordic nutrition recommendations 2004*, p. 13.

10. Lars Ovesen: *Kødindtaget i Danmark og dets betydning for ernæring og sund-
hed* (Copenhagen: Fødevaredirektoratet 2002).

11. M. Kjøller, K. Juel, F. Kamper-Jørgensen (ed.): *Folkesundhedsrapporten
Danmark 2007* (Copenhagen: Statens Institut for Folkesundhed 2007).

12. Clara Westman and Marie Skans: *Val av lunchrätt* (Stockholm: Livsmedelsverket 2001).

13. *FAO statistical yearbook 2005–2006* (Rome Food and Agriculture Organization, 2006).

14. M. Kjøller et al.: *Folkesundhedsrapporten Danmark 2007*.

15. Jan L. Pedersen, Aage Tverdal, Bente Kirkhus: "Kostendringer og døde-
lighetsutvikling av hjerte- og karsykdommer i Norge," *Tidsskrift for Den norske
legeforening 2004*, no. 11 (Oslo: Den norske legeforening 2004), p. 1532. English
summary: www.tidsskriftet.no/index.php?seks_id=1027613.

16. *Forbruksundersøkelsen 2004–2006*, Norwegian Statistical Bureau: www.ssb.no.

17. *Fødevareundersøgelsene 1995 og 2001*, Fødevareinstituttet: www.dfvf.dk.

18. *Levekårsundersøkelsen 2005*, Statistisk Sentralbyrå: www.ssb.no.

19. "Norske spisefakta 2006." Synovate MMI. Oslo 2006.

20. Bryggeriforeningen (The Brewers' Association), Copenhagen, January 15, 2007: www.bryggeriforeningen.dk.

21. "Fetma—problem och åtgärder." Report 160. Stockholm: Statens beredning för medicinsk utvärdering (SBU) 2002) pp. 40–41.

22. Lars Johansson: *Utviklingen i norsk kosthold 2007* (Oslo: Sosial og helsedirektoratet 2007), p. 15.

23. Claude Marcus: "Varför drabbas mitt barn av övervikt?": www.growing people.se.

24. *The challenge of obesity in the WHO European Region and the strategies for response* (Copenhagen: WHO Regional Office for Europe 2007).

25. *Food, nutrition, physical activity, and the prevention of cancer: A global perspective* (London: World Cancer Research Fund 2007).

26. M. R. Law et al.: "By how much does fruit and vegetable consumption reduce the risk of ischaemic heart disease?" *European Journal of Clinical Nutrition* (1998): 549–56.

27. *Consumption of vegetables, potatoes, fruit, bread and fish in the Nordic and Baltic countries*, The Norbagreen 2002 study, TemaNord 2003:556 (Nordic Council of Ministers 2003). The statistical data in this section are taken from this study.

28. Johansson: *Utviklingen i norsk kosthold 2007*, p. 14.

29. Ida Husby: "Madkultur og ernæringsoplysning," *Rapport om den danske madkultur*: www.kum.dk.

30. Finland also has this system.

31. "Högstadieelevernas måltidsvanor 2000," *Vår Föda*, no. 1 (Stockholm: Livsmedelsverket 2002).

32. Livsmedelsverket: www.slv.se.

33. Lyngø: *Vitaminer!* pp. 115–49.

34. *Skolemåltidet i grunnskolen* (Oslo: Kunnskapsdepartementet 2006), p. 16.

35. Annechen Bahr Bugge: *Ungdoms skolematvaner—refleksjon, reaksjon eller interaksjon?* (Oslo: SIFO 2007), p. 141.

36. Bugge: *Ungdoms skolematvaner*, p. 138.

37. René Bühlmann and Stig Püschl: *Madpakken* (Copenhagen: Fremad 1991), pp. 48–55.

38. Sundhedsstyrelsen: www.sundhedsstyrelsen.dek; Fødevarestyrelsen: www.foedevarestyrelsen.dk; and Danmarks fødevareforskning: www.dfvf.dk.

Glossary

æbleflæsk   Fried bacon with fried apples.

æbleskiver   Apple fritters.

akevitt   Spirits made from grains or potatoes.

blande/blanda   Mixture of water and fermented whey or buttermilk.

brisling   Sprat.

brunede kartofler   Caramelized potatoes.

brunkål   Browned white cabbage.

dravle   Curdled milk dish.

falukorv   Smoked pork and beef sausage.

fårikål   Stew with cabbage and mutton.

fenalår   Cured leg of lamb.

finker   Dish of chopped offal and spices.

franskbrød   White bread from wheat flour.

frikadeller   Danish meatballs.

frokost   The word for breakfast in Norwegian and Swedish, for lunch in Danish.

gammelost   Cheese made without rennet.

geitost   Goat cheese.

gløg/glögg   Hot spiced drink.

gomme   Curdled milk dish.

gravlaks   Cured (in Swedish gravat, graved) salmon.

gullbrød   Flatbread coated with a mixture of milk and egg.

hakkebøf   Minced beef and pork patties.

hangikjöt   Smoked lamb.

jomfruhummer   Norwegian lobster (Dublin Bay prawn).

kåldolmas   Cabbage rolls with meat and rice.

kålruletter   Cabbage rolls with minced meat.

kalvost/kalvedans/kalvesuss   Jellylike dish of meat from newborn calves.

kams   Porridgelike dish of flour and fat.

kjöttbullar   Swedish meatballs.

kjøttkaker   Norwegian meatballs.

klippfisk   Dried, salted cod.

knäckebröd   Thin, crisp leavened bread.

knettir   Large fish balls.

kransekage   Pyramid cake of marzipan rings.

kringle   Pretzel.

laufabrauð   Icelandic leaf (lace) bread.

lefse   Soft, thin unleavened bread.

leverpostej   Liver paste.

limpa   Bread.

löjrom   Vendace roe made as caviar.

lussekatter   Saffron buns.

lutefisk   Dried cod (stockfish) soaked in lye.

madpakke/matpakke   Lunch pack.

medisterpølse   Sausage of lean and fat pork.

mulle/mölja/mylja   Dish with bread, stock, and fat.

øllebrød   Soup of beer and bread.

ostkaka   Cheesecake made from curds.

plukfisk   Dish with mashed fish and potatoes.

Þorrablót   Icelandic winter food festival.

rakefisk   Fermented fish.

remoulade   A mayonnaise-like sauce.

rødgrød   Sweet red porridge from berries.

rømme   Sour cream.

rømmegrøt   Porridge of rømme and flour.

rompalt   Roe balls.

rugbrød   Rye bread.

rygost   Smoked cheese.

skyr   Icelandic yogurt-like curd.

smørbrød/smørrebrød/smörgås   Open sandwich.

sod   Meat soup.

spettkaka   Pyramid cake.

stockfish   Dried cod.

suassaat   Greenlandish meat soup.

surströmming   Fermented Baltic herring.

sylte   Head cheese.

syltemælk/syltemjölk   Dish of boiled sour milk.

tätmjölk, tettemjølk   Milk curdled with bacteria culture.

tunnbrød   Thin, unleavened bread, crisp or soft.

tvebak   Hard bread, baked twice.

västkustsallad   Seafood salad.

vispebröd   Flatbread coated with egg white.

wienerbrød   Danish pastry.

Resource Guide

SUGGESTED READING

Christiansen, Ingrid Marie, Rudolf Jensen, Julie McDonald, and John Zug. *Definitely Danish: Denmark and Danish Americans: History, culture, recipes.* Iowa City, IA: Penfield Press, 1993.

Davidson, Alan. *North Atlantic seafood.* New York: Harper & Row, 1989.

Doub, Siri Lise. *Tastes & tales of Norway.* New York: Hippocrene Books, 2002.

Hansen, Stig. *Cooking Danish.* Nashville, TN: Favorite Recipes Press, 2007.

Henderson, Helene: *The Swedish table.* Minneapolis: University of Minnesota Press, 2005.

Ojakangas, Beatrice. *The great Scandinavian baking book.* Minneapolis: University of Minnesota Press, 1999.

——— *Scandinavian cooking.* Minneapolis: University of Minnesota Press, 2003.

———. *Scandinavian feasts: Celebrating traditions throughout the year.* Minneapolis: University of Minnesota Press, 2001.

Roalson, Louise, and Joan Liffring-Zug Bourret. *Norwegian touches: History, recipes, folk arts.* Iowa City, IA: Penfield Books, 2003.

Rögnvaldardóttir, Nanna. *Icelandic food and cookery.* New York: Hippocrene Books, 2000.

Rosenberg, Judith Pierce. *A Swedish kitchen: Recipes and reminiscences.* New York: Hippocrene Books, 2004.

Sarvis, Shirley, and Barbara Scott O'Neil. *Best of Scandinavian cooking: Danish, Norwegian, and Swedish.* New York: Hippocrene Books, 1997.

Viestad, Andreas. *Kitchen of light: New Scandinavian cooking.* New York: Artisan, 2003.

WEB SITES

Denmark

Danish Fitness and Nutrition Council, http://www.meraadet.dk/uk/default.
    asp?id=1337.
Danish recipes from Consulate General of Denmark, New York, http://www.
    gknewyork.um.dk/en/menu/InfoDenmark/Danish+Cooking.
Det Danske Gastronomiske Akademi, http://www.gastronomisk-akademi.dk/
    index.htm.
Ministry of Food, Agriculture and Fisheries, http://www.uk.foedevarestyrelsen.
    dk/Forside.htm.
National Food Institute, http://www.vet.dtu.dk/Default.aspx?ID=2227.

Iceland

Ministry of Fisheries and Agriculture, http://eng.sjavarutvegsraduneyti.is.
Ministry of Health, http://eng.heilbrigdisraduneyti.is.

Norway

Culinary Institute of Norway, http://www.gastronomi.no/en.
Ministry of Agriculture and Food, http://www.regjeringen.no/en/dep/lmd.
    html?id=627.
National Institute for Consumer Research, SIFO, http://www.sifo.no.
Norwegian Directorate of Health, http://www.shdir.no.
Norwegian Institute of Public Health, http://www.fhi.no/eway/?pid=238.

Scandinavia

New Nordic Food, http://www.nordicinnovation.net/article.cfm?id=1–853–487.

Sweden

Food from Sweden, http://www.foodfromsweden.com.
Gastronomiska Akademin, http://www.gastronomiskaakademien.com/index_
    ga.html.
Måltidens Hus i Norden, http://www.maltidenshus.com.
Ministry of Agriculture, http://www.sweden.gov.se/sb/d/2064.
National Food Administration, http://www.slv.se/default.aspx?id=231&epslangu
    age=EN-GB.
Statens folkhälsoinstitut, http://www.fhi.se.
Sveriges Hotel & Restaurang företagare, http://www.shr.se.

FILMS

Babette's Feast (1987). Dir. Gabriel Axel. Danish film based on an Isak Dinesen story. French feast but Jutland setting.

Cabin Fever (*Når nettene blir lange*) (2000). Norway. Directed by Mona J. Hoel. Christmas in a cabin in the mountains, with contrast between idyllic Christmas traditions and alcoholism.

The Celebration (*Festen*) (1996). Denmark. Directed by Thomas Vinterberg. Rich businessman and family patriarch gives a dinner for his 60th birthday, but old conflicts erupt and make the celebration less merry than planned.

Fanny and Alexander (*Fanny och Alexander*) (1982). Sweden. Directed by Ingmar Bergman. A sumptuous Christmas feast in an early twentieth-century Stockholm, Sweden wealthy household is depicted.

The Wild Duck (*Vildanden*) (1963). Norway. Directed by Tancred Ibsen. Tancred Ibsen is the grandson of Henrik Ibsen, whose play the film is based on. It begins with references to a great dinner in a rich man's house, then a middle-class morning meal with herring salad.

Selected Bibliography

GENERAL

Amilien, Virginie, and Erling Krohg (ed): *Den kultiverte maten*. Bergen: Fagbokforlaget, 2007.

————: *What do we mean by traditional food?* Lysaker, Norway: National Institute of Consumer Research (SIFO), 2001.

Bringéus, Nils-Arvid: *Man, food and milieu: A Swedish approach to food ethnology*. East Linton, Scotland: Tuckwell Press, 2001.

Elg, Ulf : *Matens metamorfos*. Stockholm: LT, 1987.

Fossgard, Eldbjørg (ed): *Nye og tradisjonelle trekk i nordisk matkultur*. Voss, Norway: Vestnorsk kulturakademi, 2005.

Genrup, Kurt: *Mat som kultur: Etnologiska kosthållsstudier*. Umeå, Sweden: Etnologiska institutionen, University of Umeå. 1988.

Jacobsen, Jan Krag, Rasmus Bo Bojesen, Helle Brønnum Carlsen, Lotte Holm, Ida Husby, and Bi Skaarup: *Den danske madkultur*. Copenhagen: Kulturministeriet 1997.

Jansson, Søren: *Maten och det sociala samspelet. Etnologiska perspektiv på matvanor*. Stockholm: Utbildningsradion, 1993.

Kayser Nielsen, Niels: *Madkultur: Opbrud og tradition*. Århus, Denmark: Klim, 2003.

Notaker, Henry: "Har vi en norsk matkultur?" *Nytt Norsk Tidsskrift 17* (2000): 345–64.

HISTORICAL OVERVIEW

Berg, Gösta, and Sigfrid Svensson: *Svensk bondekultur*. Stockholm: Bonnier 1969.

Boyhus, Else-Marie, Hallgerdur Gisladottir, Niels Kayser Nielsen, Grith Lerche, and Bi Skaarup: *Mad og skik: frembringelse, forarbejdning og servering af fødevarer*. Bol og by 2002:2. Odense, Denmark: Landbohistorisk Selskab, 2002.

Bringéus, Nils-Arvid: *Mat och måltid*. Stockholm: Carlsson, 1988.

Fjellström, Christina: *Drömmen om det goda livet: Livskvalitet och matvanor i ett uppväxande industrisamhälle: Stocka sågverk 1870–1980*. Stockholm: Almqvist & Wiksell International, 1990.

Fjellström, Phebe: *Samernas samhälle: I tradition och nutid*. Stockholm: Norstedt, 1986.

Fossgard, Eldbjørg (ed): *Tradisjon, opplysning og verkelegheit i norsk matkultur*. Voss, Norway: Vestnorsk kulturakademi, 2002.

Genrup, Kurt: *Matrike Norrland*. [Bjästa, Sweden]: CeWe förlaget, 2001.

Gísladóttir, Hallgerður: *Íslensk matarhefð*. Reykjavik: Mál og menning, 1999.

Grewe, Rudolf: "An early 13th century Northern European cookbook." In *Current research in culinary history*. Boston: Culinary Historians of Boston, 1986.

Grøn, Fredrik: *Om kostholdet i Norge indtil aar 1500*. Oslo: Gyldendal Norsk Forlag, 1926.

Højrup, Ole: *Landbokvinden*. Copenhagen: Nationalmuseet, c. 1966.

Keyland, Nils: *Svensk allmogekost*. Stockholm: Carlsson, 1989.

Kulturhistorisk leksikon for nordisk middelalder. Vols. 1–21. Oslo: Det Norske Videnskaps-akademi/Jacob Dybwad, 1956–1977.

Nordström, Ingrid: *Till bords*. Stockholm: Carlsson 1988.

Nørgaard, Else, and Claus Bjørn (ed): *Det Danske landkøkken*. Copenhagen: Dansk familielandbrug, 1989.

Notaker, Henry: *Mat og måltid*. Oslo: Aschehoug, 2006.

Olaus Magnus: *Historia om de nordiska folken*. Hedemora, Sweden: Gidlunds, 2001.

Olsson, Alfa: *Om allmogens kosthold*. Lund, Sweden: Gleerup, 1958.

Pedersen, Ragnar: "Hverdagskosten i Hedmarksbygdene." *Norveg* 28 (1985): 81–127.

Rehnberg, Mads: *Svenska gästabud från alla tider*. Stockholm: Forum, 1963.

Siggaard, Niels: *Fødemidlerne i ernærings-historisk belysning*. Copenhagen: Nilsen & Lydiche, 1945.

Skovgaard, Mette: *Bondens køkken*. Copenhagen: Nationalmuseet, 1984.

Steenstrup, Axel: *Dagligliv i Danmark i det syttende og attende århundrede: 1620–1720*. Copenhagen: Nyt Nordisk Forlag, 1969.

Stigum, Hilmar, and Kristofer Visted: *Vår gamle bondekultur*. Vol. 2. Oslo: Cappelen, 1971.

Troels-Lund, Troels: *Dagligt Liv i Norden i det sekstende Aarhundrede*. Vol. 5. Copenhagen: Gyldendalske Boghandel, s.a.

MAJOR FOODS AND INGREDIENTS

Berg, Per, and Astri Riddervold: *Spekemat*. Oslo: Damm, 2004.

Boyhus, Else-Marie: *Grisen: En køkkenhistorie*. Copenhagen: Gyldendal, 1998.

Boyhus, Else-Marie, and Jørgen Fakstorp: *Gastronomisk leksikon*. Copenhagen: Gyldendal, 1998.

Campbell, Åke: *Det svenska brödet*. Stockholm: Svensk bageritidsskrift, 1950. English summary included.

Consumption of vegetables, potatoes, fruit, bread and fish in the Nordic and Baltic countries. The Norbagreen 2002 study. TemaNord 2003:556. Nordic Council of Ministers, 2003.

Davidson, Alan: *North Atlantic seafood*. New York: Harper & Row, 1989.

Food: From farm to fork statistics. Brussels: European Commission. 2006.

Heuch, Halvor. and Astri Riddervold: *Rakefisk*. Oslo: Damm, 1999.

Nordic statistical yearbook 2007. Copenhagen: Nordic Council of Ministers, 2007.

Notaker, Henry: *Appetittleksikon*. Oslo: Gyldendal, 1997.

Ränk, Gustav: *Från mjölk till ost*. Stockholm: Nordiska museet, 1966.

Riddervold, Astri: *Lutefisk, rakefisk and herring in Norwegian tradition*. Oslo: Novus, c. 1990.

Rønn, Edith Mandrup: *Klipfisk, spegesild og ansjoser*. Roskilde, Denmark: Roskilde Museums Forlag, 1986.

Swahn, Jan-Öjvind: *Fil, fläsk och falukorv*. Lund, Sweden: Histoiska media, 2000.

————: *Mathistorisk uppslagsbok*. Bromma, Sweden: Ordalaget, 2003.

World drink trends 2005. Henley-on-Thames, England: World Advertising Research Center, 2005.

Web Sites

Denmark: Ministry of Food, Agriculture and Fisheries: http://www.uk.foedevar estyrelsen.dk/Forside.htm.

Iceland: Ministry of Fisheries and Agriculture: http://eng.sjavarutvegsradune yti.is.

Nordic Statistical Yearbook: http://www.norden.org/pub/ovrigt/statistik/sk/N200 7001.pdf.

Norway: Ministry of Agriculture and Food: http://www.regjeringen.no/en/dep/ lmd.html?id=627.

Sweden: Ministry of Agriculture: http://www.sweden.gov.se/sb/d/2064.

Statistics Denmark (Danmark Statistik): http://www.dst.dk.

Statistics Iceland: http://www.statice.is.

Statistics Norway (Statistisk Sentralbyrå): www.ssb.no.

Statistics Sweden (Statistiska Centralbyrån): http://www.scb.se.

COOKING

Börjesson, Karl-Johan: *Landskapsbröd*. Gothenburg, Sweden: Warne, 2004.

Fjällström, Phebe: *Samernas kostvanor: Människan och naturen*. Stockholm: Wahlström & Widstrand, 2001.

Holm, Lotte: *Kostens forandring*. Copenhagen: Akademisk Forlag, 1991.

Joensen, Jóan Pauli: *Færøsk madkultur: En oversigt*. Tórshavn, Faroe Islands: Faroese Research Council, 2003.

Kjærnes, Unni (ed.): *Eating patterns: A day in the lives of Nordic peoples*. Lysaker, Norway: National Institute of Consumer Research (SIFO), 2001.

Larsen, Finn: *Food in southern Greenland for 1000 years*. Højbjerg, Denmark: Hovedland, c. 2000.

Lou Mortensen, Stig: *Danske egnsretter: snysk, kjylar og mikmuskage*. Copenhagen: Bios, 2005.

Metzger, Jonathan: *I köttbullslandet: Konstruktionen av svenskt och utländskt på kulinariska fältet*. Stockholm: University of Stockholm, 2005.

Web Sites

Denmark: Danish Gastronomic Academy: http://www.gastronomisk-akademi.dk/index.htm,

Sweden: Gastronomic Academy: http://www.gastronomiskaakademien.com/index_ga.html.

TYPICAL MEALS

Aarflot Fagerli, Rønnaug: *Endringer i nordmenns matvaner på 80- og 90-tallet*. Lysaker, Norway: National Institute of Consumer Research (SIFO), 1999.

Bugge, Annechen: *Å spise middag: En matsosiologisk analyse*. Trondheim, Norway: Tapir, 2006.

Bugge, Annechen, and Reidar Almås: "Domesic Dinner: Representations and practices of a proper meal among young suburban mothers." *Journal of Consumer Culture* 6, no. 2 (2006): 203–29.

Bugge, Annechen, and Runar Døving: *Det norske måltidsmønsteret: Ideal og praksis*. Lysaker, Norway: National Institute of Consumer Research (SIFO), 2000.

Ejder, Bertil: *Dagens tider och måltider*. Lund, Sweden: Gleerup, 1969.

Fagt, Sisse, and Anja Biltoft-Jensen: *Populære middagsretter*. Copenhagen: The Danish Institute for Food and Veterinary Research, 2006.

Fürst, Elisabeth: *Vår matkultur: Konflikt mellom det tradisjonelle og det moderne*. Lysaker, Norway: National Institute of Consumer Research (SIFO), 1985.

Hazelton, Nika: *The art of Scandinavian cooking*. New York: Macmillan, 1965.

Holm, Lotte (ed): *Mad, mennesker og måltider: Samfundsvidenskabelige perspektiver*. Copenhagen: Munksgaard, 2003.

Kjærnes, Unni (ed): *Eating patterns. A day in the lives of Nordic Peoples*. Lysaker, Norway: National Institute of Consumer Research (SIFO), 2001.

Rögnvaldardóttir, Nanna: *Icelandic food and cookery*. New York: Hippocrene Books, 2000.
Wandel, Margareta, Annechen Bugge, and Jorun Skoglund Ramm: *Matvaner i endring og stabilitet*. Lysaker, Norway: National Institute of Consumer Research (SIFO), 1995.

Web Sites

Denmark: National Food Institute: http://www.vet.dtu.dk/Default.aspx?ID=2227.
Norway: National Institute for Consumer Research, SIFO: www.sifo.no.
Sweden: National Food Administration: http://www.slv.se/default.aspx?id=231 &epslanguage=EN-GB.

EATING OUT

Bugge, Annechen Bahr, and Randi Lavik: *Å spise ute*. Oslo: National Institute of Consumer Research (SIFO), 2007.
Grathwohl, Jan Ulrik: "På restaurant og værtshus." In Georg Nellemann et al., *Dagligliv i Danmark i vor tid*. Vol. 2. Copenhagen: Nyt Nordisk Forlag, 1989.
Hedlund, Oscar: *Fullständiga rättigheter*. Stockholm: Prisma, 2002.
Qvistorff, Helge V.: *Gjæstgiveriets historie i Danmark*. Skørping, Denmark: Jysk lokalhistorisk forlag, 1984.
Tellström, Richard: *The construction of food and meal culture for political and commercial ends: EU-summits, rural businesses and world exhibitions*. Örebro, Sweden: Örebro University, 2006.
Westman, Clara, and Marie Skans: *Val av lunchrätt*. Stockholm: Livsmedelsverket, 2001.

Web Sites

The Culinary Institute of Norway: http://www.gastronomi.no/en.
New Nordic Food: http://www.nordicinnovation.net/article.cfm?id=1–853–487.
Swedish Hotel and Restaurant Owners: http://www.shr.se.
Sweden: House of the Meal: http://www.maltidenshus.com.

SPECIAL OCCASIONS

Bjørnsson, Arni: *Icelandic feasts and holidays*. Reykjavik: Iceland Review, 1980.
Bringéus, Nils-Arvid: *Årets festseder*. Stockholm: LTs förlag, 1976.
———: *Livets högtider*. Stockholm: LTs förlag, 1987.
Ellekilde, Hans: *Vor danske jul gennem tiderne*. Copenhagen: Gad, 1943.
Fjellström, Christina, and Håkan Liby: *Det svenska julbordet. Rötter, riter, rätter från år 1000 till 2000*. Stockholm: Carlsson, 2003.

Hodne, Ørnulf: *Jul i Norge, nye og gamle tradisjoner*. Oslo: Cappelen, 2007.

Ojakangas, Beatrice: *Scandinavian feasts: Celebrating traditions throughout the year*. Minneapolis: University of Minnesota Press, 2001.

Piø, Iørn: *Den Gamle Jul i tekst of billeder*. Copenhagen: Sesam, 1999.

Salomonsson, Anders: *Året om med skånsk mat och kultur*. Stockholm: Arena, 2001.

DIET AND HEALTH

Becker, W., N. Lyhne, A. N. Pedersen, A. Aro, M. Fogelholm, I. Þórsdottír, J. Alexander, S. A. Anderssen, H. M. Meltzer, and J. L. Pedersen: *Nordic nutrition recommendations 2004: Integrating nutrition and physical activity*. Copenhagen: Nordic Council of Ministers, 2004.

Bugge, Annechen Bahr: *Ungdoms skolematvaner: Refleksjon, reaksjon eller interaksjon?* Oslo: National Institute of Consumer Research (SIFO), 2007.

Bühlmann, René, and Stig Püschl: *Madpakken*. Copenhagen: Fremad, 1991.

The challenge of obesity in the WHO European Region and the strategies for response. Copenhagen: World Health Organization (WHO) Regional Office for Europe, 2007.

Consumption of vegetables, potatoes, fruit, bread and fish in the Nordic and Baltic countries. The Norbagreen 2002 study. TemaNord 2003:556. Nordic Council of Ministers, 2003.

Diet, nutrition and the prevention of chronic diseases. Technical report series 916. Geneva: World Health Organization (WHO), 2003.

Fødevareundersøgelsene. København. Fødevareinstituttet 1995, 2001: www.dfvf.dk.

Food, nutrition, physical activity, and the prevention of cancer: A global perspective. London: World Cancer Research Fund, 2007.

Johansson, Lars: *Utviklingen i norsk kosthold 2007*. Oslo: Helsedirektoratet, 2007.

Kjøller, M., K. Juel, and F. Kamper-Jørgensen (ed): *Folkesundhedsrapporten Danmark 2007*. Copenhagen: Statens Institut for Folkesundhed, 2007.

Lyngø, Inger Johanne: *Vitaminer! Kultur og vitenskap i mellomkrigstidens kostholdspropaganda*. Oslo: Universitetet i Oslo, 2003.

Wandel, Margareta, and Annechen Bugge: "Nutrition in the market: Food labelling as an aid to the consumer." *Journal of Consumer Studies and Home Economics* 20 (1996): 215–28.

Web Sites

Danish Fitness and Nutrition Council: http://www.meraadet.dk/uk/default. asp?id=1337.

Iceland: Ministry of Health: http://eng.heilbrigdisraduneyti.is.

Norwegian Directorate of Health: http://www.shdir.no.

Norwegian Institute of Public Health: http://www.fhi.no/eway/?pid=238.

Sweden: Public Health Institute: http://www.fhi.se.

Index

About the Author

HENRY NOTAKER is a writer and journalist at NRK, the Norwegian national television network. He has written a number of books and essays on Scandinavian food and cookbooks.